THE WORLD OF SOUTHEAST ASIA

THE
WORLD
OF
SOUTHEAST
ASIA

SELECTED HISTORICAL READINGS

HARRY J. BENDA

YALE UNIVERSITY

JOHN A. LARKIN

STATE UNIVERSITY OF NEW YORK AT BUFFALO

HARPER & ROW, PUBLISHERS
NEW YORK · EVANSTON · LONDON

THE WORLD OF SOUTHEAST ASIA: *Selected Historical Readings*

Library of Congress Catalog Card Number: 67-23444

Contents

PREFACE, XI

PART I. *Early Travelers*

1. The Perilous Journey of Fa-hsien, 3
2. A Seventh-Century Visit to Sumatra, 5
3. An Early Chinese Description of the Philippines, 7
4. The Travels of Marco Polo in the Southern Seas, 10
5. Two Fifteenth-Century Descriptions of Malacca, 13
6. The *Suma Oriental* of Tomé Pires, 18
7. First European Glimpses of Mindanao and the Visayan Islands, 24

PART II. *Indigenous Accounts*

8. The Oath of Allegiance to a Khmer Sovereign, 33
9. Theravada Kingship in Pagan, 34
10. The Magical World of a Javanese Chronicle, 37
11. The Rām Khamhāēng Inscription, 40
12. The Legendary Grandeur of Majapahit, 45
13. Sino-Vietnamese Relations, 47
14. Pomp and Circumstance at the Malaccan Court, 49
15. Javanese History According to the *Babad Tanah Djawi,* 52
16. Kingship in Acheh, 59

v

17. From the Domesday Book of Burma, 62
18. The Glass Palace Chronicle, 68

PART III. *The Western Presence,*
from Periphery to Dominance

19. The Portuguese Seizure of Malacca, 77
20. The First Dutch Voyage to the Indies, 80
21. Louis XIV and the King of Tonkin, 84
22. A Complaint from Jacarta to the Gentlemen Seventeen, 87
23. The Conquest of the Philippines, 90
24. A Description of Siam in the Seventeenth Century, 92
25. The Dutch East India Company's Trade in Southeast Asia, 94
26. Dutch Accounts of the Court of Mataram, 98
27. Philippine Social and Economic Problems in the Eighteenth Century, 102
28. The First Nguyen Emperor Through European Eyes, 104
29. Letter from the Court of Ava to the Governor-General of India, 108
30. Before Imperialism: The British in Malaya (1810), 110
31. John Crawfurd's Mission to the Courts of Cochinchina and Siam, 114
32. Siamese Kingship in the Nineteenth Century, 119
33. *Max Havelaar* and the Cultivation System, 124
34. Early French Imperialism in Cochinchina, 128
35. The Birth of the Federated Malay States, 132
36. Dutch Colonial Policy in the Twentieth Century, 134
37. In Defense of the *Mission Civilisatrice* in Indochina, 137
38. An Official View of Rebellion in Burma, 141

PART IV. *The Southeast Asian Response to the West*

39. A Muslim Boyhood in Malaya, 149
40. Nineteenth-Century Dynastic Rivalries in Mainland Southeast Asia, 152
41. Messianic Currents in Java's "Little Tradition," 155

42. Prince Diponegoro as Islamic Deliverer, 157
43. A Nationalist Condemnation of British Rule in Burma, 160
44. Peasant Unrest in the Philippines, 164
45. King Chulalongkorn on Slavery and Education, 169
46. A Filipino Critique of Spanish Colonialism, 173
47. Conservative Nationalism in Vietnam, 179
48. Radical Nationalism in Vietnam, 182
49. The 1932 Revolution in Thailand, 185
50. Sukarno's *Indonesia Accuses,* 189
51. Sutan Sjahrir on the Dilemma of the Intellectual, 193
52. Manuel Luis Quezon's "New Deal for the Laboring Classes in the Philippines," 196
53. The Indian Minority in Burma, 199
54. Minority Nationalism: The Karens in Burma, 202
55. The Jews of the East, 204
56. In Defense of the Chinese, 211

PART V. *The Era of Decolonization*

57. The Japanese Blueprint for Southeast Asia, 219
58. Java Under the Japanese Occupation, 224
59. The Burmese Declaration of Independence (1943), 227
60. The Philippines During the War Years, 235
61. French Indochina in the Co-Prosperity Sphere, 242
62. The Oratory of President Sukarno, 244
63. Islam Versus the Secular State in Indonesia, 250
64. A Communist Interpretation of the Indonesian Revolution, 254
65. "The Philippines First," 260
66. A Communist View of American Rule in the Philippines, 264
67. The Declaration of Independence of the Republic of Vietnam, 270
68. Ho Chi Minh Interprets the Geneva Conference, 274
69. Problems of Nation-Building in Independent Burma, 277
70. Malayan Independence, 280
71. Thai Foreign Policy in the 1960s, 283

PART VI. *The Modern Traveler*

72. City and Country in Modern Thailand, 289
73. Patterns of Malay Life in Singapore, 292
74. A Village in Contemporary South Vietnam, 294
75. The Plural Society in Malaya, 298
76. Lao Rice Planting Rituals, 301
77. Religious Life in Java, 304
78. Upland and Lowland in Modern Burma, 308
79. Among the Hanunóo of Mindoro, 311
80. A Sumbawan Village, 313

SUGGESTED READINGS, 319
INDEX, 325

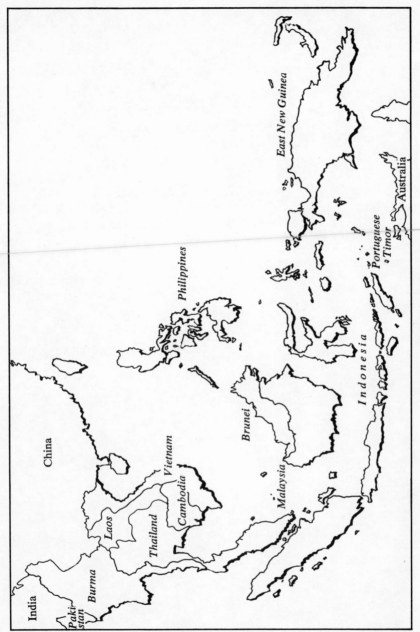

SOUTHEAST ASIA

Preface

IT MAY BE WELL to state our objectives in compiling this book. We did not, of course, aim at putting together a documentary history of Southeast Asia, something that cannot be encompassed in a short volume, given the vast complexity of the area. Rather, we have from the very outset envisaged these readings as a teaching tool, and, as such, complementary to the standard texts in Southeast Asian history. Their prime purpose, then, is to serve the beginner rather than the scholar.

As a quick glance at the table of contents will show, the emphasis is rather heavier on the modern period, reflecting to a large extent our own special interests and also the orientation of most college courses devoted to Southeast Asia. At the same time, however, this is not a reader in contemporary Southeast Asian affairs preceded by a diminutive historical "background" section. On the contrary, we have included a fairly large sampling from materials on premodern Southeast Asia since these are, so we feel, of crucial importance to the entire course of the region's history. From that variegated history we have purposely chosen to dwell on the internal developments of the different Southeast Asian societies rather than on their "international" relations. And since our emphasis is almost exclusively on these societies, we have reduced to a bare minimum documents relating to the affairs of foreigners, especially during the long centuries when these foreigners, particularly Europeans, did not directly impinge on the native societies themselves, however important their place in Asian commerce might have been. For the same reason, we have exluded any documentation pertaining to the drawn-out quarrels and struggles for mercantile dominance among European powers in that part of the world. It is only when Westerners assumed more or less direct control of parts of Southeast Asia and started to affect the lives of the region's inhabitants, especially from the nineteenth century on, that we have focused on their activities as major agents in Southeast Asian history.

In spite of its modern orientation, this collection is primarily intended as an "Asian-centric" contribution to the study of Souheast Asian history, an effort to get away from the still prevalent notion that the history of that area is somehow an extentsion of European history. We have striven to look into Southeast Asian societies, both in their organizational and ideological aspects, and to chart some of the changes to which they have been subjected in the course of time. For this purpose, considerable detail on the original socio-political systems was required while, on the other hand, the sheer forward march of chronology as such could be relegated to a place of less importance. Such a procedure is, as we well know, not without dangers and problems, and the reader must therefore be reminded that this short book should not be read in isolation. Its purpose is to illustrate, to highlight, to supply something of the flavor of Southeast Asian history, albeit in rigorously limited if not tantalizingly brief dosages. Of equal importance, we hope, should be the fact that we have selected Asian voices wherever we could, especially to throw some light on the problems of Southeast Asian historiography, that is, on the way in which some of the cultural entities in the area gave expression to their views of human society and of history itself. Even then, however, we have of course by no means ignored the foreigner; we have used him in order to provide us with the kind of information that is otherwise difficult to come by—for insights are nobody's monopoly—and we have also used him when, in his own right, he was an important molder of Southeast Asia's fate. But wherever possible, we have taken our stand beside, or perhaps behind, the native actors, looking over their shoulders, so to speak, at events and, also, at the foreigner. Our readers must judge whether our effort to avoid the pitfalls of "Europocentrism" has succeeded.

No compilation of this kind can please everyone; it certainly does not entirely satisfy us. Some degree of arbitrariness has been unavoidable, both in the choice of individual documents and the ordering of the selections into categories. But like all historians, we have followed, consciously or otherwise, our own preferences reinforced by our teaching experience. In the course of over two years, we have made many changes, deleting, reluctantly in some cases, documents that had been originally included. More important, there must be literally hundreds of sources that have not come to our attention. Yet if some of our original selections have dropped by the wayside, the blame (or praise) belongs in no small measure to the reactions of Yale undergraduate and graduate students to the documentary readings assigned them in the classroom.

Two additional factors regarding the problem of selectivity deserve mention. We have here and there exluded materials reasonably well known, if not actually oft-quoted in the standard works; sometimes we have decided to exclude a better known piece (or author) in order to allow the inclusion of a lesser known document, especially when it seemed to us that such a decision would provide a better balance.

We were faced, too, with the perennial problem of securing equitable representation for the various constituent parts of Southeast Asia. We confess that this problem has proved particularly difficult, even discounting the rather obvious desire of both authors to "push" their areas of specialized training to the foreground. On the whole, however, we have endeavored to let all major parts of the region speak with adequate clarity, though admittedly allocating them uneven numbers of pages. No patriot will, we know, agree that justice has been done to his particular country, let alone the "unrepresented minorities" for whom we have not been able to find room in these few pages. To some extent we have been guided by considerations of the sheer size and population of each area. In the end, we have done our best to be fair, but no one knows better than we that the best may not be good enough.

The book is divided into six parts, each preceded by a short prefatory statement stressing some of the significant underlying themes of the documentary readings included in that section. While the documents of the first parts are chronologically arranged, the remainder are grouped together topically or geographically; this format was dictated by the subject matter covered. Each individual document is introduced by a short editorial note, identifying its background and, where possible, its author. These have been purposely kept to a minimum, since— we should repeat—the volume is not meant to be read in isolation; general texts will usually provide the wider setting and other details.

We have similarly limited our explanatory notes to the clarification of foreign terms. Weights and measures have been rendered in their modern equivalents only where so doing would prove meaningful; the same holds for geographical and other terms, titles, etc. With regard to transliterations, we have as a rule followed those adopted in the various documents, even though this has inevitably led to lack of consistency as, especially, between Indonesian and Malay renderings of identical words. We have adopted a policy of using brackets for our own explanatory editorial notes, reserving parentheses for insertions made either by the original authors and/or editors or our own translators in the body of the texts. In the introductory notes, we have used parentheses throughout. Ellipses are used to indicate all textual deletions. Authors' and original editors' footnotes have been dropped, since they are of importance primarily to advanced scholars.

Finally, a few words of appreciation. First and foremost, to the undergraduate and graduate students in Southeast Asian history at Yale, who for two years have expressed their preferences and ideas and thus helped to shape the final contours of this book. At the early stages, Sydney W. Mayer rendered a great deal of help. Colleagues and friends, at Yale and elsewhere, have been most generous throughout. We should like to single out for special thanks Dr. Truong Buu Lam, who has helped us greatly in making the final selections of Vietnamese documents, in addition to translating some items personally. Others in this country include John F. Cady, Harold C. Conklin, William S. Cornyn, Theodore Friend III, Thomas W. Gething, John P. Heiman, Rufus S. Hendon, James R. Irikura, John K. Musgrave, Jr., and Arthur F. Wright. Two Dutch scholars, Dr. J. Noorduyn and Professor A. A. Teeuw, have been most helpful, the latter in particular having undertaken the burdensome task of preparing a virtually new English rendition of a stanza from the *Nagarakertagama*. Mrs. Margaret W. Broekhuysen deserves our gratitude for her skillful translations of both Dutch and French sources. To the staffs of the Yale University Library and the Quezoniana Collection of the National Library of the Philippines we should like to express our gratitude for many and courteous services.

Jeffrey J. Parish, George E. Marcus, and especially Victor B. Lieberman have rendered much painstaking and time-consuming spade work, without which our labors would have dragged on for a long time. And to Ruth Borel, Janice Soboleski, Lida Boyko, Jan Sayre, Helen Balestrino, and Pamela Russell our sincerest thanks for having manned the typewriters with fortitude and good humor from slow beginnings to the rushed end.

Without the financial support from Yale University's Southeast Asia Studies program, this documentary collection could never have seen the light of day, and we wish to record our indebtedness for the continued generosity that allowed us to prepare it, first as teaching materials and subsequently as a finished manuscript for the publisher.

We are indebted to the various publishers who have kindly allowed us to reproduce materials originally published by them. Specific acknowledgments for their permissions are shown in the source notes accompanying the individual documents in the text.

In addition, we should like to thank the following scholars whom we have asked to grant us their own permission: Teodoro A. Agoncillo, Prachoom Chomchai, Harold C. Conklin, Raymond Firth, Judith Freedman, Clifford Geertz, Peter R. Goethals, J. de Graaf, D. G. E. Hall, Joel M. Halpern, Gerald C. Hickey, Harold R. Isaacs, Kenneth Perry Landon, E. R. Leach, David R. Sturtevant, Georges Taboulet, and Paul Wheatley.

Our wives, Eva Benda and Judith Larkin, have graciously managed to gloss over our departures from normal family routine. The latter, indeed, has done far more than passively tolerating the birth of the book, having assisted in innumerable ways in its delivery, most notably in compiling the index.

H. J. B.
J. A. L.

New Haven, Conn.

THE WORLD OF SOUTHEAST ASIA

PART I

Early Travelers

HISTORICAL INFORMATION about early Southeast Asia stems from two kinds of sources: travel accounts by foreigners and indigenous materials. The former provide us with the first glimpses of the area and sometimes serve as a check on the information contained in the latter.

In general, the travel accounts in this part describe the Southeast Asian realms closest to the coasts, since all journeys had to be accomplished by sea, there being no major overland roads in the early centuries. The narratives of these travelers reflect more accurately their own motivations and interests than they provide a reasonably complete or adequate picture of the Southeast Asian regions they describe. In fact, many of those voyagers were not primarily concerned with Southeast Asia, but were visiting the area en route to or from China. The information they convey is spotty and very likely far from reliable in several respects. Thus, Fa-hsien and I-tsing, both Buddhist monks, concerned themselves with the state of religion in southern Sumatra rather than with other aspects of what presumably was a highly developed emporium (Documents 1 and 2). Chao Ju-kua and Tomé Pires, commercial representatives of the Chinese and Portuguese governments respectively, wrote on matters of trade in Southeast Asia, neglecting important social and political

1

factors in the countries about which they wrote (Documents 3 and 6). The other four spokesmen in this part, Marco Polo, Fei-Hsin, Ma-Huan, and Pigafetta—essentially all adventurers—focused their attention on the idiosyncrasies of local dress and custom (Documents 4, 5, and 7).

These seven short extracts, spanning some eleven centuries, yield only a few isolated and incidental insights into the contacts between foreign visitors and Southeast Asians. They offer, for example, just a fleeting glance of the close relations, particularly through trade, between the Chinese Empire and the dynastic coastal states to the south. The documents do, however, provide concrete details recorded nowhere else in the literature of the region.

1

The Perilous Journey of Fa-hsien

*Fa-hsien (ca. 334—?), whose original name was Kung, was ad-
mitted to the Buddhist order at the age of three, at which
time his new name, meaning "Law Manifest," was given to
him. He set out from China for India in* A.D. *399, accompanied by nine or ten other monks. The return from his four-
teen-year journey took him to Sumatra, the very brief description of which is presented here. This travel account is
the first of its kind available in written form to the scholar.*

THE HOMEBOUND VOYAGE

Having obtained ... Sanskrit books [in Ceylon], he [Fa-hsien]
set sail on a large merchant ship which carried about two hundred
passengers. A small boat trailed behind, for use in case the large
vessel should be wrecked, as sailing on this sea was most hazar-
dous. They had sailed eastward with a fair wind for two days only,
when they were caught up in a typhoon and the ship sprang a leak,
through which the water rushed in. The merchants wanted to take
to the smaller boat; but the men already in it severed the cable,
for fear lest they be swamped. Then the terrified merchants believed
their end was at hand, and in an endeavour to stop the ship from
sinking they threw their coarser merchandise into the sea. Fa-hsien
also cast overboard his pitcher, washbasin and some other possessions. Dreading lest the merchants should throw his sacred books
and drawings of images into the sea, he invoked Avalokitesvara in
all sincerity, as well as the monks of China who had embraced the
faith.

"I have come so far to search for the Law," he prayed. "Carry
me back with your spiritual power to my destination!"

Fa-hsien, *A Record of the Buddhist Countries,* trans. Li Yung-hsi (Pe-
king: The Chinese Buddhist Association, 1957), pp. 87–90.

3

The hurricane lasted for thirteen days and nights, but finally they reached the shore of an island. When the tide ebbed, they found the leak and repaired it, then sailed on again.

That sea is infested with pirates, and none who meet them can escape alive. The great ocean stretches on every side without end, and one cannot tell east from west. Only by looking at the sun, the moon and the stars, can mariners tell their direction. On dull or rainy days, their vessel simply drifted before the wind. On dark nights, all they could see were great billows beating one against the other and shining like fire, with huge turtles, sea monsters and other amazing creatures in them. The bewildered seamen did not know in what direction they were sailing, but since the ocean was unfathomable there was nowhere to cast anchor; so not until the weather cleared could they distinguish the direction and set the right course. Had they happened to strike a reef, they would have been lost. After voyaging in this way for about ninety days, they reached the country called Yavadvipa [Sumatra].

THE COUNTRY OF YAVADVIPA

In this country heretical Brahmanism flourishes, and there are very few Buddhists.

After staying here for five months, Fa-hsien embarked on another great merchant ship which also carried about two hundred men. They provided themselves with fifty days' provisions, and set sail on the sixteenth day of the fourth month. Fa-hsien observed the summer retirement on board this vessel, which sailed towards the northeast, bound for Kwangchow.

After sailing for about one month, at the second watch one night it suddenly blew a black squall, and the rain pelted down. Sailors and passengers alike were terror-struck. Once more Fa-hsien in all sincerity invoked Avalokitesvara and the monks in China, and thanks to their protection he was able to live through that night. . . .

Owing to the continuous rain, the pilot charted a wrong course.

Thus they sailed for more than seventy days till their provisions and water were nearly exhausted. They had to use salt water from the sea for cooking, and each man's ration of fresh water was two pints. Soon the fresh water was nearly used up, and the seamen took counsel together.

"Usually," they said, "it takes only fifty days to reach Kwang-chow. But we have been sailing now for many more days than that. We must have been off our course." So they steered towards the northwest to look for land.

2

A Seventh-Century Visit to Sumatra

> *An admirer of Fa-hsien, I-tsing (635–713), like his predecessor, was admitted to a Buddhist order at an early age, devoting the first thirty-seven years of his life to scholarly and monastic pursuits. In 671, I-tsing left for India, and in the course of his twenty-five year journey stopped at several points in Southeast Asia on the return voyage to China. The following travel account is one of the major reports of Indianized Southeast Asia during the period of the T'ang Dynasty in China (618–907).*

... This [East India] is the place where we embark when returning to China. Sailing from here two months in the south-east direction we come to Ka-cha [Acheh]. By this time a ship from Bhoga [Palembang] will have arrived there. This is generally in the first or second month of the year. But those who go to the Simhala Island (Ceylon) must sail in the south-west direction. They say that that island is 700 yoganas off. We stay in Ka-cha till winter, then start on board ship for the south, and we come after a month

I-tsing, *A Record of the Buddhist Religion as Practised in India and the Malay Archipelago,* trans. J. Takakusu (Oxford: Clarendon, 1896), pp. xxxiv-xxxv.

to the country of Malayu, which has now become Bhoga; there are many states (under it). The time of arrival is generally in the first or second month. We stay there till the middle of summer and we sail to the north; in about a month we reach Kwang-fu (Kwang-tung). The first half of the year will be passed by this time.

When we are helped by the power of our (former) good actions, the journey everywhere is as easy and enjoyable as if we went through a market, but, on the other hand, when we have not much influence of Karma, we are often exposed to danger as if (a young one) in a reclining nest. I have thus shortly described the route and the way home, hoping that the wise may still expand their knowledge by hearing more.

Many kings and chieftains in the islands of the Southern Ocean admire and believe (Buddhism), and their hearts are set on accumulating good actions. In the fortified city of Bhoga Buddhist priests number more than 1,000, whose minds are bent on learning and good practices. They investigate and study all the subjects that exist just as in the Middle Kingdom (Madhya-desa, India); the rules and ceremonies are not at all different. If a Chinese priest wishes to go to the West in order to hear (lectures) and read (the original), he had better stay here one or two years and practice the proper rules and then proceed to Central India.

At the mouth of the river Bhoga I went on board the ship to send a letter (through the merchant) as a credential to Kwang-chou (Kwang-tung), *in order* to meet (my friends) and ask for paper and cakes of ink, which are to be used in copying the Sûtras in the Brahma-language, and also for the means (cost) of hiring scribes. Just at that time the merchant found the wind favourable, and raised the sails to their utmost height. I was in this way conveyed back (although not myself intending to go home). Even if I asked to stop, there would have been no means of doing so. By this I see it is the influence of Karma that can fashion (our course), and it is not for us, men, to plan it. It was on the twentieth day of the seventh month in the first year of the Yung-ch'ang period (689) that we reached Kwang-fu. . . .

3

An Early Chinese Description of the Philippines

James A. Robertson wrote of Chao Ju-kua, author of the following excerpt: "He was inspector of the salt gabel in the province of Fo-kien, and his title was probably Shih-po, which means 'Superintendent of Sea Trade.' As this post existed in Fo-kien only during the years 1277–1287, it is probable that those dates fix the period of Chao Ju-kua. His work is called the Chu-fan-chï *(A Description of Barbarian Peoples), and the greater part of his notes are copies from older records. His position, however, gave him opportunity to gather information personally from the traders who anchored at his port. At that time more foreign traders frequented Chinese ports than either before or after, and it would be comparatively easy to gather information. The* Chu-fan-chï *contains more geographical information than do the court records"* (The Philippine Islands, *Vol. XXXIV, pp. 183–184).*

The country of Ma-i [Philippine archipelago] is to the north of P'o-ni [Borneo]. Over a thousand families are settled together along both banks of a creek (or, gully). The natives cover themselves with a sheet of cotton cloth, or hide the lower part of the body with a loincloth.

There are bronze images of gods, of unknown origin, scattered about in the grassy wilderness. Pirates seldom come to this country.

When trading ships enter the anchorage, they stop in front of the officials' place, for that is the place for bartering of the country. After a ship has been boarded, the natives mix freely with the

Chao Ju-kua, His Work on the Chinese and Arab Trade in the Twelfth and Thirteenth Centuries, entitled Chu-fan-chï, trans. F. Hirth and W. W. Rockhill (St. Petersburg: Printing Office of the Imperial Academy of Sciences, 1911), pp. 159–162.

ship's folk. The chiefs are in the habit of using white umbrellas, for which reason the traders offer them as gifts.

The custom of the trade is for the savage traders to assemble in crowds and carry the goods away with them in baskets; and, even if one cannot at first know them, and can but slowly distinguish the men who remove the goods, there will yet be no loss. The savage traders will after this carry these goods on to other islands for barter, and, as a rule, it takes them as much as eight or nine months till they return, when they repay the traders on shipboard with what they have obtained (for the goods). Some, however, do not return within the proper term, for which reason vessels trading with Ma-i are the latest in reaching home. . . .

The products of the country consist of yellow wax, cotton, pearls, tortoise-shell, medicinal betel-nuts and *yü-ta* cloth [abaca textiles]; and (the foreign) traders barter for these porcelain, trade-gold, iron censers, lead, coloured glass beads, and iron needles. . . .

The San-sü (or "Three Islands"), belong to Ma-i; their names are Kia-ma-yen [Calamián Island Group between Mindoro and Palawan], Pa-lau-yu [Palawan], and Pa-ki-nung [Busuanga Island, largest of the Calamián Islands], and each has its own tribes scattered over the islands. When ships arrive there, the natives come out to trade with them; the generic name (of these islands) is San-sü.

Their local customs are about the same as those of Ma-i. Each tribe consists of about a thousand families. The country contains many lofty ridges, and ranges of cliffs rise steep as the walls of a house.

The natives build wattled huts perched in lofty and dangerous spots, and, since the hills contain no springs, the women may be seen carrying on their heads two or three jars one above the other in which they fetch water from the streams, and with their burdens mount the hills with the same ease as if they were walking on level ground.

In the remotest valleys there lives another tribe called Hai-tan [negritos]. They are small in stature and their eyes are round and yellow (brown), they have curly hair and their teeth show (between their lips). They nest in tree tops. Sometimes parties of three or five lurk in the jungle, from whence they shoot arrows on passers-by without being seen, and many have fallen victims to them. If thrown a porcelain bowl, they will stoop and pick it up and go away leaping and shouting for joy.

Whenever foreign traders arrive at any of the settlements, they live on board ship before venturing to go on shore, their ships being moored in mid-stream, announcing their presence to the natives by beating drums. Upon this the savage traders race for the ship in small boats, carrying cotton, yellow wax, native cloth, cocoanut-heart mats, which they offer for barter. If the prices (of goods they may wish to purchase) cannot be agreed upon, the chief of the (local) traders must go in person, in order to come to an understanding, which being reached the natives are offered presents of silk umbrellas, porcelain, and rattan baskets; but the foreigners still retain on board one or two (natives) as hostages. After that they go on shore to traffic, which being ended they return the hostages. A ship will not remain at anchor longer than three or four days, after which it proceeds to another place; for the savage settlements along the coast of San-sü are not connected by a common jurisdiction (i.e., are all independent).

The coast faces south-west, and during the south-west monsoon the surge dashes against the shore, and the rollers rush in so rapidly that vessels cannot anchor there. It is for this reason that those who trade to San-sü generally prepare for the return trip during the fourth or fifth moon (i.e., in May or June).

The following articles are exchanged in barter: porcelain, black damask and various other silks, (glass?) beads of all colours, leaden sinkers for nets, and tin.

P'u-li-lu [Polillo Island near Luzon] is connected with San-sü, but its settlements are more populous; most of the people are of a cruel disposition and given to robbery. The sea thereabout is full of bare ribs of rock with jagged teeth like blasted trees, their points and edges sharper than swords and lances; when ships pass by they tack out in time in order to steer clear of them; from here come coral-trees . . . but they are very difficult to get.

The local customs and commercial usages are the same as in San-sü.

4

The Travels of Marco Polo in the Southern Seas

> *The famous Venetian traveler, Marco Polo (1254–1324), was the first European to have recorded his journey to the Far East and Southeast Asia. The following passage, in which he discusses his observations in Java, Sumatra (Java the Less), and Champa, has been a subject of controversy among historians, many of whom contend that he never visited Java though he may have spent several months on the island of Sumatra. Marco Polo is reputed to have stopped in the Kingdom of Champa on his voyage back to Europe from China. Upon his return to Italy at the turn of the fourteenth century, Marco Polo's half-believed travel account sparked a renascence of interest of intellectual Europe in Asia.*

CHAPTER V. OF THE GREAT COUNTRY CALLED CHAMBA [CHAMPA]

You must know that on leaving the port of Zayton[1] you sail west-south-west for 1500 miles, and then you come to a country called CHAMBA, a very rich region, having a king of its own. The people are Idolaters and pay a yearly tribute to the Great Kaan [Emperor of China], which consists of elephants and nothing but elephants. And I will tell you how they came to pay this tribute.

It happened in the year of Christ 1278 that the Great Kaan sent a Baron of his called Sagatu with a great force of horse and

The Book of Ser Marco Polo, trans. Henry Yule (London: John Murray, 1903), Vol. II, pp. 266–268, 272–274, 284–285. By permission of John Murray (Publishers), Ltd.

[1] Ch'üan-chow, in Fukien Province. In Polo's time a great port for the South Seas trade.

foot against this King of Chamba, and this Baron opened the war on a great scale against the King and his country.

Now the King (whose name was Accambale) was a very aged man, nor had he such a force as the Baron had. And when he saw what havoc the Baron was making with his kingdom he was grieved to the heart. So he bade messengers get ready and despatched them to the Great Kaan. And they said to the Kaan: "Our Lord the King of Chamba salutes you as his liege-lord, and would have you to know that he is stricken in years and long hath held his realm in peace. And now he sends you word by us that he is willing to be your liege-man, and will send you every year a tribute of as many elephants as you please. And he prays you in all gentleness and humility that you would send word to your Baron to desist from harrying his kingdom and to quit his territories. These shall henceforth be at your absolute disposal, and the King shall hold them of you."

When the Great Kaan had heard the King's ambassage he was moved with pity, and sent word to that Baron of his to quit that kingdom with his army, and to carry his arms to the conquest of some other country; and as soon as this command reached them they obeyed it. Thus it was then that this King became vassal of the Great Kaan, and paid him every year a tribute of 20 of the greatest and finest elephants that were to be found in the country.

But now we will leave that matter, and tell you other particulars about the King of Chamba.

You must know that in that kingdom no woman is allowed to marry until the King shall have seen her; if the woman pleases him then he takes her to wife; if she does not, he gives her a dowry to get her a husband withal. In the year of Christ 1285, Messer Marco Polo was in that country, and at that time the King had, between sons and daughters, 326 children, of whom at least 150 were men fit to carry arms.

There are very great numbers of elephants in this kingdom, and they have lignaloes [fragrant wood] in great abundance. They have also extensive forests of the wood called *Bonús* [ebony], which is jet-black, and of which chessmen and pen-cases are made. But there is nought more to tell, so let us proceed.

CHAPTER VI. CONCERNING THE GREAT ISLAND OF JAVA

When you sail from Chamba, 1500 miles in a course between south and south-east, you come to a great Island called Java. And the experienced mariners of those Islands who know the matter well, say that it is the greatest Island in the world, and has a compass of more than 3000 miles. It is subject to a great King and tributary to no one else in the world. The people are Idolaters. The Island is of surpassing wealth, producing black pepper, nutmegs, spikenard [fragrant ointment], galingale [aromatic herb], cubebs [medicinal berry], cloves, and all other kinds of spices.

This Island is also frequented by a vast amount of shipping, and by merchants who buy and sell costly goods from which they reap great profit. Indeed the treasure of this Island is so great as to be past telling. And I can assure you the Great Kaan never could get possession of this Island, on account of its great distance, and the great expense of an expedition thither. The merchants of Zayton and Manzi[2] draw annually great returns from this country.

CHAPTER IX. CONCERNING THE ISLAND OF JAVA THE LESS. THE KINGDOMS OF FERLEC [PERLAK] AND BASMA [PASAI]

When you leave the Island of Pentam and sail about 100 miles, you reach the Island of JAVA THE LESS. For all its name 'tis none so small but that it has a compass of two thousand miles or more. Now I will tell you all about this Island.

You see there are upon it eight kingdoms and eight crowned kings. The people are all Idolaters, and every kingdom has a language of its own. The Island hath great abundance of treasure,

[2] Man-tzu, Polo's name for the old Southern Sung region centered on Hangchow Island.

with costly spices, lignaloes and spikenard and many others that never come into our parts.

Now I am going to tell you all about these eight kingdoms, or at least the greater part of them. But let me premise one marvellous thing, and that is the fact that this Island lies so far to the south that the North Star, little or much, is never to be seen!

Now let us resume our subject, and first I will tell you of the kingdom of FERLEC.

This kingdom, you must know, is so much frequented by the Saracen merchants that they have converted the natives to the Law of Mahommet—I mean the towns-people only, for the hill-people live for all the world like beasts, and eat human flesh, as well as all other kinds of flesh, clean or unclean. And they worship this, that, and the other thing; for in fact the first thing that they see on rising in the morning, that they do worship for the rest of the day.

Having told you of the kingdom of Ferlec, I will now tell of another which is called BASMA.

When you quit the kingdom of Ferlec you enter upon that of Basma. This also is an independent kingdom, and the people have a language of their own; but they are just like beasts without laws or religion. They call themselves subjects of the Great Kaan, but they pay him no tribute; indeed they are so far away that his men could not go thither. Still all these Islanders declare themselves to be his subjects, and sometimes they send him curiosities as presents. . . .

5

Two Fifteenth-Century Descriptions of Malacca

The oldest remaining accounts of the great fifteenth-century Muslim commercial center at Malacca were written by two Chinese. Both authors served the famous eunuch, Cheng-Ho, who made a series of naval expeditions to the Indian Ocean during the Ming period. Fei-Hsin, a junior officer, compiled

his Hsing-ch'a Sheng-lan (Description of the Starry Raft) *in
1436. Ma-Huan, a Muslim interpreter on several of the voy-
ages, wrote the* Ying-yai Sheng-lan (Description of the Coasts
of the Ocean) *in 1451.*

FROM FEI-HSIN'S DESCRIPTION OF THE STARRY RAFT [1436]

This place did not formerly rank as a kingdom. It can be
reached from Palembang on the monsoon in eight days. The
coast is rocky and desolate, the population sparse. The country
(used to) pay an annual tax of 40 taels of gold to Siam. The
soil is infertile and yields low. In the interior there is a mountain from (the slopes of) which a river takes its rise. The (local)
folk pan the sands (of this river) to obtain tin, which they melt
into ingots called *tou.* These weigh 1 kati 4 taels standard weight.
(The inhabitants) also weave banana fibre into mats. Apart from
tin, no other product enters into (foreign) trade. The climate is
hot during the day but cool at night. (Both) sexes coil their hair
into a knot. Their skin resembles black lacquer, but there are
(some) white-complexioned folk among them who are of Chinese
descent. The people esteem sincerity and honesty. They make a
living by panning tin and catching fish. Their houses are raised
above the ground. (When constructing them) they refrain from
joining planks and restrict the building to the length of a (single)
piece of timber. When they wish to retire, they spread their
bedding side by side. They squat on their haunches when taking
their meals. The kitchen and all its appurtenances is (also) raised
(on the stilts). The goods (used in trading at Malacca) are blue
and white porcelain, coloured beads, coloured taffetas, gold and
silver. In the seventh year of Yung-lo (1409), the imperial envoy,
the eunuch Cheng-Ho, and his lieutenants conferred (on the
ruler), by Imperial command, a pair of silver seals, and a head-

Paul Wheatley, *The Golden Khersonese* (Kuala Lumpur: University of
Malaya Press, 1961), pp. 321–324. By permission of the author and the
University of Malaya Press.

dress, girdle and robe. They also set up a tablet (stating that) Malacca had been raised to the rank of a kingdom, but at first Siam refused to recognize it. In the thirteenth year (of Yung-lo) (1415), the ruler (of Malacca, desirous of) showing his gratitude for the Imperial bounty, crossed the ocean and, accompanied by his consort and son, came to court with tribute. The Emperor rewarded him (appropriately), whereupon (the ruler of Malacca) returned to his (own) country.

FROM MA-HUAN'S DESCRIPTION OF THE COASTS OF THE OCEAN [1451]

Formerly (Malacca) was not styled a kingdom but was known as the Five Isles, because there were that number of islands off that part of the coast. It had no king, but only a chieftain. The country was under the rule of *Hsien-lo* (Siam), to which it paid an annual (tribute) of 40 taels of gold. Default (in this matter) would have provoked an attack. In the seventh year of the ssŭ-ch'ou (period) of the Yung-lo (Emperor) the eunuch Cheng-Ho, (in his capacity) as an imperial envoy, conveyed (to Malacca) the commands of the Emperor, (in token of which) he bestowed on the chieftain of that country a pair of silver seals, a head-dress, a girdle and a long robe. He raised the place to the status of a city, since when it has been known as the Kingdom of Malacca. Henceforth the Siamese dared not venture to attack it, and the ruler, now by the imperial favour (styled) king, proceeded in company with his consort to the capital (of China), where he expressed his gratitude and offered products of his country as tribute. The Emperor then assigned him a ship in which to return home so that he might (continue to) govern his land. To the south-east (of this country) is the ocean, to the north-west the mainland, which is continued as a chain of mountains. The soil is sandy and saline. Temperatures are hot during the day, but cool at night. The infertile fields yield little rice, so that the people are not greatly concerned with agriculture. A sizeable stream flows by the royal palace before entering the sea. Over this the King has built a bridge, on which he has constructed some twenty booths for the sale of all kinds of commodities. Both the King and his subjects revere the laws of Islam, and observe its fasts and penances. The King wears a white turban of fine local cloth, a long floral robe of fine green calico, and leather shoes. He fares abroad in a palanquin. Among the (common) people the men wear square, cotton kerchiefs round their heads, and the women dress their hair in chignons. The bodies (of the people) are rather dark (in colour). They wrap a length of white cotton round their loins and wear short bajus of cotton print. Their customs and usages are pure and simple. Their houses are raised on one-storey platforms and lack a layer of planks (against the ground), but a floor of split coconut-palms is erected and lashed with rattan—exactly as if it were a sheep-pen—at a height of about four feet. On this floor (the people) spread their beds and mats, on which they sit cross-legged, and (on this floor) they also eat, sleep and cook. Most of the inhabitants (of Malacca) are occupied in fishing, for which they venture out to sea in boats hollowed from a single tree(trunk). Local products include *Coptis teeta* (rhizomes), ebony, damar, tin and suchlike. Damar in its original state is the sap of a tree which flows into the ground and is then dug up. It oozes from the tree in gouts in the same way as the resin of the pine does. When lit, it continues to burn, and the native people use it for lighting purposes. When they have finished building a boat, they smear this substance along the seams to render them waterproof. The people gather a great deal (of damar) for sale to other countries. A superior variety, which is clear, transparent and resembles amber, is called *sun-tu-lu-ssŭ*. The local people make it into beads for tĕngolok. These beads, which they sell, are known as water amber. Tin occurs in two localities in the mountains, and the King (of Malacca) has appointed officials to control (these districts). Men wash (the tin) in sieves, smelt it and cast it into ingots of disk-like shape, the standard weight of which is either 1 kati 8 taels or 1 kati 4 taels. Ten ingots bound together with rattan constitute a small bundle, forty ingots a large bundle. In all their trade transactions (the people) use (these ingots of) tin. The language, the books and the marriage ceremonies (of Malacca) closely resemble those of *Chao-wa* (Java). In the mountainous wilderness (of the interior) is a palm known as the sago. The country folk pound the bark (of this palm), which resembles the root of the Chinese bean, soak it in water, (allow it) to settle and strain it. The flour obtained in this way is moulded into pellets of the size of green peas, which are dried in the sun and sold as food. On the low ground bordering the sea there grows a palm whose fronds are as long as those of the kajang. When its sword-like leaves first appear they are (as pliable) as young bamboo shoots. The fruits have the appearance of lichees, and are of the size of hen's eggs. The people use them to ferment a liquor, which they call kajang wine and which has the power of intoxication. The local folk interweave the leaves of this plant with bamboo to make fine quality mats which, although only two feet wide, exceed ten feet in length. These they offer for sale. There are sugarcane, plantains, jack-fruit, wild lichees and suchlike. The vegetables include onions, ginger, leeks, mustard, gourds, watermelons and so forth. Cattle, goats, fowls and ducks are few, and therefore costly, a head of buffalo being priced at a kati of silver. . . . When this place (Malacca) is visited by Chinese merchant vessels (the inhabitants) erect a barrier (for the collection of duties). There are four gates in the city wall, each furnished with watch- and drum-towers. At night men with hand-bells patrol (the precincts). Inside the walls a second small enclosure of palisades has been built where godowns have been constructed for the storage of specie and provisions. When the government ships were returning homewards, they visited this place in order both to repair (their vessels) and to load local products. Here they waited for a favourable wind from the south, and in the middle of the fifth month they put out to sea on their return voyage. The King (of Malacca), accompanied by his consort, his son and some of his headmen, laid in products of his country and followed (our) fleet (to China), where he came to court and presented tribute.

6

The Suma Oriental *of Tomé Pires*

Perhaps the most important and complete account of South-east Asia produced in the first half of the sixteenth century was the Suma Oriental *of Tomé Pires (c. 1468–c. 1539). Pires visited India and many places in the Indonesian Archipelago and possibly traveled to Cochinchina, Siam, and Cambodia. His knowledge of Luzon came from traders at Malacca where Pires worked for the Portuguese government. Because of his great ability as a factor, writer, and drug merchant, Pires, the commoner apothecary, was appointed first Portuguese ambassador to China in 1516, after the* Suma *was completed.*

(SIAM)

There are three ports in the kingdom of Siam on the Pegu side, and on the Pahang and *Champa* side there are many. They all belong to the said kingdom and are subject to the king of Siam. The land of Siam is large and very plenteous, with many people and cities, with many lords and many foreign merchants, and most of these foreigners are Chinese, because Siam does a great deal of trade with China. The land of Malacca is called a land of Siam, and the whole of Siam, *Champa* and thereabouts is called China.

The kingdom of Siam is heathen. The people, and almost the language, are like those of Pegu. They are considered to be prudent folk of good counsel. The merchants know a great deal about merchandise. They are tall, swarthy men, shorn like those of Pegu. The kingdom is justly ruled. The king is always in resi-

Armando Cortesão, ed. and trans., *The Suma Oriental of Tomé Pires and the Book of Francisco Rodrigues* (London: Cambridge University Press for The Hakluyt Society, 1944), Vol. I, pp. 103–104, 107–109, 112, 114–115, 133–134. By permission of The Hakluyt Society.

dence in the city of Odia [Ayuthia]. He is a hunter. He is very ceremonious with strangers; he is more free and easy with the natives. He has many wives, upwards of five hundred. On the death (of the king) it has as king a person of the blood (royal), usually a nephew, the son of a sister, if he is suitable, and if not there are sometimes agreements and assemblies (to decide) who will be the best. Secrets are closely kept among them. They are very reserved. They speak with well-taught modesty. The important men are very obedient to the king. Their ambassadors carry out their instruction thoroughly.

Through the cunning (of the Siamese) the foreign merchants who go to their land and kingdom leave their merchandise in the land and are ill paid; and this happens to them all—but less to the Chinese, on account of their friendship with the king of China. And for this reason less people go to their port than would (otherwise) go. However, as the land is rich in good merchandise, they bear some things on account of the profit, as often happens to merchants, because otherwise there would be no trading.

There are very few Moors in Siam. The Siamese do not like them. There are, however, Arabs, Persians, Bengalees, many Kling [Indians], Chinese and other nationalities. And all the Siamese trade is on the China side, and in Pase, Pedir and Bengal. The Moors are in the seaports. They are obedient to their own lords, and constantly make war on the Siamese, now inland and now in Pahang. They are not very warlike fighting men. The said Siamese wear bells like the men of Pegu, and no less but just as many. The lords wear pointed diamonds and other precious stones in their privy parts in addition to the bells—a precious stone worn is according to the person or his estate. . . .

There is a great abundance of rice in Siam, and much salt, dried salt fish, *oraquas* [arrack], vegetables; and up to thirty junks a year used to come to Malacca with these.

From Siam comes lac, benzoin, brazil [sappanwood], lead, tin, silver, gold, ivory, cassia fistula [laxative]; they bring vessels of cast copper and gold, ruby and diamond rings; they bring a large quantity of cheap, coarse Siamese cloth for the poor people.

They say that the chief merchandise they take from Malacca to Siam are the male and female slaves, which they take in quantities, white sandalwood, pepper, quicksilver, vermilion, opium, . . . cloves, mace, nutmeg, wide and narrow muslins, and Kling cloths in the fashion of Siam, camlets [near waterproof garments], rosewater, carpets, brocades from Cambay, white cowries, wax, Borneo camphor, pachak which are roots like dry rampion [a European edible root], gall-nuts . . . and the merchandise they bring from China every year is also of value there.

The Siamese have not traded in Malacca for twenty-two years. They had a difference because the kings of Malacca owed allegiance to the kings of Siam, because they say that Malacca belongs to the land of Siam—They say that it is theirs and that twenty-two years ago this King lost Malacca, which rose up against this subjection. They also say that Pahang rose against Siam in the same way, and that, on account of the relationship between them, the kings of Malacca favoured the people of Pahang against the Siamese, and that this was also a reason for their disagreement.

They also say that it was about the tin districts which are on the Kedah side, and which were originally under Kedah, and were taken over by Malacca; and they quarrelled for all these reasons, and they say that the chief reason was the revolt against subjection. After this the Siamese sailed against Malacca, and the Siamese were routed by the Malays, and (they say) that the *Lasamane* [Laksamana] was the captain—who has therefore been held in great honour ever since.

The Siamese trade in China—six or seven junks a year. They trade with Sunda and Palembang . . . and other islands. They trade with Cambodia and Champa and Cochin China . . . and with Burma . . . and . . . [Chiengmai] on the main land, when they are at peace.

On the Tenasserim side Siam also trades with Pase, Pedir, with Kedah, with Pegu, with Bengal; and the Gujaratees come to its port every year. They trade richly outside and liberally inside the country, but they are great tyrants.

(CAMBODIA)

Leaving Siam on the way to China along the sea-coast, is the kingdom of Cambodia, which is bounded along the said way by *Champa*. The said king is a heathen and knightly. This country extends far into the hinterland. He is at war with the people of Burma and with Siam, and sometimes with *Champa,* and he does not obey anyone. The people of Cambodia are warlike.

The land of Cambodia possesses many rivers. There are many lancharas [sailboats] on them, which sail to the coast of Siam on the Lakon side, and they often form into armadas against friends and foes (?). The land of Cambodia produces quantities of food-stuffs. It is a country with many horses and elephants.

The land of Cambodia produces quantities of rice and good meat, fish and wines of its own kind; and this country has gold; it has lac, many elephants' tusks, dried fish, rice.

Fine white cloths from Bengal, a little pepper, cloves, vermilion, quicksilver, liquid storax [medicine], red beads.

In this country the lords burn themselves on the death of the king—as do the king's wives and the other women on the death of their husbands. And they go shorn around their ears as a sign of elegance.

(COCHIN CHINA)

The king of Cochin China is king of a larger and richer country than *Champa*. The kingdom is between *Champa* and China. He is a powerful warrior in the land. He has a great many lancharas and thirty or forty junks. The country contains large navigable rivers. There are no settlers by them; near the sea (there are) many. His country extends a long way inland. In Malacca his country is called Cochin China. . . .

The king is a heathen, and so are all his people. They are not friendly to Moors. They do not sail to Malacca, but to China and to *Champa*. They are a very weak people on the sea; all their achievement is on land. They have great lords. This king is joined to the king of China by marriages; and as this king does not make war with China, he always has an ambassador at the king of China's court, even though the king of Cochin China be unwilling, or though it breed discontent in him, because he is his vassal. . . . Cochin China is a land of many horses.

This king is much given to war, and he has countless musketeers, and small bombards. A very great deal of powder is used in his country, both in war and in all his feasts and amusements by day and night. All the lords and important people in his kingdom employ it like this. Powder is used every day in rockets and all other pleasurable exercises, as we shall see in the merchandise which is of value there.

Chiefly gold and silver, much more than in *Champa;* the calambac [fragrant wood] is not so much as in *Champa.* They have porcelain and pottery—some of great value—and these go from there to China to be sold. They have better, bigger and wider and finer taffeta of all kinds than there is anywhere else here and in our (countries). They have the best raw (?) silks in colours, which are in great abundance here, and all that they have in this way is fine and perfect, without the falseness that things from other places have, and also seed pearls and not much.

At the head of the merchandise appreciated in Cochin China is sulphur, and (they would take) twenty junks of this if they would send them as many as these; and sulphur from China is greatly valued. A very great deal comes to Malacca from the islands of Solor beyond Java . . . and from here it goes to Cochin China.

A large quantity of saltpetre is also of value, and a large quantity comes there from China, and it is all sold there. Rubies, diamonds, sapphires and all other fine precious stones are of value, and some opium, but little, a little pepper, and so with the other things that are of value in China. Liquid storax is of fair value.

They rarely come to Malacca in their junks. They go to China, to Canton . . . which is a large city, to join up with the

Chinese (?); then they come for merchandise with the Chinese in their junks, and the chief thing they bring (to Malacca) is gold and silver and things they buy in China.

The money they use for buying food is the cash from China, and for merchandise gold and silver.

(PHILIPPINES)

The *Luçōes* [people of Luzon] are about ten days' sail beyond Borneo. They are nearly all heathen; they have no king, but they are ruled by groups of elders. They are a robust people, little thought of in Malacca. They have two or three junks, at the most. They take the merchandise to Borneo and from there they come to Malacca.

The Borneans go to the lands of the *Luçōes* to buy gold, and foodstuffs as well, and the gold which they bring to Malacca is from the *Luçōes* and from the surrounding islands which are countless; and they all have more or less trade with one another. And the gold of these islands where they trade is of a low quality —indeed very low quality.

The *Luçōes* have in their country plenty of foodstuffs, and wax and honey; and they take the same merchandise from here as the Borneans take. They are almost one people; and in Malacca there is no division between them. They never used to be in Malacca as they are now; but the *Tomunguo* [regent] whom the Governor of India appointed here was already beginning to gather many of them together, and they were already building many houses and shops. They are a useful people; they are hard-working.

7

First European Glimpses of Mindanao and the Visayan Islands

Antonio Pigafetta (1491?–1536?), a Venetian nobleman, joined the Magellan expedition (1519–1522) with the permission of the King of Spain, Charles V. Not only did Pigafetta write the only first-hand account of this pioneering voyage around the world, but he also produced the first Western eyewitness report of the Philippine Islands. He made the following observations during his travels to Mindanao and the Visayan Islands in 1521.

In the midst of that archipelago, at a distance of eighteen leguas from the island of Zzubu [Cebu], at the head of the other island called Bohol, we burned the ship "Conceptione," for too few men of us were left (to work it). We stowed the best of its contents in the other two ships, and then laid our course toward the south southwest, coasting along the island called Panilongon, where black men like those in Etiopia live. Then we came to a large island (Mindanao), whose king [datu] in order to make peace with us, drew blood from his left hand marking his body, face, and the tip of his tongue with it as a token of the closest friendship, and we did the same. I went ashore alone with the king in order to see that island. We had no sooner entered a river than many fishermen offered fish to the king. Then the king removed the cloths which covered his privies, as did some of his chiefs; and began to row while singing past many dwellings which were upon the river. Two hours after nightfall we reached the king's house. The distance from the beginning of the river

Antonio Pigafetta, *Magellan's Voyage Around the World,* trans. James A. Robertson (Cleveland, Ohio: A. H. Clark, 1906), Vol. II, pp. 13, 17, 19, 21, 25.

where our ships were to the king's house was two leguas. When we entered the house, we came upon many torches of cane and palm leaves.... Until the supper was brought in, the king with two of his chiefs and two of his beautiful women drank the contents of a large jar of palm wine without eating anything. I, excusing myself as I had supped, would only drink but once.... Then the supper, which consisted of rice and very salt fish, and was contained in porcelain dishes, was brought in. They ate their rice as if it were bread, and cook it after the following manner. They first put in an earthenware jar like our jars, a large leaf which lines all of the jar. Then they add the water and the rice, and after covering it allow it to boil until the rice becomes as hard as bread, when it is taken out in pieces. Rice is cooked in the same way throughout those districts. When we had eaten, the king had a reed mat and another of palm leaves, and a leaf pillow brought in so that I might sleep on them. The king and his two women went to sleep in a separate place, while I slept with one of his chiefs. When day came and until the dinner was brought in, I walked about that island. I saw many articles of gold in those houses but little food. After that we dined on rice and fish, and at the conclusion of dinner, I asked the king by signs whether I could see the queen. He replied that he was willing, and we went together to the summit of a lofty hill, where the queen's house was located. When I entered the house, I made a bow to the queen, and she did the same to me, whereupon I sat down beside her. She was making a sleeping mat of palm leaves. In the house there was hanging a number of porcelain jars and four metal gongs—one of which was larger than the second, while the other two were still smaller-for playing upon. There were many male and female slaves who served her. Those houses are constructed like those already mentioned. Having taken our leave, we returned to the king's house, where the king had us immediately served with refreshments of sugarcane.... The afternoon having waned, I desired to return to the ships. The king and the other chief men wished to accompany me, and therefore we went in the same balanghai [native boat]. As we were returning along the river, I saw on the summit of a hill at the right, three men suspended from one tree, the branches of which had been cut away. I asked the king what was the reason for that, and he replied that they were malefactors and robbers. Those people go naked as do the others above mentioned. The king's name is Raia Calanao. The harbor is an excellent one. Rice, ginger, swine, goats, fowls, and other things are to be found there. . . . It is fifty leguas from Zzubu, and is called Chipit [on northeastern Mindanao]. Two days' journey thence to the north-west is found a large island called Lozon [Luzon], where six or eight junks belonging to the Lequian people [from the Ryukyu islands] go yearly.

Leaving there and laying our course west southwest, we cast anchor at an island not very large and almost uninhabited. The people of that island are Moros and were banished from an island called Burne [Brunei]. They go naked as do the others. They have blowpipes and small quivers at their side, full of arrows and a poisonous herb. They have daggers whose hafts are adorned with gold and precious gems, spears, bucklers, and small cuirasses of buffalo horn. They called us holy beings. Little food was to be found in that island, but (there were) immense trees. . . .

About twenty-five leguas to the west northwest from the above island we found a large island, where rice, ginger, swine, goats, fowls, figs one-half braza [fathom] long and as thick as the arm (i.e. bananas) (they are excellent; and certain others are one palmo [eight inches] and less in length, and are much better than all the others), cocoanuts, camotes [sweet potatoes] . . . , sugar-cane and roots resembling turnips in taste, are found. Rice is cooked there under the fire in bamboos or in wood; and it lasts better than that cooked in earthen pots. We called that land the land of promise, because we suffered great hunger before we found it. We were often on the point of abandoning the ships and going ashore in order that we might not die of hunger. The king made peace with us by gashing himself slightly in the breast with one of our knives, and upon bleeding, touching the tip of his tongue and his forehead in token of the truest peace, and we did the same. . . . (It is called) Pulaoan [Palawan].

Those people of Pulaoan go naked as do the others. Almost all of them cultivate their fields. They have blowpipes with thick wooden arrows more than one palmo long, with harpoon points, and others tipped with fishbones, and poisoned with an herb; while others are tipped with points of bamboo like harpoons and are poisoned. At the end of the arrow they attach a little piece of soft wood, instead of feathers. At the end of their blowpipes they fasten a bit of iron like a spear head; and when they have shot all their arrows they fight with that. They place a value on brass rings and chains, bells, knives, and still more on copper wire for binding their fishhooks. They have large and very tame cocks, which they do not eat because of a certain veneration that they have for them. Sometimes they make them fight with one another, and each one puts up a certain amount on his cock, and the prize goes to him whose cock is the victor. They have distilled rice wine which is stronger and better than that made from the palm.

PART II

Indigenous Accounts

THIS PART CONTAINS the other major source of information on early Southeast Asia—native writings. Unlike the Chinese and European reporters in the foregoing section, the Southeast Asian authors do not seem primarily concerned with descriptions of the world of fact. Rather, they tend to convey an ideal, or idealized, way of life. Their most important function is to inform us about the cultural environment in which they lived and the ways and values of that environment. Virtually all of them focused their attention on the royal courts, which were not only centers of terrestrial authority, but above all magico-religious microcosmic copies of the universe as well.

This preoccupation with royalty reveals itself most clearly in the documents about kingdoms where Indian culture had its greatest influence. Many of these realms were located in interior, lowland, wet-rice-growing regions. The function and role of the king is the dominant theme in the oath of allegiance to Sūryavarman I of Angkor, the Shwegugyi Pagoda Inscription of Pagan, the Rām Khamhāēng Inscription of Sukhothai, as well as the excerpts from the Javanese *Nagarakertagama* and the Burmese *Glass Palace Chronicle* (Documents 8, 9, 11, 12, and 18). Unquestionably, these five documents show that

29

absolute kingship was widespread geographically in Southeast Asia over a long period of time.

Not all kingship in Southeast Asia was absolute in nature, however. Whether the "Indianized" monarchy was subject to at least a measure of ecclesiastical censure, if not control, is a tantalizing question raised in the passages from the *Pararaton* from thirteenth-century Java (Document 10). A later Javanese document raises the problem of religion and politics in another context, Islamic (Document 15). And the Pagan Inscription (Document 9) clearly shows the importance of religious piety in a Buddhist realm.

But there were other types of principalities, mostly located on the coasts, seaward-looking and based economically not on sedentary peasantries but on trade and commerce. In such environments, kingly absolutism flourished less. Even though in style and ceremony the monarch might approximate his landlocked cousins, as is suggested in the *Sejarah Melayu* (Document 14), the matter-of-factness with which the Achehnese chronicler tells of the fate of the rulers in that northernmost part of Sumatra is a clear indication of the very real power possessed by the "aristocracy" of the coastal sultanate (Document 16). The *An-nam chi-luoc* describes yet another type of political authority, the "Sinicized" monarchy of Vietnam, in which the king depended for his strength upon the goodwill and recognition of the Chinese emperor (Document 13).

All the preceding documents tell much about the nature of kingship in various parts of Southeast Asia over an impressively long span of time. Yet, too few of them examine the day-to-day mechanics of government, the tissues that hold these political communities together. Even the detailed accounts in the *Sejarah Melayu*, though refreshingly concrete, concern the elaborate proceedings at the court itself, not how that court actually administered its territory. None the less, ordinary administrative functions had to be performed even by the most exalted and "other-worldly" states; if nothing else, taxes had to be collected to permit their functioning. It is for this reason that the systematic survey in the Burmese "Domesday Book" constitutes such an important supplementary source for this section (Document 17).

Finally, another aspect of political reality, the conduct of war, is taken up in the *Babad Tanah Djawi* in the account of the Javanese siege of Batavia (Document 15).

8

The Oath of Allegiance to a Khmer Sovereign

Lawrence Palmer Briggs writes, "Having subdued all the [Khmer] Empire, Sūryavarman I [1002–1011] called on all the officials to come to the Royal Palace and to take the oath of allegiance to him. Eight inscriptions, in Khmer, containing the oath, are found on the pillars of the Gopura of the Royal Palace, in which about 4,000 names may be counted. Here is the oath" (The Ancient Khmer Empire, p. 151).

In 933c* (A.D. 1011)... August-September... This is the oath which we, belonging to the body of *Tamvrac* (guard) of the first (second, third, or fourth) category, swear, all, without exception, cutting our hands, offering our lives and our devotion gratefully, without fault, to H. M. Srī Sūryavarmadeva, who has been in complete enjoyment of sovereignty since 924c* (A.D. 1002), in the presence of the sacred fire, of the holy jewel, the brahmans and the *ācāryas* [teachers]. We will not revere another king, we shall never be hostile (to our king), and will not be accomplices of any enemy, we will not try to harm him in any way. All actions which are the fruit of our thankful devotion to H. M. Srī Sūryavarmadeva, we pledge ourselves to perform them. If there is war, we promise to fight and to risk life, with all our soul, in devotion towards our King. If there is no war and we die by suicide or sudden death, may we obtain the recompense of people devoted to their masters. If our existence remains at the service of His Majesty up to our death, we will perform our task with devotion to the King, whatever may be the time and circumstances of our

Lawrence Palmer Briggs, *The Ancient Khmer Empire* (Philadelphia, Pa.: The American Philosophical Society, 1951), p. 151. By permission of The American Philosophical Society.

* The designation "c" means that the date in this inscription was reckoned in the Śaka system of computations, introduced into Indochina from India about the fifth century.

death. If His Majesty orders us to go far away, to obtain information on any matter, we will try to learn the thing in detail and each of us to keep this promise in whatever concerns us. If all of us who are here in person do not keep this oath with regard to His Majesty, may He still reign long, we ask that He inflict on us royal punishment of all sorts. If we hide ourselves in order not to keep this oath strictly, may we be reborn in the thirty-second hell as long as the sun and the moon shall last. If we fulfil this promise without fault, may His Majesty give orders for the maintenance of the pious foundations of our country and for the sustenance of our families, because we are devoted to our master, His Majesty, Sūryavarmadeva, who has enjoyed complete sovereignty since 924 śaka (A.D. 1002); and may we obtain the recompense of people devoted to our masters, in this and the other world.

9

Theravada Kingship in Pagan

> *The Shwegugyi Pagoda Inscription, the last part of which is here transliterated and translated, was found at Shwegugyi Pagoda, Pagan, and printed in Burmese characters. It was in Pali verse of great poetical merit. The inscription, dated 503 B.E. (A.D. 1141), was set up by the famous Pagan King Alaung-sithu, also known as Lansu I (A.D. 1112–1187), a monarch presented as the prototype of a saintly Theravada Buddhist ruler. Gordon H. Luce has put his translation into blank verse.*

By this my gift, whatever boon I seek,
It is the best of boons, to profit all;
By this abundant merit I desire
Here nor hereafter no angelic pomp
Of Brahma, Suras, Maras; nor the state

Gordon H. Luce, trans., "The Shwegugyi Pagoda Inscription," *Journal of the Burma Research Society*, Vol. X (1920), pp. 72–74. By permission of the Burma Research Society.

And splendours of a monarch; nay, not even
To be the pupil of the Conqueror.
But I would build a causeway sheer athwart
The river of Samsara, and all folk
Would speed across thereby until they reach
The Blessed City. I myself would cross
And drag the drowning over. Ay, myself
Tamed, I would tame the wilful; comforted,
Comfort the timid; wakened, wake the asleep;
Cool, cool the burning; freed, set free the bound.
Tranquil and led by the good doctrines I
Would hatred calm. The three immoral states,
Greed, hate, delusion, rooted all in self,
O may they die, whenever born in me!
Won not by oppression may my wealth remain
Nor yield to fire nor robbers, life by life,
Longings of sense for all delicious things,
Sounds, sights, and touches, odours, relishes,
Pregnant of immorality, begone!
May sense of shame, fear of reproach (declared
By the Sun's kinsman Guardians of the world)
Cover me always. As the best of men
Forsaking worldly wealth and worthless fame
Fled, for he saw their meaning—so would I
All worldly wealth forsaking draw me near
Religion and the threefold course ensue.

　　I would fulfil hereafter, great and small,
Those rules the Teacher gave for our behoof.
Borne through the element the spotless moon
Outdazzles all the constellated stars:
So I delighting in the Master's lore,
The saint's religion, virtuously yoked,
Would shine among disciples. I would know
Sutta [passages or chapters in Buddhist scriptures],
And Abhidhamma [transcendent doctrine],

Vinaya [rules of the order],
The Master's mind, his ninefold doctrine fraught
With words and meaning. By the Conqueror's Law
I would do good to others and myself.
What the Great Sage forbids I would not do.
May I be always conscious and aware
Of kindness done me. Union of ill friends
be far from me. Beholding man's distress
I would put forth mine energies and save
Men, spirits, worlds, from seas of endless change.

By merit of this act I would behold
Mettayya, captain of the world, endued
With two and thirty emblems, where he walks
Enhaloed on a rainbow pathway fair
Like Mèru King of mountains, and sets free
Samsara's captives by his holy words.
There might I hear good Law, and bending low
Offer the four things needful to the Lord
And all his monks, till clad in virtues eight,
Informed by such a Teacher, I become
A Buddha in the eyes of spirits and men.

Tathagata by men and spirits adored
Shines bright in virtues manifold; so I
Would shine and be by men and spirits adored.

The twenty four infinities he saved
From bondage of Samsara, compassed all
A Buddha's duties, mercifully taught
The fourscore and four thousand points of Law
For good of all hereafter, blazed abroad
With his disciples like a ball of fire,
Set forth the transcience of conditioned things,
Wrecking the notion of dull fools who deemed
"All things are stable," and at last attained
The city of Nirvana, safe retreat

Where is not age nor death.—O might I thus
Compass a Buddha's duties and attain
That city lavish of abounding bliss! . . .

This is the stone inscription of the king
Siritibhuvanadiccapavaradhammaraja
Brave, thoughtful, keen, and prudent, who ensues
The elements of wisdom, the Three Gems
Adores, and seeks Nirvana. He began
On Sunday the fourth waxing of Kason
In the five hundred and third year to build
At an auspicious moment. That same year
On Thursday eleventh waning of Nadaw
'Twas done, with effigies of guardian spirits.

10
The Magical World of a Javanese Chronicle

*The following excerpts are taken from one of the earliest
Javanese writings of quasi-historical content, the* Pararaton
*(Book of Kings). It tells the life story of King Angrok of
Singosari and his successors, as well as the beginnings of the
realm of Majapahit, the last of the great Hindu-Javanese empires, in the fourteenth century. The episodes reproduced here
recount the struggle between Singosari and Kediri, though
very likely without any intention of conveying historically
accurate data.*

King Angrok then set out for Mount Leyar, and when Black
Wednesday . . . had arrived, he went to the meeting place. He hid
in a refuse pile, where he was covered with grass. . . . Then the
seven sounds let themselves be heard: rolling peals of thunder and

J. L. A. Brandes, ed. and trans., *Pararaton (Ken Arok) of het Boek der
Koningen van Tumapel en van Majapahit* (The Hague: Nijhoff; Batavia:
Albrecht, 1920), pp. 55–56, 62–64. English translation from the Dutch by
Margaret W. Broekhuysen. By permission of Martinus Nijhoff.

short ones, earthquake, lightning, heat-lightning, whirlwinds and wind storms; rain fell at a time when it could not be expected; rainbows were constantly to be seen in the east and at the same time in the west, and after that, without any lapse of time, voices were heard, noisy and boisterous . . . "Who shall make the island of Java firm and strong? . . ." and "Who is to become king of the island of Java?" they [the gods] asked. Bhatâra Guru [the god Brahma] answered: "Know, ye gods, that I have a son who was born a human being of a woman of Pangkur; he shall make the land of Java firm and strong." Now King Angrok emerged from the refuse pile, and when they had seen him the gods approved of him and confirmed that his name as king was to be Bhatâra Guru; thus they decided amidst loud and general acclaim.

Now it so happened that as by God's direction, the king of Daha [Kediri], Prince Dangdang Gendis, said to the clergy in Daha, "Clerical gentlemen of the Çivaite doctrine as well as of the Buddhist doctrine, how is it that you do not make a *sembah* [obeisance] before me, since I am Bhatâra Guru?" The clergy, not a single one of those from Kediri excepted, answered, "Lord, there has never been a cleric yet who made a *sembah* before a king." Thus all of them spoke. Dangdang Gendis said, "Well, if this has not been done so far, you make a *sembah* before me now; if you do not realize my magic power I shall give you proof of it." He placed a spear with its stem into the ground, sat down on its point and said, "See, you gentlemen of the clergy, what magic power I possess," and he showed himself with four arms and three eyes, just like Bhatâra Guru. But the clergy of Daha, now obliged to make a *sembah* before him, still did not wish to perform it, but resisted and fled to King Angrok at Tumapel. This was the beginning of Tumapel's withdrawal from [the control of] Daha.

Then King Angrok was recognized as the Prince of Tumapel which is another name for the realm of Singosari, and homage was paid him by the Çivaite and Buddhist clergy from Daha. . . .

. . . Singosari was very prosperous, [and] general peace was enjoyed there.

After the rumor had been spreading for some time that Ken

Angrok had become king, a report was brought to Prince Dang-dang Gendis that [Ken Angrok] wanted to march against Daha. Prince Dangdang Gendis said, "Who could destroy my country? Only if Bhatâra Guru himself were to descend from heaven, it could perhaps be achieved." This was reported to Ken Angrok. The latter then said, "Approve, gentlemen of the clergy, that I assume the name of Bhatâra Guru." He then called himself thus with their approval. Then he attacked Daha. Prince Dangdang Gendis . . . said, "Woe unto me, for Angrok has the favor and the support of the gods." Between the armies of Tumapel and Daha it came to an encounter . . . an equally heroic battle was waged on both sides and considerable losses were sustained, but Daha lost. A younger brother of Dangdang Gendis, the *ksatriya* [warrior] Raden Mahisa walungan, died a hero's death, as did one of his *mantris* [ministers] called Gubar Baleman; they were both overpowered by the people of Tumapel, but the fighting was furi-ous. . . . When their chief had been overpowered, the Daha army took to flight; they fled like bees who swarm off . . . it was impossi-ble to remedy the situation. Then also Prince Dangdang Gendis withdrew from battle; he fled to a place of worship and hanged himself up in the air with [his] horse and shield bearer [and] with [his] *payung* [umbrella] bearer and *sirih* [betel] bearer, his water page and the page who carried his mat. . . . And when his wives, Dewi Amisani, Dewi Hasin and Dewi Paya, learned that Prince Dangdang had lost the battle and was adrift in the realm of the gods, they, too, disappeared with the *kraton* [royal palace] and everything else, becoming invisible.

Ken Angrok's victory over Daha was complete. Now that he had vanquished his adversary he returned to Tumapel, having changed the state of affairs on Java.

11

The Rām Khamhāēng Inscription

> *The Sukhothai kingdom flourished in what is now central Thailand from the middle of the thirteenth century until it was overshadowed by the new Thai kingdom established at Ayuthia a century later. Rām Khamāēng was the greatest of the Sukhōthai kings, and after his death in 1317, the kingdom declined rapidly. The following passage is taken from the Rām Khamhāēng Inscription of 1292.*

My father was named Sī Intharāthit, my mother was named Nāng Süang, and my elder brother was named Bān Müang. There were five of us children, born of the same womb: three boys and two girls. Our first-born brother died when he was still small. When I had grown up and attained the age of nineteen, Khun Sām Chon, chieftain of the city of Chōt, came to attack the city of Tāk. My father went into combat on Khun Sām Chon's left. Khun Sām Chon made a massive charge; my father's men fled and dispersed in a complete rout. But as for me, I did not take flight. I mounted the elephant "Anekphon" and I urged it on before my father. I engaged Khun Sām Chon in an elephant duel: I rode in quickly against Khun Sām Chon's elephant, "Māt Müang," and put him out of combat. Khun Sām Chon fled. Then my father conferred upon me the title Phra Rām Khamhāēng because I had defeated Khun Sām Chon's elephant.

During my father's life I served my father and I served my mother. If I got a bit of meat or a bit of fish, I took it to my father; if I had any sort of fruit, sour or sweet, anything delicious and good to eat, I took it to my father. If I went on an elephant hunt and caught any, I took them to my father. If I went to attack

Georges Coedès, *Recueil des inscriptions du Siam* (Bangkok: Bangkok Times Press, 1924), pp. 44–48 [French version]; pp. 55–58 [Thai version]. English translation by Thomas W. Gething.

a village or a city and collected some elephants and ivory, men and women, silver and gold, I gave them to my father. Then my father died—only my elder brother remained. I continued to serve my elder brother, as I had served my father. When my elder brother died the kingdom in its entirety fell to me.

During the life of King Rām Khamhāēng this city of Sukhōthai has prospered. In the water there are fish; in the fields there is rice. The lord of the country levies no tolls on his subjects as they travel along the roads, driving cattle to go trade, riding horses to go sell. Whoever desires to trade elephants does so; whoever desires to trade horses, does so; whoever desires to trade silver or gold does so. If a commoner, a nobleman, a chieftain, or anyone at all falls ill, dies, and disappears, the house of his ancestors, his clothing, his elephants, his family, his granaries, his servants, his ancestors' areca and betel orchards are transmitted as a whole to his children. If some commoners, nobles, or chieftains are in disagreements, (the king) makes a true inquiry, and settles the matter for his subjects in an equitable fashion; he is never in collusion with practicers of thievery and deceit. If he sees someone else's wealth he does not interfere. He accords aid and assistance to whomever comes riding an elephant to find him, requesting his protection for their country. If they have neither elephants nor horses, neither male servants nor female, neither silver nor gold, he gives them some and helps them to lay out their own villages and cities. If he captures some enemy soldiers or warriors he neither kills them nor beats them. In the (palace) doorway a bell is suspended —if an inhabitant of the kingdom has any complaint or any matter which irritates his stomach and torments his mind, and he desires to expose it to the king it is not difficult: he has only to ring the bell that the king has hung there. Every time that King Rām Khamhāēng hears the sound of the bell he questions (the complainant) on his case and settles it in an equitable fashion. Consequently the inhabitants of this city of Sukhōthai admire him.

There are areca and betel orchards in all areas of the country. There are many coconut orchards in this country, many jack-fruit orchards in this country, many mango orchards in this country,

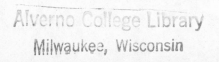

and many tamarind orchards in this country. Whoever starts an orchard is permitted to do so by the king. In the middle of this city of Sukhōthai there is a marvelous well, with clean and delicious water like that of the Mekong during the dry season. Around this city of Sukhōthai there is a triple rampart measuring 3,400 wā (= 20,400 feet). The inhabitants of this city of Sukhōthai are fond of almsgiving, charity, and the maintenance of the precepts. King Rām Khamhāēng, the sovereign of this city of Sukhōthai, the princes as well as the princesses, the men as well as the women, the nobles, and the chieftains, all without exception, without distinction of rank or of sex, practice the religion of the Buddha with devotion and observe the precepts during the rainy season retreat.[1] At the close of the rainy season, the Kathin ceremonies take place, lasting one month.[2] At the time of the Kathin ceremonies offerings are made of stacks[3] of cowry shells, of stacks of areca, of stacks of flowers, of cushions, and of pillows. The Kathin offerings made each year amount to two million. Chanting, (the people) go off to perform the Kathin ceremonies at the monastery of the Aranyik, and when they return to the city the procession forms at the monastery of the Aranyik and stretches as far as the border of the plain. There everyone prostrates himself, while lutes and guitars, hymns and songs resound. Whoever wants to play, plays; whoever wants to laugh, laughs; whoever wants to sing, sings. This city of Sukhōthai has four main gates—each year a great crowd presses against them in order to enter and see the king light candles and gesture with the fire. And this city of Sukhōthai is filled with people to the bursting point!

In the middle of this city of Sukhōthai there are sanctuaries. There are some gold statues of the Buddha, there is a statue of the Buddha which measures eighteen cubits, there are some statues of the Buddha which are large, and there are some which are of

[1] The period when young men in particular temporarily join the monkhood.

[2] An observance involving the weaving, sewing, and offering of new vestments to the monks.

[3] It should be noted that the containers for these stacks are of a special conical shape.

moderate size. There are large sanctuaries, and there are moderate-sized ones; there are monks, both theras and mahātheras.[4]

To the west of this city of Sukhōthai is found the monastery of the Aranyik. King Rām Khamhāēng founded it and offered it to the patriarch, to the chief monk, a scholar who has studied completely the Three Scriptures and who is more learned than all the other monks of the country, having come from Nakhōn Sī Thammarāt. In the middle of this monastery of the Aranyik there is a great, lofty sanctuary, beautifuly situated, which contains a statue of the standing Buddha, with a height of eighteen cubits.

To the east of this city of Sukhōthai there are sanctuaries and monks. There is a large lake, areca and betel orchards, dry fields and paddy fields, hamlets, large and small villages, and there are mango and tamarind orchards. All of this is as beautiful as in a picture.

To the north of this city of Sukhōthai there is a market, there is a Buddha image, and there is a prāsāt.[5] There are areca and jackfruit orchards, dry fields and paddy fields, hamlets, and villages large and small.

To the south of this city of Sukhōthai there are hermitages and sanctuaries, and monks who live there. There is a dam; coconut, jack-fruit, mango, and areca orchards; and there is a spring from a hillside. There is Phra Khaphung—the spirit and divinity of this mountain, superior to all the spirits of the country. If a prince, whoever he might be, governing this city of Sukhōthai deals with (the spirit's) cult in a dignified way and presents ritual offerings to him, then this country is stable and prospers; but if (the sovereign) does not follow the prescribed cult and does not present ritual offerings properly then the spirit of this mountain no longer protects nor respects this country which [consequently] falls into decadence.

In 1214, the year of the dragon, King Rām Khamhāēng, sovereign of the cities of Sī Satchanālay and Sukhōthai, who had had

[4] Two categories of senior monks.
[5] An official governmental building. Perhaps a castle or temple in Khmer style.

sugar palms planted fourteen years earlier, ordered some artisans to cut a stone slab (a dais) and place it in the midst of these sugar palms. On the day of the new moon, the eighth day of the waxing moon, the day of the full moon, and the eighth day of the waning moon a group of monks, theras and mahātheras, mounts and sits down upon that dais, and recites the Law there to the laity and to the assembly of the faithful, observing the precepts. On days other than those for the recitation of the Law, King Rām Khamhāēng, sovereign of the cities of Sī Satchanālay and Sukhōthai, mounts the stone dais and sits down, and together with the assembled nobles and dignitaries governs the affairs of the country. On the days of the new moon and the full moon the king has the white elephant Rūcāsī harnessed . . . and the right (and left) tusks all decorated with gold and ivory. The king then mounts it and goes to make his devotions to the venerable chief of the Aranyik, then he returns.

There is an inscription in the city of Chaliang situated near the holy Sī Ratanathāt relic. (Also) there is an inscription in the cave called "King's Cave" situated on the bank of the Samphāy River. (In addition) there is an inscription in the Ratanathān Cave.

In the middle of the sugar palm (grove) there are two pavilions: One is called "The Pavilion of the Gold Buddha," the other "The Pavilion of the Buddha." The stone dais is called Manangkhasilā-bāt—it has been put in that place so that everyone can see (it).

King Rām Khamhāēng, the son of King Sī Intharāthit, is the sovereign of the cities of Sī Satchanālay and Sukhōthai, as well as the Mā, the Kāw, the Lao, and the Thai who live under the celestial vault. Both the river Thai of the U River and the river people of the Khōng have submitted and pay him homage. In 1207, the year of the pig, he had the holy relics exhumed so that everyone could contemplate them. He worshiped and venerated these relics for one month and six days, then he had them buried in the middle of the city of Sī Satchanālay; there he erected a cetiya (or "chadi") which was finished in six years; he surrounded the Great Relic with a stone fort which was built in three years.

This alphabet for writing Thai did not exist previously. In 1205, the year of the goat, King Rām Khamhāēng with great concentration and meditation devised this alphabet for writing Thai, and this Thai alphabet exists because the king developed it.

This king, Rām Khamhāēng, seeks to be the chief and the sovereign of all the Thai. He is the master who instructs all of the Thai so that they may know about merit and the true Law. Among all the men who live in this Thai country none is his equal in knowledge and in wisdom, in bravery and in hardiness, in force and in energy. He has vanquished the crowd of his enemies who possess broad cities and numerous elephants. . . .

12

The Legendary Grandeur of Majapahit

> *The following document reproduces in free translation the first five stanzas of Canto 83 of the rhymed panegyric* Nagarakertagama, *composed by the court poet, Prapança, in 1365, to glorify King Hayam Wuruk of Majapahit (1350–1389). It was accidentally found in 1894 during the Dutch occupation of the island of Lombok, and has since that time become an invaluable, though controversial, source for Javanese historiography.*

Such is the excellence of His Majesty the Prince who reigns at Majapahit as absolute monarch. He is praised like the moon in autumn, since he fills all the world with joy. The evil-doers are

The English translation, prepared by Professor A. A. Teeuw of Leiden University, is based on Theodore G. Th. Pigeaud's version, *Java in the 14th Century: A Study in Cultural History* (The Hague: Nijhoff, 1960), Vol. III, pp. 97–98. An earlier Dutch translation by H. Kern was also used, especially for the explanatory note: "De Nagarakertagama. Oudjavaansch lofdicht op Koning Hayam Wuruk van Majapahit," in *Verspreide Geschriften* (The Hague: Nijhoff, 1918), Vol. VIII, pp. 95–97. By permission of Koninklijk Institut voor de Taal-, Ldan- en Volkenkunde.

like the red lotus, the good—who love him wholeheartedly—are like the white lotus.[1] His retinue, treasures, chariots, elephants, horses, etc., are (immeasurable) like the sea.

The land of Java is becoming more and more famous for its blessed state throughout the world. "Only Jambudwipa [India] and Java," so people say, "are mentioned for their superiority, good countries as they are, because of the multitude of men experienced in the doctrine . . . ; whatever 'work' turns up, they are very able to handle it."

First comes the Illustrious Brahmaraja, the excellent brahmin, an irreproachable, great poet and expert of the religious traditions; he has complete knowledge of the speculative as well as all the other philosophies, . . . the system of dialectical (logic), etc. And (then) the holy Bhamana, very pious, virtuous, experienced in the Vedas and the six pure activities. And also the Illustrious Vishnu, powerful in Samaveda incantations, with which he aims to increase the country's prosperity.

For this reason all kinds of people have continually come from other countries, in multitudes. There are Jambudwipa, Kamboja [Cambodia], China, Yawana [Annam], Champa, Karnataka [in South China], etc., Goda [Gaur] and Siam—these are the places whence they come from. They come by ship with numerous merchants; monks and brahmins are the principal ones who as they come are regaled and are well pleased during their stay.

And in each month of *Phalguna* [February-March] His Majesty the Prince is honored and celebrated in his residence. Then the high state officials come from all over Java, the heads of districts, and the judicial officials . . . ; also the (people from) other islands, Bali, etc., all come with tributes so numerous that they are uninterrupted, to honor him. Traders and merchants fill the market in dense crowds with all their wares in great variety.

---

[1] Red lotuses open during the day but close at night, while white lotuses open at night, displaying themselves to the moon. Evil-doers shrink from the moon, i.e., from the prince.

13
Sino-Vietnamese Relations

> *The* An-nam chi-luoc, *or* Essay on Annam, *was written in the fourteenth century by a Vietnamese named Le-Tac. Composed originally in Chinese, the* Essay *offers a compendium of information, historical and geographical, about Vietnam prior to 1339. Below are two documents taken from this work. Part I is a letter from General Le-Hoan, posing as the legal heir to the Vietnamese throne, seeking investiture in 980 from the Sung emperor. Part II consists of a letter of congratulations from the ruler of Annam to Emperor Ch'engtsung (Timur Khan) of the Yüan Dynasty upon the latter's ascent to the throne of China in 1295. It expresses in barely veiled terms the fervent hope that the new emperor would inaugurate a peaceful reign, in sharp contrast to that of his immediate predecessor, Kublai Khan, who had invaded and devastated the coastal regions of Vietnam without succeeding in subjugating the country.*

[I]

My ancestors have received favors from the Imperial Court. Living in a far away country at a corner of the sea [Annam], they have been granted the seals of investiture for that barbarian area and have always paid to the Imperial ministers the tribute and respect they owed. But recently our House has been little favored by Heaven; however, the death of our ancestors has not prevented us from promptly delivering the tribute. . . .

But now the leadership of the country is in dispute and investiture has not yet been conferred by China.

My father, Pou-ling, and my eldest brother, Lienn, formerly

Le-Tac, *An-nam chi-luoc* (Hué: University of Hué, 1961), pp. 134–135, 126 [Vietnamese version]; pp. 83–84, 80 [Chinese version]. English translation by T. B. Lam. By permission of the University of Hué.

enjoyed the favors of the Empire [China], which endowed them with the titles and functions of office. They zealously and humbly protected their country, neither daring to appear lazy or negligent, nor having the opportunity to win great merit in the eyes of the Emperor for performing their duty. Suddenly events changed our fate. While still in mourning clothes, the good fortune of our House began to crumble. The mandarins [officials], the army, the people, the court elders, and members of my family, all who came to my home to mourn, entreated with me to lead the army. I refused repeatedly, but they begged me with all the more force and insistence. It seemed to me that to appeal to the Emperor would delay a solution even more. My people, who are wild mountain-dwellers [i.e., uncultured, rather than real inhabitants of the mountains], have unpleasant and violent customs; they are a people who live in caves and have disorderly and impetuous habits. I feared that trouble would arise if I did not yield to their wishes. From prudence I therefore assumed power temporarily, assuming the role of supervisor of the military affairs of the country. I hope that His Majesty will place my country among His other tributary states by granting me the investiture. He will instill peace in the heart of His little servant by allowing me to govern the patrimony my parents left me. Then shall I administer my barbarian and remote people. I shall take care of the land of the bronze column. I shall send tributes of precious stones and ivory, and before the Golden Gate I shall express my loyalty.

May His Majesty only have indulgence for my shortcomings and may He grant me His pardon.

[II]

The Dragon flies in the heavens; new life has come to the Golden Throne. Many embassies have flocked to the Palace to express their sincere congratulations.

One man has ascended the Throne and ten thousand kingdoms are at peace. In great awe I observe that, under His Imperial Majesty's rule, peace and culture flourish within the Empire. His benevolence and virtue permeate the lands beyond the sea as they do at home. Always faithful to the kingly way, He embraces with the same kindness far lands and near. He lays aside military concerns and promotes cultural achievements. He restrains the ardor of His troops and puts an end to all combat. He enlarges His own indulgence and benevolence. He illuminates the virtue and merit of His Ancestors. The sound of thunder has ceased; it has changed into a rain of Imperial blessings. His investiture of tributary kings has been granted with a heavenly generosity. For the people it is a true rebirth, for the Universe a true springtime. I and my people happily live in peace and rejoice to hear the news of His ascendance to the Throne. My glances are directed toward the Northern sky; my heart also turns toward the extreme North, toward the Imperial Dwelling. From this country so remote in the South which I govern, I wish and desire that the longevity of the Emperor may be as great as the mountains of the South are high.

14
Pomp and Circumstance at the Malaccan Court

Perhaps the best known account of life and customs in fifteenth-century Malacca is the Sejarah Melayu (History of Malaya), *or, inexactly translated,* The Malay Annals. *While much of this literary work was written in about 1535, it was compiled, with later additions, by one of the descendants of the Malacca* Bendaharas *(Viziers) in about 1612. Although the* Annals *are historically inaccurate, particularly with reference to specific dates and events, they do present a graphic description of the social climate of Malay Malacca.*

When the king gave audience, principal ministers, senior war-chiefs and courtiers occupied the body of the hall of audience:

C. C. Brown, trans., "The Sejarah Melayu" (Malay Annals), *Journal of the Malayan Branch of the Royal Asiatic Society,* Vol. XXV, pts. 2 and 3 (October, 1952), pp. 54–55, 57–59. By permission of the Malaysian Branch of the Royal Asiatic Society.

princes of the blood royal occupied the gallery on the left and knights the gallery on the right: heralds and young war-chiefs stood at the foot of the dais bearing swords, the heralds on the left being descendants of ministers eligible for the appointments of Bendahara, Treasurer or Temenggong, and the chief herald on the right being descended from a war-chief eligible for the appointment of Laksamana [Admiral] or Sri Bija 'diraja: he who bore the title of Sang Guna was Laksamana-designate: and he who bore the title of Tun Pikrama was Bendahara-designate. At the paying of homage the chief of the four or five heralds took precedence of the courtiers who sat in the body of the audience hall and of everybody except principal ministers. Cham shipmasters of high standing and young nobles (who held no office) occupied the balcony of the hall of audience. The Raja's personal requisites, such as his cuspidore, goglet and fan (and shield and bow) were put in the passage, though the betel set was placed in the gallery. The sword of state was borne by the Laksamana or the Sri Bija 'diraja, whose position was in the gallery on the left. If envoys came, the letter was received by the chief herald on the right, while the Raja's reply to the envoys was announced by the herald on the left. The ceremonial prescribed for the arrival or departure of envoys was that a large tray and a salver were to be brought in by a slave from the palace; and the large tray was to be received by the herald on the right and set down as near to the throne as the Bendahara's seat. The shoulder-cloth and the salver were given to the bearer of the letter. If it was a letter from Pasai . . . it was received with full ceremonial equipment . . . , trumpet, kettledrums and two white umbrellas side by side and the elephant was brought alongside one end of the audience hall. For the Rajas of those two countries (Pasai and Haru) were regarded as equal (to the Raja of Malaka in greatness) and however they (the three) might stand to each other in point of age, it was "greetings" (not "obeisance") they sent to each other. To a letter from any other state less respect was accorded, only the big drum, the clarionet and a yellow umbrella being used. The letter was borne on elephant or on horseback as circumstances might demand, and it was taken down (from the elephant or horse as the case might be) outside the outer gate. If (it was a letter from) a Raja of some standing, the trumpet might be used and two umbrellas, one white and one yellow, and the elephant made to kneel outside the inner gate. . . .

If the Raja left the palace, on days that the litter was used the Treasurer held the head of the litter, with the Temenggong holding it on the right and the Laksamana on the left, while the rear end of the litter was held by the two chief heralds. Opposite the chain near the Raja's knee the Laksamana (sic) held the litter on the right and the Sri Bija 'diraja held it on the left. Heralds and war-chiefs marched in front of the litter, each carrying the insignia assigned to him. The regalia were borne by men marching in front of the Raja; and there was one state lance on the right and one on the left. In front of the Raja went . . . the heralds bearing the swords of state (and?) in front (of them?) those who carried spears. What was called the "standard" was in front of the Raja, as were the drums and kettledrums on the Raja's right and the trumpets on his left. For in a procession the right ranked higher than the left, whereas in regard to seating the left ranked higher than the right, which applied also when an audience was given. (In a procession), of those who marched in front of the Raja it was those of lower rank who led the way. In front of all went the lances and pennons followed by the musical instruments of every description. Behind the Raja went the Bendahara with the chief ministers and judges. . . .

For the festival of the night of the twenty-seventh of Ramdlan [Ramadan, month of fasting] the following was the procedure. While it was still day the (?Laksamana took the) royal praying-mat in procession to the mosque, the Temenggong sitting on the head of the elephant. To the mosque too were taken the betel bowl and other personal requisites of the Raja, and the drums(?). Then when night had fallen, the Raja proceeded to the mosque, the ceremonial being as for days when the Raja assisted at the evening prayers, followed by the special vespers of the fasting month. When the prayers were concluded, the Raja returned to the palace. On the following day the Laksamana took the royal turban in procession, for it was the custom that Malay Rajas going to the mosque should wear the turban and the cassock. These were the privilege of royalty and could not be worn for weddings except by special permission of the Raja, when they might be worn. . . .

Throughout his long reign Sultan Muhammad Shah [Sri Maharaja, A.D. 1424–1444] shewed a high degree of justice in his treatment of his subjects, and Malaka became a great city. Strangers flocked thither and its territory stretched westward as far as Bruas Ujong and eastward as far as Trengganu Ujong Karang. And from below the wind to above the wind Malaka became famous as a very great city, the Raja of which was sprung from the line of Sultan Iskandar Dzu'l-Karnain: so much so that princes from all countries came to present themselves before Sultan Muhammad Shah, who treated them with due respect bestowing upon them robes of honour of the highest distinction together with rich presents of jewels, gold and silver.

God knoweth the truth. To him do we return.

15
Javanese History According to the Babad Tanah Djawi

The Babad Tanah Djawi *was a panegyrical history of the traditional Javanese type, apparently first composed during the reign of Sultan Agung of Mataram (1613–1645). The Dutch historian, B. H. M. Vlekke, writes that "recent studies have shown that this history of Mataram has been revised and enlarged several times during the seventeenth and eighteenth centuries. . . . [It] recapitulates the older history of Java in such a way as to . . . prove, not only that Mataram was a continuation of the last Hindu-Javanese kingdom, but also that its ruling family was directly descended from that of Majapahit" (Nusantara: A History of Indonesia, rev. ed., pp. 145–146. Cited by permission of W. van Hoeve, The Hague). The first excerpt is of importance to the history of Islam*

in Java; the second illustrates the Javanese interpretation of
the struggle against the Dutch East India Company.

[I]

Prince Bra-Widjaja heard the report that many people submitted to Giri. *Patih* [chief minister] Gadjah-Mada was then sent
out to march against Giri. The Giri population got into a tumult
and fled to the palace. At that moment the *sunan* [ruler] of Giri
was busy writing and became frightened when he heard of the
enemy's arrival, who intended to destroy Giri. He threw down
the pen with which he was writing and prayed to God. The
thrown-down pen changed into a *kris* [dagger], which of its own
accord proceeded to the attack. Many from Madja-Pait died in
battle. Those remaining fled back to Madja-Pait.

After the enemy's retreat the *kris* returned of its own accord,
spattered with blood, and placed itself before the priest-prince.
At the sight of the blood-spattered *kris* the priest-prince prayed
that his wrong behavior might be forgiven him. . . .

After some time the *sunan* of Giri died and was succeeded by
his grandson, under the name *Sunan* Parapèn. At that time prince
Bra-Widjaja had received word of the death of the *sunan* of Giri
and of the succession of the latter's grandson, called Parapèn.

Prince Bra-Widjaja then commanded the chief minister
Gadjah-Mada and his sons to conquer Giri. *Sunan* Parapèn
marched against the Madja-Pait army, but was defeated. Then he
fled to the seashore. After that the capital of Giri was completely
reduced to ashes. The sons of the prince of Madja-Pait went to
the grave of the deceased previous *sunan*. The guardians of the
grave were two cripples. The command was given to excavate the
grave. The soldiers of Madja-Pait started digging at once, but

I. J. Meinsma, ed., *Babad Tanah Djawi in proza Javaansche geschiedenis
loopende tot het jaar 1647 der Javaansche jaartelling,* trans. W. L. Olthof
(The Hague: Nijhoff, 1941), pp. 28–31, 141–143. English translation from
the Dutch by Margaret W. Broekhuysen. By permission of Koninklijk
Instituut voor de Taal-, en Volkenkunde.

fell to the ground. Then the two cripples were told to dig. If they did not want to do it they were threatened that the *krisses* would be tried on them. So the two cripples quickly started digging. The soil in the grave had been excavated and the boards with which the coffin had been closed were taken away. A countless number of bees came out of the grave, flew upward and filled the atmosphere. It made a sound as if the sky fell down. Then they attacked the Madja-Pait troops, all of which fled to save their lives. Arrived in the capital Madja-Pait, they were still pursued by the bees. Prince Bra-Widjaja and his army left the capital and fled far away, because they did not consider themselves capable of resisting the attack of the bees. After this the bees returned to their own country.

When the bees weren't there anymore Prince Bra-Widjaja returned with his army to the capital Madja-Pait and did not intend to do any more harm to the *sunan* of Giri.

The two cripples who guarded the grave were cured of their disease. They hastened to inform the *sunan* of Giri, who had fled to the seashore, and told him that the enemies had been wiped out because they had been attacked by bees, and they reported the cause of their [own] cure.

When *Sunan* Parapèn heard the news from the two men he returned to Giri. After some time Giri was again just as prosperous as before and had no more enemies.

At that time Prince Bra-Widjaja again remembered his son, who had settled in Bintara. He asked the *adipati* [lord] of Terung: "What is this about your brother, that he has not paid his respects for such a˜long time? He had made an agreement with me that he would come and pay his respects every year, and it is three years already that he has not been here. Does he so much enjoy luxury that he does not think of me anymore? Therefore go to Bintara now, and ask your brother what is the reason that he does not come to pay me his respects."

The *adipati* of Terung immediately went on his way to Bintara with ten thousand men. He visited his brother and conveyed the king's commands. Radèn Patah answered that he was very grateful for Prince Bra-Widjaja's affection. Now the reason that he did not come to pay his respects was the interdiction of his religion which does not permit a Muslim to pay his respects to an infidel. It had been prophesied that Bintara would become an independent realm, from whence the conversion of the Javanese to Islam would begin.

The *adipati* of Terung understood the intention and was afraid to return to Madja-Pait, unless his brother accompanied him. Then he kept after Radèn Patah so that his plans would soon be carried out. The *adipati* of Terung was to assist him in battle. Then they agreed to bring together all Islamites with their weapons in Bintara. The Regent of Madura, Arja Tédja of Tuban, the Regent of Sura-Pringga and the priest-prince of Giri assembled with their troops in Bintara. Also the *walis* [holy men] and the faithful assembled. Then all departed for Madja-Pait. The number of troops was countless. Then the capital of Madja-Pait was enclosed. Many inhabitants of Madja-Pait submitted to the *adipati* of Bintara and no one dared to combat him. The *adipati* of Bintara and the *adipati* of Terung then went on the *alun-alun* [square in front of the royal palace]. The *adipati* of Bintara sat down on the throne on the *pagelaran* [mat], while the warriors were respectfully squatting before him.

Patih Gadjah-Mada informed the prince that they were being attacked by the enemy from Bintara, and that at that moment the *adipati* of Bintara was seated on the throne on the *pagelaran*.

When Prince Bra-Widjaja heard that his son was on the *pagelaren,* he climbed on the *panggungan* [lookout tower] in order to look at his child. After Prince Bra-Widjaja had seen his son he ascended to heaven with the troops that had remained faithful to their prince. At the same moment that Prince Bra-Widjaja ascended to heaven, something like a ball of fire was seen which came from the palace of Madja-Pait, looked like a bolt of lightning and sounded like terrible thunder, and which fell down in Bintara.

The *adipati* of Bintara then entered the palace. He was very surprised not to meet anyone. In his heart he wept. Then he left the *kraton* [palace] and returned to Bintara with his collaborators and their troops. On their arrival at Bintara the *sunan* of Ampel-Denta said to the *adipati* of Bintara that he should become prince of Madja-Pait, which was due him as his heritage. But the *sunan* of Giri first had to be prince of Madja-Pait for forty days as a means to make the traces left by an infidel prince disappear. This advice was followed.

When the forty days had passed the *sunan* of Giri transferred the princely dignity to Radèn Patah. Radèn Patah now was prince of Demak and reigned over the whole of Java under the name Sénapati Djimbun Ngabd'ur-Rahman Panembahan Palémbang Saidin Panatâgama. Ki Wana-Pala was elevated to *patih* under the name *patih* Mangu-Rat. The Javanese were all submissive and embraced Islam. Then it was agreed to erect a mosque in Demak. The *walis* divided the work among themselves. All were ready. Only the *sunan* of Kali-Djaga lagged behind; his task was not yet done because he was just making a pilgrimage to Pemantingan. On his return in Demak the mosque would be erected. *Sunan* Kali-Djaga hastily collected a few chips which he tied together. That same night the bunch of chips changed into a column. The next day, on the first of the month Dulkangidah, the mosque was erected, in the year 1428. The longitudinal direction of the mosque pointed to the *kaäba* in Mecca. . . .

[II]

The servants of the Company noticed that they would be attacked and arranged their soldiers, to the number of four brigades, in battle-array. The cannon were set up in a quadrangle. Grenades and bombs were being readied. And the commanders of the Dutch who were armed with guns were, for each company: a captain, two lieutenants and an ensign. . . . Everything was arranged. They had divided the activities among themselves and had promised to assist each other to the end. They stood arranged on the square with their backs to each other. Those who stood in the southwest got most of the reinforcements. . . . Everywhere one saw the gleaming of the firelocks. . . .

Pangéran [Prince] Mandura-Radja gave the signal for the attack. The Javanese marched forward shouting, in closed ranks, intending to storm the fortress. The Dutch repelled the attack. The cannon were fired repeatedly with a sound as if the mountains collapsed. Cannon balls fell like rain, there were some like lumps of fire. Many Javanese died and fell down all around, many also were wounded. Some crawled on hands and feet. Those who continued to advance were annihilated. Then they retreated, overtaken by the darkness. The next morning *Pangéran* Mandura-Radja commanded the (troops) who were on the ships to attack the fortress simultaneously with the land-forces. So (they), too, fired their cannon from the ships. The artillery battle was violent. From the Dutchmen one captain, two lieutenants and three corporals had died in battle, whereas many of the soldiers were wounded and the number of the dead could not be counted.

Panembahan [another lordly honorific] Purbaja had already arrived by sea off Djakarta and began the battle with the Dutch who were on the ships. The Dutch were defeated and fled. The *panembahan* then went ashore in order to land. There the artillery battle was still raging and the thunder of the cannon sounded from all sides. The Dutch trained their cannon on that of the Javanese and hit the mouth so that a piece broke off. Many ships were destroyed. Many Javanese died in battle. And also many Dutchmen died. The Dutch already began to lack gunpowder and cannon-balls. And then it happened that they used muck to shoot with. Many Javanese had to vomit because they were hit by the muck. As regards *Panembahan* Purbaja, he had come to the center of the battlefield with only three followers. The Dutch noticed that *Panembahan* Purbaja arrived and had learned that he had extraordinary magical power and could fly. So they overwhelmed him with gunfire. They shot at him from [in? tr.] the air, but the *panembahan* was not hit and smoking at his ease he approached the fortress. The *panembahan* spoke in a loud voice: "Well, you Dutchmen, how you are shooting at me! Do you trust the solidity of your fortress?" And while speaking he pointed to the fortress. In the walls of the Dutch fortress a hole the size of a man appeared. When the *panembahan* had thus given proof of his magic power he returned to his ship in order to go back to Mataram. However, *Panagéran* Mandura-Radja continued the battle with great force, but he could not get closer to the fortress because he could not stand the stench of the muck. His clothes were all dirtied by the muck. The number of those who died in battle . . . was larger than that of the survivors and no one could continue because of the stench of the muck. After they had retreated from the battle they all sat down in the river to clean themselves.

At that time the battle had lasted already a considerable time. The surviving Javanese deserted partly to return to their land, completely undone by fright. And of the Dutch, three brigades had died in battle and only one brigade survived. All trembled with fear and none of them thought they would escape with their lives.

Panembahan Purbaja had returned to Mataram, paid his respects to the Prince, and told his experiences from beginning to end, saying: "As regards the war in Djakarta, it would be best to stop it, since the Dutch have only come here to trade."

His Highness the Sultan was pleased to hear this and spoke calmly: "Uncle, you are right. Besides, it is Allah's established will that at a later time the Dutch will help my descendants who will be princes. When one of my descendants later on will suffer defeat in battle, the Dutch will surely help him. My only reason for starting this war was that I wanted to set an example, so that in the future they would be afraid. . . ."

When the Dutch learned that the Mataramese army had retreated they were all very happy. They all surmised that this had happened according to the will of His Highness the Sultan, who had pardoned the Dutch. The Dutch then sent an envoy to Mataram in order to offer a large number of different gifts.

16
Kingship in Acheh

The following excerpt is taken from the Hikayat Acheh (The History of Acheh) *which, its title notwithstanding, was in fact a panegyric of this North Sumatran sultanate's best-known ruler, Sultan Iskandar Muda (1607–1636). It was very likely composed during his life time. The passages below refer, of course, to two of Iskandar Muda's predecessors, and they provide an interesting insight into the nature of kingship in that part of Indonesia.*

After the kingdom of Acheh Dar as-Salam with all its subject territories had been handed over to Sultan Seri 'Alam, he acted very generously. He would sit in state in the Friday annex every day from midday until almost sunset.

Then the various rulers, judges, important chiefs, lawyers, courtiers ... and all their attendants would stand paying homage in the courtyard of the royal palace. While they were all paying homage, Sultan Seri 'Alam would endow them with gold, silver and luxurious clothing, according to each one's rank. Thus they became rich because of the Sultan's many gifts.

Now it happened at that time that the Maharaja, the judges and prominent persons did not approve of this behavior in the Sultan. So one day the various rulers, judges and important chiefs gathered. Maharaja and Malik az-Zahir said, "Oh chiefs, why are we permitting our lord to behave like this, daily taking money from the State treasury and throwing it away on the undeserving? After all we do not know what may happen next. Only Almighty God knows that. If at any time an enemy should come from the west

Teuku Iskandar, ed., "De Hikajat Atjeh," *Verhandelingen van het Koninklijk Instituut voor de Taal-, Lande en Volkenkunde*, Vol. XXVI (The Hague: Nijhoff, 1958), pp. 95–98. English translation by R. O. Robson. By permission of Koninklijk Instituut voor de Taal-, Land- en Volkenkunde.

or the east, what could we spend on the military operations, because our lord Sultan Seri 'Alam is as lacking in wisdom and counsel as a queen? We and the chiefs, on the other hand, must think hard before all the money has been used up on gifts for the rulers and chiefs in the land of Fansur [present-day Barus, a town on the east coast of Sumatra]." The chiefs and prominent men replied, "We and the senior chiefs are all in the same boat, and if it sinks we shall all go down together. So we will agree to whatever you both propose." Maharaja and Malik az-Zahir said, "It is our opinion that we should depose our lord Seri 'Alam, and that we should transfer the kingship to our lord Sultan Zainal, son of Sultan Ghori, in order to preserve the continuity of succession in the kingdom of Acheh Dar as-Salam from the line of Sayyid al-Marhum."

Then Sultan Seri 'Alam was deposed and Sultan Zainal was installed.

The former had occupied the throne for one year before passing away. He passed away in the year 995 (A.H.) [A.D. 1617]. In that same year Sultan Zainal-'Abidin, son of Sultan Ghori who was a brother of Sultan 'Ali Ri'ayat Shah, was installed. . . .

After the kingdom of Acheh Dar as-Salam and all its subject territories had been handed over to Sultan Zainal-'Abidin, he would always go out on to the arena and would have rutting elephants as well as ones which were not rutting charge each other, and as a result several people were gored to death by them, and the Bunga Setangkai palace was rammed and then collapsed in ruins together with its annexes. He pitted very small elephants against each other, and had buffaloes and bullocks fight, as well as rams. When he had the buffaloes fight a number of people were either killed, had bones broken, or were crippled or blinded. He would order men to beat each other and to duel with staves and shields, and would order Achehnese champion fencers to compete with Indian ones, so that several of the Achehnese and Indian fencers were killed and some were wounded. And he would order men to wrestle and to throw each other to the ground and to practice *penchak* (a dance consisting of a stylized representation of the

movements of combat). He would order men from Pigu to do war-
dances, and some had their faces smashed and their cheeks blown
out. He would order men from Tiku and men from Periaman to
fight with the long *kris* (Indonesian dagger), and some of them
were injured. He would order Javanese to fight with lances, to
perform *wayang* (shadow-theatre) and play the *gender* (Javanese
xylophone-like musical instrument), and others to dance Javanese
dances and Sundanese dances, and he would always be ordering
people to sing, play the *harbab* (violin-like instrument), *kechapi*
(four-stringed lute) and *bangsi* (flageolet), and give all kinds of
performances.

This was the Sultan's constant practice: whether he was seated
in state in the Bunga Setangkai palace in the square or was leaving
for the river, if he saw a buffalo or bullock he ordered it to be
cut down, and if he saw a sheep or a goat he would order that
too to be killed. He would even instruct the Bujang Khayyal Allah
and Bujang Dandani to catch a dog if it should happen to pass by
while the Sultan was sitting in state in the Bunga Setangkai palace.
But if they could not find it, he would become angry with them
as a result; when he ordered people to hunt deer or pigs, if these
should escape from anyone's reach this person would also fall
into disfavor.

If the Sultan were holding audience in a certain place all the
chiefs were instructed to sit in homage in the hot sun or in the
rain without distinction between the good or the evil.

If the Sultan should spur on his horse when setting out and the
chiefs could not keep up with it and were left behind, then they
too would incur his wrath.

When the chiefs noticed these habits of the Sultan, and observed
that they were growing worse day by day, they said to each other,
"What should we do about our lord, for if his oppression of us
is like this while he is still young, what will it be like when he
is older? According to us, if he continues to be ruler everything
will certainly fall in ruins about our ears." Then Sharif al-Muluk
Maharaja Lela said, "If that is how it is, it would be best for us
to depose our lord the Sultan."

After the chiefs had reached agreement on this matter, one evening the Sultan summoned persons to recite texts in praise of God, and the chiefs were summoned along with them. On that occasion they were reciting texts in the Friday annex. The Sultan was then put on an elephant and was taken to Makota 'Alam. When he arrived at Makota 'Alam ... [where he was done to death][1] ... the Sultan had occupied the throne for two years when he passed away. He passed away in the year 997 (A.H.) [A.D. 1619]. In that same year Sultan 'Ala ad-Din Ri'ayat Shah Marhum Sayyid al-Mukkamil was installed.

17

From the Domesday Book of Burma

> *Perhaps the greatest ruler of the Konbaung dynasty of Burma was Bodawpaya (1782–1819). Quite early in his reign, he ordered a survey of the population, property, and tax system in his kingdom, and followed it up by another, between 1801 and 1803. Many of the original records have been preserved in native paper books called* parabaiks *or in palm leaf manuscripts, including the following two selections concerning towns in the Pegu area of southern Burma.*

THE RECORD OF PAUNGLIN TOWNSHIP 1164

The record of the examination of Nga Tha Ye, birthday-6-, aged 28, the Thugyi [headman] of Paunglin Township one of the 32 provinces of Hanthawaddy, taken on the ninth waxing of Tawthalin 1164 [1803].*

[1] There is a lacuna in the text, but the Sultan's assassination can be inferred from the context.

J. S. Furnivall, trans., "Some Historical Documents," *The Journal of the Burma Research Society,* Vol. VIII (1918), pp. 41–42; Vol. IX (1919), pp. 33–36. By permission of the Burma Research Society.

* The inconsistencies of spelling and punctuation in this document are in the original translation.

Sir:

During the reign of the King who came to Hanthawaddy my great-grand-father Nga Kyaw Gaing was the governor in charge; after my great-grand-father Nga Kyaw Gaing was no more my grand-father Nga Kyaw Hla was governor in charge; after the death of my grand-father Nga Myat Le was the governor in charge; after Nga Myat Le was no more as I was the son who inherited his dignities I continue to govern and am in charge. . . .

Within these boundaries by four and eight these are Mahura Uyin village, Kya-in village, Akhabyin village, Wanetchaung village, Malit village, Moksonyaungbin village, and Sitpin village. In these villages there are 93 house-holds of the cultivating class; 24 households of rent paying Yuns; 102 of revenue paying Yabeins; the total of the three is 219; there are 349 households of their offspring; the total of the two is 768 *(sic)*. There are 537 adult males and 528 adult females 131 boys and 106 girls, the total of them all is 1302.

The revenue paying Karens and Sabeins nine tolas and two *mat* of revenue and supplementary revenue four tolas and two *mat;* the two together making fourteen tolas and two *mat (sic)* a head. They have to bring it in and pay it to the Akunwun and the revenue clerks.

The cultivators within the area have to measure out, bring in and pay 55 baskets of paddy to the Keepers of the Royal Granary for each yoke of buffalo. The fisheries lakes streams channels dykes and ditches are not worth taxing, no revenue has to be paid in on their account, the inhabitants can make their living from them.

Written by Nga Tha.

THE RECORD OF RAMMAWADI TOWNSHIP 1164

The Record of the examination of Nga Ke, born on the first day of the week aged 37, the Thugyi of Rammawadi Township taken on the second waning of the second Waso in the year 1164.

I am the ruler and guardian. . . .

Within these boundaries thus laid down by four and eight there are the Myoma Town, the villages of Tonywa, Kyaukchauk, Kandaing, Kandaw, Kinywa, Zinchaung, Minyat, Thin chaung, Alèchaung, Yanbauk, Yanbet, Yanbye-ngè, Ledaung, Thandaung, Nyaungbinhla, Mayasein, Kunchaung-Kyunthaya, Myochaung, Kyauklet, in all twenty small villages. . . .

In the Myoma there is the Tadaung daw pagoda, the benefaction of Sandathu Dhamma Raza, the glebe land is worked by 18 pairs of buffalo, 525 Arakanese quarter baskets are sown; in Kandaing village is the Namwedaw Pagoda the benefaction of Sandathu Dhamma Raza Saw Maing gyi, the glebe lands are in Yanbauk village so much as 7 pairs of buffalo work 210 Arakanese quarter baskets being sown, and in Kandaing village so much as one pair works 30 quarter baskets being sown; in Kankaw village there is the Kankawdaw pagoda the benefaction of Sandathu Dhamma Raza, the glebe land is in Alèchaung so much as two pairs of buffalo work, 60 quarter baskets being sown; in Alèchaung village there is the Na on daw Pagoda, the benefaction of Si taya min, the glebe land is in the Thabyu valley of Mayasein, so much as four pairs of buffalo work, 120 quarter baskets being sown; in Lèdaung village is the Li-yo-daw pagoda, the benefaction of Sandathu Dhamma Raza, the glebe land is so much as 5 pairs of buffalo work, 170 quarter baskets being sown, and in Yan bet village so much as one pair of buffalo works 40 quarter baskets being sown; in Hon village there is the Pakondaw Pagoda, the benefaction of Sandathu Dhamma Raza, the glebe land is so much as 16 pairs of buffalo work and 655 quarter baskets are sown; in the same village is the Letthandaw pagoda the benefaction of Sandathu Dhamma Raza, the glebe land is so much as four pairs of buffalo work, and 120 quarter baskets are sown; in the same village is the San U Thein Pagoda, the benefaction of Sandathu Dhamma Raza, the glebe land is so much as 18 pairs of buffalo work, 240 quarter baskets being sown; in the Yanbye nge village is the Hnokkandaw pagoda the benefaction of Sandathu Dhamma Raza, the glebe land is so much as seven pairs of buffalo work, 280 quarter baskets being sown; in the same village is Seitsadaw kyaung the benefaction of Sandathu Dhamma Raza the glebe land is so much as eight pairs of buffalo work, 320 quarter baskets being sown; in the same village are the Thein and Pagoda the benefaction of the Queen of Sandathu Dhamma Raza and her sister Mi Nyo Hla, the glebe land is so much as 12 pairs of buffalo work and 360 quarter baskets are sown.

In Yan the village there is Athèdaw Pagoda, the benefaction of Sandathu Dhamma Raza, the glebe land is so much as 20 pairs of buffalo work and 620 quarter baskets is sown, and in Yan bauk village so much as 6 pairs of buffaloes work, 240 quarter baskets being sown and in the Myoma there is glebe land of the same pagoda so much as 2 pairs work, 60 quarter baskets being sown; in Kinywa village there is Kamokdaw pagoda the benefaction of Sandathu Dhamma Raza, the glebe land is so much as a pair of buffalo work, 30 baskets being sown. So far as Nyaungbin hla pyi village there is the Teikdaw pagoda the benefaction of Sandathu Dhamma Raza glebe land being so much as a pair of buffalo works and 30 quarter baskets being sown. In all there are 11 Pagodas, three *theins* [ordination hall] and one monastery, the glebe land attaching to all three kinds being so much as 133 pairs of buffalo work, and 4110 quarter baskets of paddy being sown. Formerly during the time of the Lord of Arakan no revenue was collected from the glebe lands of the monasteries and pagodas and none was paid in.

As for the revenue that was regularly paid the people of the 18 villages paid as bee's wax revenue 720 pieces of silver, for places where there was water 470 pieces of silver, at the Thingyan Festival 417 pieces of silver, at the close of [Buddhist] *Lent* 368 pieces of silver; the company of iron workers 800 pieces of silver as revenue on the iron; the *kalas* [Indians] who lived in the town pay as poll tax 750 pieces of silver and at the time of their festival 118 pieces, the kala fisherman pay as revenue for their nets 55 pieces of silver, it is the custom to present the revenue once every year to the Lord of Arakan.

It is the custom to collect one piece of silver on every hundred "tas" [cubit] of bamboo of high land worked by the villagers a distance of ten bamboos, twelve cubits long in length and three bamboos in breadth being reckoned as a hundred "tas." From the people who work san hemp gardens it is the custom to collect one piece of silver on every 100 "tas," 10 lengths of bamboo, 12 cubits long in length and 10 lengths in breadth being reckoned as 100 "tas." It is the custom to collect revenue from people who cultivate tobacco in gardens 10 lengths of bamboo 12 cubits long, in length and 10 broad. The tobacco is strung on split bamboo and one piece of silver is charged for each bamboo according to the number of strings.

From unmarried sons and unmarried daughters if they ought to possess a house it is the custom to collect two pieces of flat copper wire and pay it to the person appointed by the Lord of Arakan. It is the custom for cultivators of paddy fields to pay on each pair of buffalo, five baskets of paddy in Arakan quarter baskets and measure and deliver it at the royal granary. It is the custom for the people to make over to the Lord of Arakan 29 boats of 7 fathoms, 8 fathoms and 9 fathoms length.

The people who put their trust in persons possessed by nats [spirits] and in offerings to nats can follow their religion if they wish to do so. No revenue has to be paid on sheds erected in honour of nats.

No revenue had to be paid to the Viceroy Nara thaman kyaw wun sin whom His Majesty appointed when he took possession of the township on its passing his dominion in the year 46 [1782]. Thereafter revenue had to be paid to the successors of Viceroys and Akunwuns [revenue officer] and officials at their assessment. According to the custom of the writing the villagers and residents of the town pay for every household one "mat" of silver, a revenue of 1944 pieces of silver, at the New Year festival of the Thingyan every household pays one "mat" of silver, 1208 pieces of silver, for wax every household pays one "mat" of silver, 1350 pieces of silver; the company of iron workers pay revenue on the iron at 2 pieces of silver for every household, 1559 pieces of silver; the kalas who dwell in the Town and the Province pay a poll tax of three pieces of silver, 749 pieces of silver, and at their time of festival one piece for every two houses; 124 pieces of silver, those of them who are fishermen for every company pay one piece of silver, a revenue of 74 pieces of silver. The cultivators of bran gardens who live in the village of the province pay one piece of silver for every 30 "ta" of bamboos; a plot in length ten bamboos 12 cubits long and in breadth three bamboos is reckoned as 30 "tas;" the san hemp cultivators pay one piece of silver on every 1000 "tas," in length 10 bamboos 12 cubits long and in breadth 10 bamboos. The cultivators of tobacco for a plot 10 bamboos 12 cubits long in length and three bamboos in breadth pay one piece of silver for every bamboo, the tobacco being strung on split bamboos, according to the number of pairs of string.

For a son and a daughter who ought to possess a house two flat pieces of copper wire are paid.

The glebe land of monasteries and pagodas pays one piece of silver for every yoke of buffalo working the land on which 40 quarter baskets is sown. The people who trust in persons possessed by nats and offerings to nats if they receive support for the nat has to pay one piece of silver.

When the Viceroy and akunwuns and officials appoint a collector they have to pay.

The cultivators of paddy land for every yoke of buffalo have to pay 3 Burman baskets of paddy and measure it and deliver it in to the royal granary in Ramawadi Town. If the Viceroy or Akunwuns or officials have occasion to use boats the headman of the quarters and the villages have to make boats 7 fathoms, 8 fathoms and 9 fathoms in length and place them at their disposal.

Within the Township of Ramawadi of which I was the true one lord and guardian there is one landing stage and watch posts for vessels to come and go; besides this there is no fishery nor landing stage nor toll booth nor ferry.

This is the deposition of Nga Kè the thugyi of the Township of Ramawadi.

18

The Glass Palace Chronicle

> *King Bagyidaw of Burma (1819–1838) appointed in 1829 a committee of monks, brahmins, and learned ministers to write an official history of the Burmese kings in the form of a chronicle. The authors, writing in the Palace of Glass, drew upon Pali texts, Burmese poetry, chronicles, and inscriptions. The following passage gives a vivid descripton of palace life as it had been and still was in part when* The Glass Palace Chronicle *was compiled.*

Because the king had become a man from the state of an ogre, he was great in wrath, haughtiness, and envy, exceeding covetous and ambitious. He had three thousand concubines and maids of honour. There were thirty chief scribes to examine the lists and registers; they failed not day nor night. The guards of the royal slumbers were staunch and loyal, and guarded day and night at the inner and the outer wall. Thus the king's rule was painful to the palace-women, insomuch that none durst trifle with a single word.

Queen Saw alone was the chief queen. The lesser queens were five: Sawlon, daughter of a master of white magic; Sawnan, daughter of queen Hpwasaw's sister; Shinhpa; Shinmauk; and Shinshwe. These five queens took each their turn to present food before the king.

The king, being one who had received the Lord's prophecy, suffered not from any of the ninety-six diseases, and never so much as sneezed or yawned; and so none was allowed to sneeze or yawn in his presence. If any one happened to sneeze or yawn he beheaded him. One day a young handmaid in the king's pres-

The Glass Palace Chronicle, trans. Pe Maung Tin and G. N. Luce (Oxford: The Clarendon Press, 1923), pp. 167–169. By permission of The Clarendon Press.

ence was exceeding fain to sneeze, and because she could not refrain it, she put her face to a great jar and sneezed, hoping that
the king would not hear. But alas! the sound was louder than if
she had sneezed openly. And the king asked: "What sound is
that?" Queen Saw spake into his ear, saying, "A girl was afraid
to sneeze openly, so she put her face to a great jar and sneezed!"
And he asked again, "How dared she sneeze?" "O king," replied
Queen Saw, "sneezing and yawning are even as the ninety-six
diseases. Only the king is free from diseases and needeth not to
sneeze nor yawn. But all other folk, who are not free from sneezing and yawning, cannot refrain themselves, but sneeze!" "Is it
even so?" quoth the king. "I knew it not ere this, but aye waxed
wroth." And he had great remorse.

Now when the king awoke from slumber his mind was not
loosened until he had thrown and hit his handmaids with aught
that was in his reach. So while he was fast asleep queen Saw removed the weapons that were near him and left only *lompani*
[eggplant] and other fruits. Once when he awoke from sleep he
threw the *lompani* fruit that was near him at a young handmaid;
whereby she swelled at the waist. Therefore the *lompani* fruit was
called *hkayan*.

In the hot season the king loved to sport at splashing water.
He made a great shade from the palace to the river wharf and
walled it in so that men might not see, and built a royal lodge
for security thereby; and taking his queens, concubines, and all
his women he was wont to go along a tunnel of cabins and sport
in the water. One day he whispered a young girl and caused her
to drench queen Sawlon with water, so that her eyes and face
and hair were wringing wet. Sawlon was chafed at heart, and she
put poison in the King's food and said, "Shinmauk, I am not well.
Prithee, take my place and offer the king his food!" And Shinmauk
thought no i!! but offered the food.

Now, just as he was about to eat, a dog below the table sneezed.
Therefore the king ate not but gave it to the dog; and when the
dog ate, that moment he died. "What is this?" cried the king, and
Shinmauk spake into his ear, "Sawlon told me she was ill and

begged me to offer the food in her stead!" So the king called
Sawlon and questioned her and because she could not hide the
matter nor jest it away, she cried, "Thou grandson of a turner!
I have done thee service and thou hast made me great; and now
that I am exalted to this high degree, lo! thou hast whispered a
young girl and she hath drenched me with water in the eyes of all,
so that my clothes and hair were wet! Therefore my heart was
warped and I plotted against thee."

Then the king called a thousand smiths and caused them to
build an iron frame and commanded her to be burnt thereon.
But Sawlon gave abundance of gold and silver to the executioners
that they might not finish the iron frame for seven days. Meanwhile she practiced piety and virtue and hearkened to the Law of
Abhidhamma night and day for full seven days, and told her
beads recalling the merits of the Three Gems, beginning each with
"Such is He . . .," with "Well expounded . . . ," and with "Well accomplished. . . ."

But when the seventh day was come the executioners called her
with fair and seemly words: "Wife of a king! The royal anger is
terrible! Tarry not, but come!" Then, telling her beads as she
recalled the merits of the Three Gems, Sawlon ascended the blaz-
ing iron frame. And lo! the fire, they say, was extinguished thrice.
After the third time she prayed, "May I be burnt and vanish in a
moment! And may the boon I ask be granted!" So she died.

Not long after Sawlon died the king at his hour of sleep raved
and shrieked aloud, "Sawlon, come and watch beside me!" Queen
Saw spake into his ear, "O king, didst thou not put to death thy
slave Sawlon?" But the king's heart was bruised and broken and
he could not sleep. When the elder, the king's chaplain, heard of
it he came and admonished him: "Lo, thou hast put her to death.
It ill beseems thee, O king, to be broken and bruised therefor.
If other kings, thy fellow builders of empire, hear thereof, they
will laugh thee to scorn. Peradventure they who visit thee hereafter will scant thee reverence. Publish not thine heart's remorse,
O king, to all the people. Remember the Law of Right Effort
preached by the Lord Omniscient: 'Strive to avert the spreading

of evil that hath arisen. Strive to avert the arising of evil that hath not arisen. Strive to aid the arising of good that hath not arisen. Strive to aid the spreading of good that hath arisen.' "

So at last the king was filled with patience and control. From that day forward he commanded his uncle Theimmazi saying, "Albeit I am angry, weigh thou and examine every matter. Tarry for a half month, for a decade of days. Let him die thereafter who deserveth to die. Who deserveth not to die, let him go free!" Theimmazi was the younger brother of the king's mother. He had been a monk, but when the king came to the throne he turned layman and received the name Theimmazi.

PART III

The Western Presence, from Periphery to Dominance

THE READINGS in this part, spanning a period of four centuries, demonstrate the changing nature of the Western presence in Southeast Asia. Gradually but relentlessly the European shifted from being an interested observer to acting as a major participant in the Asian scene. The following documents, arranged chronologically, view the Westerner from four different vantages, at the same time revealing much about Southeast Asia as it evolved from an independent to a dependent area.

The European is first seen as a keen observer of the area, often with a substantial interest in the establishment of trade and diplomatic relations. Since these relations almost invariably involved the royal courts, the narrators provide details about kingship missing in the early native chronicles. Three early Dutch voyagers record information about the Portuguese, the court of Mataram and the place of Islam in that kingdom, and seventeenth-century Siam and its flourishing Buddhist monkhood (Documents 20, 26, and 24). Two British observers, John Crawfurd and the well-known governess Anna Leonowens, describe the semi-despotic court of nineteenth-century Siam (Documents 31 and 32). Crawfurd's observations on the Thai social system are especially acute, but his notes on Cochinchina pale before the sympathetic sketch drawn

73

earlier by his compatriot, Sir John Barrow, of Emperor Gia-Long, founder of the Nguyen dynasty of Vietnam (Document 28).

From a second vantage the European appears in the more active role of establishing or attempting to establish spheres of influence in Southeast Asia by peaceful or forceful means. The earliest and most dramatic armed encounter was the Portuguese seizure of Malacca in 1511, recorded by Afonso de Albuquerque, conquering Viceroy of India (Document 19). The Dutch East India Company acquired Jacarta (Batavia) as its center of commercial operations; from small beginnings Batavia soon grew into a dominant port city in insular Southeast Asia (Documents 22 and 25). The setting up of diplomatic relations between Europeans and Southeast Asian potentates is recorded in the documents relating to Mataram, to Burma, and to Kedah in Malaya (Documents 26, 29, 30). The last item shows a native ruler seeking, rather than a European power forcing upon him, protection for his own political purposes. Louis XIV's letter to the king of Tonkin was yet another attempt to further relations, doomed to failure because of the Sun King's insistence on propagating Christianity in Vietnam (Document 21). Only in the Philippines did Christianity spread under the aegis of the Spaniards; some of the means by which they attained success are rather humorously described by a friar in Document 23.

A third vantage presents the European in his position as colonial official and Southeast Asia under the full impact of modern colonialism. From the late nineteenth century on, the Westerner spoke with the voice of authority, often condescending, and the "native" was forced into the background. Where formerly the ruler of Kedah had requested protection, a British official summoned Malay rulers into a Western-conceived federation (Document 35). And where in the seventeenth century the king of

France had deferentially addressed his counterpart in Tonkin, Francis Garnier forcefully argued the case for outright French annexation and retention of Cochinchina (Document 34). But the fullest flavor of modern colonialism in action, of the imperious colonial attitude that pervaded most of Southeast Asia until the onset of the Pacific War, is provided in two gubernatorial speeches, one made in French Indochina and the other in British Burma, and in the short extract from a governmental commission's report in the Netherlands East Indies (Documents 37, 38, and 36).

The final vantage reveals the European in his role of critic of colonialism and recorder of its detrimental effects on the social fabric of indigenous Southeast Asian societies. The two critics represented here both served in the colonial establishments of their respective countries. The first was no less a figure than a Spanish governor-general in the late eighteenth century (Document 27); the other, a middle-rank Dutch official writing eighty years later, became one of the giants of Dutch literature and at the same time a major influence on Dutch colonial policy in the Indies (Document 33). Such criticisms of colonial rule by Europeans, though always exceptional, were certainly not infrequent. But it was only when the main critics ceased to be Westerners that Southeast Asian nationalism was born.

19

The Portuguese Seizure of Malacca

After the conquest of Goa in 1510 and the establishment of Portuguese rule on the Indian subcontinent, Afonso de Albuquerque, viceroy of the new colony, sought for the second time to assert Portuguese supremacy over the Straits of Malacca and the valuable spice trade that flowed from the Straits region. In 1511 Albuquerque's fleet appeared before the great trading center at Malacca. He reportedly gave the following speech to the officers and men of his ships on the eve of the second (and successful) assault of the Muslim fortress.

Sirs, you will have no difficulty in remembering that when we decided upon attacking this city, it was with the determination of building a fortress within it, for so it appeared to all to be necessary, and after having captured it I was unwilling to let slip the possession of it, yet, because ye all advised me to do so, I left it, and withdrew; but being ready, as you see, to put my hands upon it again once more, I learned that you had already changed your opinion: now this cannot be because the Moors have destroyed the best part of us, but on account of my sins, which merit the failure of accomplishing this undertaking in the way that I had desired. And, inasmuch as my will and determination is, as long as I am Governor of India, neither to fight nor to hazard men on land, except in those parts wherein I must build a fortress to maintain them, as I have already told you before this, I desire you earnestly, of your goodness, although you all have already agreed upon what is to be done, to freely give me

The Commentaries of the Great Afonso Dalboquerque, Second Viceroy of India, trans. Walter de Gray Birch (London: Cambridge University Press for The Hakluyt Society, 1880), First Series, No. 62, Vol. III, pp. 115–119. By permission of The Hakluyt Society.

again your opinions in writing as to what I ought to do; for inasmuch as I have to give an account of these matters and a justification of my proceedings to the King D. Manuel, our Lord, I am unwilling to be left alone to bear the blame of them; and although there be many reasons which I could allege in favour of our taking this city and building a fortress therein to maintain possession of it, two only will I mention to you, on this occasion, as tending to point out wherefore you ought not to turn back from what you have agreed upon.

The first is the great service which we shall perform to Our Lord in casting the Moors out of this country, and quenching the fire of this sect of Mafamede so that it may never burst out again hereafter; and I am so sanguine as to hope for this from our undertaking, that if we can only achieve the task before us, it will result in the Moors resigning India altogether to our rule, for the greater part of them—or perhaps all of them—live upon the trade of this country and are become great and rich, and lords of extensive treasures. It is, too, well worthy of belief that as the King of Malaca, who has already once been discomfited and had proof of our strength, with no hope of obtaining any succour from any other quarter—sixteen days having already elapsed since this took place—makes no endeavour to negotiate with us for the security of his estate, Our Lord is blinding his judgement and hardening his heart, and desires the completion of this affair of Malaca: for when we were committing ourselves to the business of cruising in the Straits (of the Red Sea) where the King of Portugal had often ordered me to go (for it was there that His Highness considered we could cut down the commerce which the Moors of Cairo, of Méca, and of Judá, carry on with these parts), Our Lord for his service thought right to lead us hither, for when Malaca is taken the places on the Straits must be shut up, and they will never more be able to introduce their spiceries into those places.

And the other reason is the additional service which we shall render to the King D. Manuel in taking this city, because it is the headquarters of all the spiceries and drugs which the Moors carry every year hence to the Straits without our being able to prevent them from so doing; but if we deprive them of this their ancient market there, there does not remain for them a single port, nor a single situation, so commodious in the whole of these parts, where they can carry on their trade in these things. For after we were in possession of the pepper of Malabar, never more did any reach Cairo, except that which the Moors carried thither from these parts, and forty or fifty ships, which sail hence every year laden with all sorts of spiceries bound to Méca, cannot be stopped without great expence and large fleets, which must necessarily cruise about continually in the offing of Cape Comorim; and the pepper of Malabar, of which they may hope to get some portion because they have the King of Calicut on their side, is in our hands, under the eyes of the Governor of India, from whom the Moors cannot carry off so much with impunity as they hope to do; and I hold it as very certain that if we take this trade of Malaca away out of their hands, Cairo and Méca are entirely ruined, and to Venice will no spiceries be conveyed except that which her merchants go and buy in Portugal.

But if you are of opinion that, because Malaca is a large city and very populous, it will give us much trouble to maintain possession of it, no such doubts as these ought to arise, for when once the city is gained, all the rest of the Kingdom is of so little account that the King has not a single place left where he can rally his forces; and if you dread lest by taking the city we be involved in great expenses, and on account of the season of the year there be no place where our men and our Fleet can be recruited, I trust in God's mercy that when Malaca is held in subjection to our dominion by a strong fortress, provided that the Kings of Portugal appoint thereto those who are well experienced as Governors and Managers of the Revenues, the taxes of the land will pay all the expenses which may arise in the administration of the city; and if the merchants who are wont to resort thither—accustomed as they are to live under the tyrannical yoke of the Malays—experience a taste of our just dealing, truthfulness, frankness, and mildness, and come to know of the instructions of the King D. Manuel, our

Lord, wherein he commands that all his subjects in these parts be very well treated, I venture to affirm that they will all return and take up their abode in the city again, yea, and build the walls of their houses with gold; and all these matters which here I lay before you may be secured to us by this half-turn of the key, which is that we build a fortress in this city of Malaca and sustain it, and that this land be brought under the dominion of the Portuguese, and the King D. Manuel be styled true king thereof, and therefore I desire you of your kindness to consider seriously the enterprise that ye have in hand, and not to leave it to fall to the ground.

20
The First Dutch Voyage to the Indies

The following document represents excerpts from the famous account of the first Dutch voyage to the Indies (1595–1597) under the command of the impetuous Cornelis van Houtman, who was killed in Sumatra on a subsequent voyage. The passages reproduced are from the comprehensive work written by Willem Lodewijcksz and originally published in 1598. They provide an account of the Dutchmen's first impressions of the port and city of Bantam (Banten) in West Java.

HOW WE CAME TO SUNDA HARBOR AND WHAT HAPPENED THERE ON ARRIVAL

Sailing slowly then (because of the unfavorable currents and also the change of wind: for after midnight the wind is from the east until 10.-A.M. and then from the west until evening, which makes it so difficult to pass through the Straits) we came, on

Willem Lodewijcksz, *De eerste schipvaart der Nederlanders naar Oost-Indië onder Cornelis de Houtman 1595–1597*, eds. G. P. Rouffaer and J. W. IJzerman (The Hague: Nijhoff, 1915), Vol. I, pp. 72–77. English translation by Margaret W. Broekhuysen. By permission of the author and publisher.

June 22nd, to Bantam Harbor and the Coast of Sunda, seeing
before us an uninhabited, green, beautiful island which is called
Pulo Panan [Pulau Pandjang, or Long Island] by the Javanese;
it is said to be a long island. To the north of it we saw about 70
small sails, which looked like a forest from afar; these were (as
we were told) all fishing-boats, which made it evident that Bantam
must be a very large, populous town. In a bay of the Java country
we saw a *iunco* [junk], which is a Javanese ship . . . and a canoe
came to us from this ship, but we could not understand what was
said, so they went back to the *iunco* and brought someone who
spoke Portuguese, who asked us where we came from. And when
we asked him to come aboard, he went back to the *iunco,* which
immediately hoisted sail and disappeared around a corner, where
we lost it (from sight). In the afternoon we measured 34 fathoms,
after that 24, and after two hours 10, so that the bottom seemed
to become drier very suddenly: for shortly afterwards we measured only 8 fathoms and our shallowest depth was 7 fathoms, but
then it became deeper again. We had the high Java mainland to
starboard, and Pulo Panjan to port, the former to the east, the
latter to the west; we measured a depth of 10 fathoms. To the
east we saw some more uninhabited islands, also straight ahead
the town of Bantam, whither the small sailboats were heading; the
wind was northeast from the sea and we sailed a course (at the
wish of our sounding-man) of southeast to south. Towards evening a *Parao* [prow] came from the town, carrying 6 Portuguese
with their slaves; they came aboard and told us they had been
sent by the Governor, who, together with all the inhabitants, was
greatly afraid of us; they asked us from whence we came, to which
we replied: from Holland, in order to trade with them, in all
friendship, their spices against our merchandise; to this they
answered that we certainly had come to the right place but at an
unsuitable time: because five days ago they had sent five *sommas*
(which are Chinese ships) to China and that the one we had seen
lying in the bay that morning was looking for cargo along the
coast; they showed us great friendship. And since we inquired
urgently about the King they told us that he had succumbed be-

fore Palimban [Palembang] (a town situated on Sumatra, which had rebelled) with many of his people, at the time that they occupied most of the town but then, because of the death of their King, they had left the town again. . . .

Through the Portuguese we offered the Governor all friendship and service. The Portuguese upon leaving our ship feigned pleasure and so sailed to the town, where they told the Governor of their experiences.

On the 24th we came somewhat closer to the island, and cast anchor at 7 fathoms close to the Island of Pulo Panjan; to the southwest of us we had another uninhabited green island, from behind which a tiny river flowed; here we stayed and our sounding-man went to the town of Bantam which we saw from afar lying 2 miles away. The naval admiral, called Tomogon Angabaya, came to our ship(s?) and talked to us through an interpreter, offering us all friendship and refreshment in the name of the Governor, and all that was in the Governor's power; (asking us) to come to the town as well as to him personally; we thanked him very much for this, telling him that if he should like to come over he would be welcome. He wanted some (ship's) biscuit, which was given him, after which we excused him, since he had some business on the long island, so he said; (but) then we saw him go back to the town without having gone to the island. . . . Shortly afterwards the Judge of the King's Tolls, called Sabander [collector of harbor dues] came, and with him the Portuguese, who offered us all friendship in the name of the King and the Council, as a proof of which they brought us many chickens, goats, and other fruits. . . .

The next day Tomongon Angabaya came with the Sabander, offering us on behalf of the Governor and themselves all that we might need, and expressing the wish that we should not trust the Portuguese because they were seeking to play us tricks and were so double(-faced) that one could never know their hearts and their manner, and that we need not be afraid: for the harbor was free for all merchants: promising also that we should receive all spices in preference to others. They wished to see some merchandise, and we showed them some, presenting them with eight

(lengths) of green *Caffa* [gauze cloth used for Moslem turbans].
After this a black man came to us on behalf of the Governor; he
was a *Quillin* [a Klingalese, from the Coromandel coast of India]
commonly called Quillin Panjan, or the tall Quillin, acquainting
us with the fact that the whole Kingdom desired a service from us,
that is, that we should sail to Palmban [Palembang] situated on
Sumatra and take it under fire from the sea; that they would march
by land in order to capture the town; they would give us all that
would be found in the town; this we refused since we had come
to trade and not to wage war; he then left our ship, just before . . .
two . . . men had come on board, who wished to see our nautical
maps, on which we showed them from how far we had come in
order to obtain their friendship and their trade, with which they
showed themselves very satisfied, the more so when they heard
that we could come thence and go back in six months; also that we
had been underway 14 months looking for the way. . . .

The next day, being the 26th of that month, (people of) several
nationalities came on board, with whom we traded in all friendship and who wished that we would not trust the Portuguese. We
showed them some merchandise which pleased them exceedingly.
We sent a manned boat to the western corner of Java, three miles
farther west than Pulo Panjan, where there was a small village,
in order to buy some cattle, but since the people were slaves they
were not allowed to sell any; so we bought a large pot of wet
indigo for three little Nuremberg mirrors. In the meantime a high
courtier (or so it seemed) came to the ship *Mauritius;* we showed
him our maps and then he left our ship again; later we understood
that he was a bad character sent by the Portuguese to spy upon us.
The Chinese brought several kinds of merchandise on board, as
porcelain, silk goods, silk and others. . . .

The 27th of that month many *Paraos* came alongside in the
morning . . . (and) the Sabandar came aboard, very urgently requesting that we should come and greet the Governor on land
and present him, according to the old customs, with some gem on
behalf of our King, in token of peace and confederation; four mid-
shipmen were sent for this purpose with a gift of beautiful crystal

glasses, a gilded mirror, and some scarlet cloth; they went with this Quillin Panjan. When they came to the harbor they found the water very low, the harbor was even dry, but from the marks on the palisade it was clear that at high tide the depth must be as much as 8 feet. On arrival they were met by the Portuguese and after a feigned *Beso las manos* [I kiss your hands] they [the midshipmen] were separated from the others and met by the Sabandar who led them to the Governor's palace; the latter was still at table and therefore they waited in the front courtyard. . . . The Governor appeared here within a short time . . . (and) they immediately presented (him) with their gifts, asking him if it might please him to come and visit their masters in order to negotiate a firm alliance and covenant; through his interpreter he answered that he would take this into consideration. From there they went to the Sabander's courtyard, who there served them some preserves, and from here they went back on board that same evening. The next day we brought all our guns on deck since we heard the news that the Governor would come and visit us the next day; we prepared everything in order to receive him well. Several gentlemen came aboard, also merchants from Coraçone [Khorasan, in northeast Persia] and many others, who honored us with gifts of clean cinnamon water and brandy. Many fruits were offered for sale, as radishes, onions, leeks, etc.

21
Louis XIV and the King of Tonkin

> The "Sun King's" letter reproduced below was entrusted to a Father Lefebvre of the French Society of Foreign Missions, who, however, failed to obtain an audience with the ruler of Tonkin, Chua Trinh-Tac. In fact, the ruler died while Lefebvre was kept waiting, and his successor refused to see the Frenchman. He had to be satisfied with the letter to Louis, which amply illustrates the king's opinion concerning relations with European powers.

LETTER FROM THE KING OF FRANCE
TO THE KING OF TONKIN
(JANUARY 10, 1681)

Most high, most excellent, most mighty and most magnanimous Prince, our very dear and good friend, may it please God to increase your greatness with a happy end!

We hear from our subjects who were in your Realm what protection you accorded them. We appreciate this all the more since we have for you all the esteem that one can have for a prince as illustrious through his military valor as he is commendable for the justice which he exercises in his Realm. We have even been informed that you have not been satisfied to extend this general protection to our subjects but, in particular, that you gave effective proofs of it to Messrs. Deydier and de Bourges. We would have wished that they might have been able to recognize all the favors they received from you by having presents worthy of you offered you; but since the war which we have had for several years, in which all of Europe had banded together against us, prevented our vessels from going to the Indies, at the present time, when we are at peace after having gained many victories and expanded our Realm through the conquest of several important places, we have immediately given orders to the Royal Company to establish itself in your kingdom as soon as possible, and have commanded Messrs. Deydier and de Bourges to remain with you in order to maintain a good relationship between our subjects and yours, also to warn us on occasions that might present themselves when we might be able to give you proofs of our esteem and of our wish to concur with your satisfaction as well as with your best interests.

By way of initial proof, we have given orders to have brought to you some presents which we believe might be agreeable to you. But the one thing in the world which we desire most, both for

Georges Taboulet, ed., *La geste française en Indochine* (Paris: Adrien-Maisonneuve, 1955) Vol. I, pp. 84–86. English translation by Margaret W. Broekhuysen. By permission of the author and Adrien-Maisonneuve.

you and for your Realm, would be to obtain for your subjects who have already embraced the law of the only true God of heaven and earth, the freedom to profess it, since this law is the highest, the noblest, the most sacred and especially the most suitable to have kings reign absolutely over the people.

We are even quite convinced that, if you knew the truths and the maxims which it teaches, you would give first of all to your subjects the glorious example of embracing it. We wish you this incomparable blessing together with a long and happy reign, and we pray God that it may please Him to augment your greatness with the happiest of endings.

Written at Saint-Germain-en-Laye, the 10th day of January, 1681,

Your very dear and good friend,
Louis

ANSWER FROM THE KING OF TONKIN TO LOUIS XIV

The King of Tonkin sends to the King of France a letter to express to him his best sentiments, saying that he was happy to learn that fidelity is a durable good of man and that justice is the most important of things. Consequently practicing of fidelity and justice cannot but yield good results. Indeed, though France and our Kingdom differ as to mountains, rivers, and boundaries, if fidelity and justice reign among our villages, our conduct will express all of our good feelings and contain precious gifts. Your communication, which comes from a country which is a thousand leagues away, and which proceeds from the heart as a testimony of your sincerity, merits repeated consideration and infinite praise. Politeness toward strangers is nothing unusual in our country. There is not a stranger who is not well received by us. How then could we refuse a man from France, which is the most celebrated among the kingdoms of the world and which for love of us wishes to frequent us and bring us merchandise? These feelings of fidelity and justice are truly worthy to be applauded. As regards your wish that we should cooperate in propagating your religion, we do not dare to permit it, for there is an ancient custom, introduced by edicts, which formally forbids it. Now, edicts are promulgated only to be carried out faithfully; without fidelity nothing is stable. How could we disdain a well-established custom to satisfy a private friendship? Today France carries to us its merchandise to be sold or exchanged; it practices justice through its wealth and exercises fidelity. . . . In this way friendship is based on justice and fidelity, and thus it may be as durable as gold or stone. Why then is it necessary that we should have the same wish?

We beg you to understand well that this is our communication concerning our mutual acquaintance. This then is my letter. We send you herewith a modest gift which we offer you with a glad heart.

This letter was written at the beginning of winter and on a beautiful day.

22

A Complaint from Jacarta to the Gentlemen Seventeen

> *Below is an excerpt from one of the "general reports" which the governor-general and the Council of the Indies in Java sent at frequent intervals to the Gentlemen Seventeen in Holland. This particular report was written on July 9, 1621, during the first governor-generalship of Jan Pieterszoon Coen, who was just then on a punitive expedition in Banda. The two authors, Pieter de Carpentier (later himself governor-general of the Indies) and Jacob Dedel, paint an interesting picture of the many problems confronting the Dutch in their first settlement in Java.*

Jaccarta, thank God, keeps growing by the day, as you may be able to see from the monthly income. On June 14th the sixth

Chinese junk arrived here from China, after it had been underway for about four months; this year these junks have not brought any merchandise (suitable for) the Netherlands (market), nothing but coarse china, iron pots, sugar, fruits, arak, some coarse, poor textiles and different other trifles but a large multitude of people. We calculate that they brought in about one thousand men.

We have granted passes to several Chinese merchants and *nachodas* [ships' captains] for 15 junks, all of whom have promised to come back here next year with rich merchandise: with God's help there will be no lack of increase (in trade), especially if you will in the near future keep this place well provided with cash, since this is the only bait that the Chinese and all these nations fly at; this should be done until the income can dispense with your annual support, which, with God's blessing, may become the state of affairs in a few short years.

We are busy enclosing the town with wooden stockades and an earthen parapet on the east side of the river.

The fortifications and buildings of the fortress proceed according to our power and not according to our wishes; the principal buttressing is entrusted to industrious experienced workmen, especially good masters; the greater part of the craftsmen, house carpenters as well as ship's carpenters, are not worth their keep, let alone their wages, so that they cause us nothing but chagrin. It almost seems that our wagon will have to roll on in this way because we have often enough written you (about) this without effect. To what avail is it that you send launches with the ships when the carpenters who are supposed to put them together stay home? We cannot by far fulfil the needs of the ships; the needs of one have no sooner been (attended to with) redoubled (efforts) before three others are waiting, each of which ought to be helped before the other. In the meantime some ships are forced to land

W. P. Coolhaas, ed., *Generale Missiven van Gouverneurs-Generaal en Raden aan Heren XVII der Verenigde Oost-Indische Compagnie* (The Hague: Nijhoff, 1960), Vol. I, pp. 110–112. English translation by Margaret W. Broekhuysen. By permission of Ministerie van Onderwijs, Kunsten en Wetenschappen, The Hague.

prematurely because it is not their turn (to be helped); the turnover is so great that actually all the workers present here are scarcely capable of maintaining the living quarters in the fort as well as the small craft as floats, frigates, boats, barges, *tingans* [Javanese launches] and others. All we can do is to let you know about this; it is up to you to provide for these needs, and in the meantime we shall do all that is in our power. We should like to request further that if any craftsmen are hired to send us men who not only have the name but also the deed; otherwise things will remain as of old.

In our previous letter we wrote you how hard we would be pressed for cash unless you were to provide the next fleet amply. This, may God help us, has come true just as we predicted; we are in dire straits these days and have not above five thousand *reals* in the till, thus we have practically exhausted ourselves to keep a minimum of trade moving, and yet requirements have nowhere been met; we have scarcely enough left to supply the rice *proas* [prows] that come in. What will happen when pepper comes in from the outside, as was the case recently, or some other useful merchandise? The English alone will get hold of it and we can look on sadly; won't that be a nice profit and reputation for the Netherlands Company?

A few days ago we sent the frigate "Ceylon" to Grissij [Gresik] to see what spare cash might be there and to bring it here. Isn't it a shabby situation when the parents must beg support from their children? God knows how long it may be until the new aid [funds] arrive.

Also as we mentioned in an earlier letter, the English would soon like to receive restitution of the 96,000 *reals* according to the agreement and your specific subsequent instruction; what is against this [what can we do but pay them]?

If Bantam, which fortunately for us is at this juncture closed, were to open up, with what should we begin to trade? Due to lack of cash we have not been able to send a single *real* to Surat this year.

The Coromandel Coast also begins to complain, (yet) so far we see no way of helping them; nor do we know what amount we shall send to Malabar with the incoming fleet next September.

As long as four months ago we should have sent a decent ship and cash to Cambodia; to our regret it could not be done.

In the trade with Cochinchina (which was offered us by the King with a junk expressly sent from thence this year) we have not been able to cover ourselves with glory either.

We have not been able to supply the needs of the trading posts of Siam, Patani, ... Androgiri, Jambi, Palembang, Acheh, the west coast of Sumatra and other small places in the neighborhood where pepper is available. And yet you write that we should expand trade, look for new places to sail to, and provide good returns, whereas we are so powerless that we cannot (even) maintain the old state of affairs.

23
The Conquest of the Philippines

> *The conquistadores brought the Philippines under the flag of Spain, but Spanish friars undertook the far more difficult task of carrying Hispanic religion and culture to the Filipinos. The efforts of the clergy, recorded in numerous chronicles, made possible more than 300 years of Spanish dominion in the Islands. The following account relates the labors of one Recollect Friar on the hostile island of Mindanao in the early seventeenth century.*

. . . Fray Juan de San Nicolàs was in Lavayan, whose inhabitants he was subduing with incredible labors; for they refused to build him a church or a house, or to supply him with food. He was supported by the fish caught by two Tagálog Indians, servants of his, while he himself was obliged to pound his rice and carry his wood. It was God's pleasure to soften the hardness of those

Emma Blair and James A. Robertson, eds., *The Philippine Islands* (Cleveland, Ohio: Clark, 1906), Vol. XXXV, pp. 63–64.

people, in a manner that appears ridiculous. I shall not hesitate to refer to it, so that the divine Providence may be seen even in what appears accidental.

Father Fray Juan de San Nicolàs fell sick of the fever, and found that he must be bled. That took place upon the occasion of a visit from an Indian chief. The latter was greatly surprised that the father allowed himself to be bled. He asked the cause of it, and the father told him that that was a good medicine for fevers, and that the Spaniards were accustomed to its use. The Indian became quiet at that, but returned the next day to see the second bleeding. Then after several days he came with his hands to his head, and asked to be bled, as he felt sick. The father endeavored to dissuade him, but he insisted so much that the father had to order that he be bled. The barber, since the chief had refused to sell him a fowl for food, or anything else, thought to be revenged, and said that he would not bleed him unless he gave him a fowl or two pullets. The Indian had to give it to him, and although father Fray Juan laughed at the bargain, he was silent and overlooked it all, as he got some food. Other Indians fell sick, and were bled, paying for the bleeding in fowls. By that means the fathers, who were suffering from severe fevers, were able to cure themselves, God taking that means for the relief of his ministers, who had no relief in any other way. Thus the Indians became fond of them and many were baptized. Let us praise God in His infinite wisdom, since He can bring about the salvation of souls by so homely opportunities. Some curious things happened among those barbarous people, but we shall omit them in order not to enlarge this narration, and because those ministries were lost through the hidden judgments of God, and with them the fruit that could be expected. . . .

24

A Description of Siam in the Seventeenth Century

> *Between 1624 and 1636, Joost Schouten, an official of the*
> *Dutch East India Company, made five separate trips to Siam,*
> *specifically to the court city of Ayuthia, on company busi-*
> *ness. He successfully carried out his trade missions by estab-*
> *lishing good relations for the Dutch with the Siamese King,*
> *Phrasat-Thong (1629–1656). On his last visit in 1636,*
> *Schouten wrote the account from which the following passages*
> *have been excerpted.*

The *Siammers,* as also the Neighbouring Nations, are all Idolaters and Heathens, so that they have every where great and little
Temples and Cloysters for the service of their Gods; and the dwellings of their Priests. These Edifices are builded of Wood and
Stone very Artificial and sumptuous, with guilded [gilded] Towers
and Pyramids; each of the Temples and Cloysters being filled with
an incredible number of *Idols,* of diverse materials and greatness,
gilded, adorned and beautified very rich and admirable; some of
the Idols are four, six, eight, and ten fathoms long; amongst
the rest there is one of an unimaginable greatness, being one
hundred and twenty foot high. In these Temples and Cloysters
there are many Priests and Religious Men disciplined, and very
obedient to their superiours, all being subject to the Arch *Flamin,*
or Prior of the great Temple of *Iudica* [Ayuthia], whose spiritual
power is vastly great, though subordinate to the Kings. All the
Clergy (whereof there are in *Iudica* alone at least thirty thousand)
are clothed, without any remarkable difference, in yellow linnen
clothes, having their heads all shorn. The learnedst amongst these
are professed Priests, out of which the Regents of their Temples
are chosen, (who are held in great esteem and reverence by the

François Caron and Joost Schouten, *A True Description of the Mighty
Kingdoms of Japan and Siam* (London: The Argonaut Press, 1935), pp. 104,
106, 109. By permission of The Argonaut Press.

People) preaching, teaching, and offering upon their Feasts and Holy daies. These are prohibited the natural use of Women, upon pain of being burned; but they may alwaies, and at pleasure, upon declaration of their frailty or weakness, quit their frocks, and betake themselves to another life, which happens often amongst them. They have their morning and evening Song, Readings and other Services, celebrated in their Cloysters every day, and frequented by their society. They live upon the Alms and bounty of the King and great Ones, as also on the fruit which their Church Lands bring forth; but principally out of the sweet [sweat] and labours of the Commonalty, who unanimously share with them, they sending every morning some Priests and Clerks out of their Cloysters, with begging bags to receive these donations and charity: Besides these Priests, there are a sort of old Nuns shorn, lodged in Chappels near the greatest Temples, who assist very devoutly in all their preachings, singings, ceremonies, and other Church services, but all voluntary, being tied to no rules or prescriptions. These Heathens do generally believe, (however differing in many particulars) that there is one upper God, with many lesser Deities in Heaven, who created all things; that the Souls of Men are immortal, and shall be rewarded or punished according to their merits and actions; the good dwelling with the God(s) in bliss, whilest the wicked are tormented by the Devils that seduced them. . . . The Priests carry themselves very moderately to those of a contrary Religion, condemning no opinions, but believe that all, though of differing tenets, living vertuously, may be saved, all services which are performed with zeal being acceptable to the great God, especially theirs, they being convinced of its truth and innocency. This constancy of theirs makes them not easily to be drawn to any other perswasion, which hath been sufficiently attempted by the *Portugals,* whose industrious Priests omitted nothing for their conversion, and by the Mohametans who are no less zealous in their way, though with little or no success by either of them, and yet the Christians, as also the Mohametans, are both permitted the free exercise of their Religions in their Countrey. . . .

Before the coming of the Netherlanders into the *Indias,* the *Portugals* had great correspondence and amity with this Kingdom, being in such esteem and honour by the King, that the Embassadours sent from their Vice-Roys, Governours, and Bishops of *Malacca* in *India,* were not only well received by his Majesty, but richly presented by him, and many of the residing *Portugals* in this Country advanced to great Offices and preferments; they had not only the free exercise of their Religion, but their chief Priest had also a monethly pension allowed him for his more splended subsistence; thus they prospered here for many years, until the Dutch Company got footing amongst them, and gained upon them from time to time, by taking their Ships and interrupting their trade . . . insomuch that they are at present very low and out of credit. . . .

25
The Dutch East India Company's Trade in Southeast Asia

The seventeenth century marked the apex of Dutch naval and commercial supremacy in Eastern waters. Throughout Southeast Asia the Dutch East India Company sought new markets, raw materials, and commercial contacts. Siam was no exception to this pattern. The following letter, dated January 8, 1655, is a typical example of the correspondence from Batavia, the center of Dutch interests in Southeast Asia, to the Gentlemen Seventeen who controlled the affairs of the Dutch East India Company from the Netherlands.

It appears that the merchant Hendrich Craijer Zalr had promised, so they say, 20 ships, which was a very rash proceeding on his part, and thereupon they made the above-mentioned expedi-

Records of the Relations between Siam and Foreign Countries in the 17th Century (Bangkok: Council of the Vajirañāna National Library, 1916), Vol. II, pp. 10–14, 17–18.

tion, which they said, if our support did not appear, would be obliged to return unsuccessful and with shame and dishonour to the crown, as was actually the case. Moreover, it happened that a writing has come unexpectedly from the governor of Tennasserim that two Dutch ships had held the harbour there for 2 months, and had prevented the entrance and departure of foreign traders, which caused great annoyance in Siam, especially at Court, and embittered everyone against us. This gave the Companies a very favourable opportunity to blacken us and to make us odious to everyone, and to change the King's feeble opposition into open enmity, the more so since the news has from time to time been confirmed and assured, and no one there doubts it any longer. Wherefore the resident Westerwolt, who was convinced of the contrary, since he would certainly have been informed before any such action was taken, finally found himself obliged to ask that certain persons, on the King's behalf and on his own, should be deputed and sent overland to Tennasserim, in order to discover on the spot the truth of the case, which request was granted by the King, and on our behalf the junior merchant, Hugo van Crujlenburgh was sent. Meanwhile the aforementioned resident Westerwolt had on various occasions made complaint of the bad and unreasonable treatment received, but got nothing by it but a summons to court, and before four Ojas or councillors was questioned on certain points to which he had to answer forthwith, and the answer was written down word for word, to be laid before the King, who sat by and waited, and every now and then asked whether one of the questions had yet been put. So that the resident was in very great embarrassment and did not know whether even his life was any longer safe. These questions were for the most part on the subject of the help asked for against Sangora, (the Siamese) professing to have gone to war with the Castellañes [the Spanish] on our account, and to have suffered much damage in the same, and that we now refused to assist his Majesty against the rebels with ships and men; whereas the beforementioned merchant, Hendrich Craijer, had definitely made him such promises. Therefore he (the

King) had sent his forces to Ligor so as to cooperate with him (Craijer) on his arrival and keep his word: But instead we had sent our ships to Tennasserim and had taken possession of the place in order to keep foreigners aways and to ruin their trade. In consequence of this (enquiry) Westerwolt was inclined to depart from Siam and so make an end of this business, as he had sometimes proposed to do, and as there were two of our ships lying ready at the bar ... he thought he could initiate and carry his proposal into execution, but was warned that no living soul would escape the power of the King since he could kill them all and trample them under foot and that his threats (of departing) were not at all to the purpose. For all which reasons the aforesaid resident could not answer the questions put to him without embarrassment: And nothing followed thereon, except that four or five days later a prohibition was published that, for the future, neither Siamese nor Peguers were to be allowed to serve the Dutch, thus putting great contempt upon the nation. From all which contemptuous proceedings the above-mentioned Westerwolt came to the conclusion that in case the long expected help could not be sent this year we should have (? trouble) in Siam; also that this same year the Japanese cargoes were likely to be unimportant, even if he were allowed to ship and dispatch them. This gave us no small concern, for now, in addition to the war with Portugal, we had come to a rupture with the new government in England, and it still continued impossible for us to spare any force in ships or men for Siam, and it was also inadvisable to continue to keep the King any longer in an uncertain hope, whereby our cause could only be made worse the longer it lasted, since it was quite uncertain whether we in the near future should have the power (to help him). Besides it is not the Company's function nor does it agree with its maxims to interpose itself in the wars of foreign potentates over questions and quarrels which do not concern it in the least. Nevertheless, it was decided and considered necessary to send thither at least one good flyboat to take the cargo for Japan, if it were allowed, or, in case of refusal, to sail to Taiwan, in order to return hither at its proper time with sugar. For which purpose the aforesaid *Gecroonde Liefde* was again employed, departing on the 21st May from this roadstead with a letter and a handsome present to the King, also one to the Oja Zebartiban above mentioned, in answer to his [letter] written to us from Ligor: In which we have made known clearly and definitely our inability to send assistance, and that it was impossible to say when it could be sent on account of the wars referred to above. That so his Majesty should therefore no longer wait for it and that we should be freed from the vexations which would otherwise probably be renewed every year. We have also sent (on the 5th September) the ship *Schiedam* in order that, all being well, it should return hither at once, laden with rice, sapan wood and other necessaries, or if it can get no cargo, to sail to the Moluccas and bring us thence as much pepper as it can take in. . . .

Last year there were two Johor vessels in Siam which the Siamese, we know not why, took for spies, treated them as such and sent them back in disgrace without allowing them to provision with rice and water for the voyage, or to get in their outstanding debts here. Whereby they being irritated, as it seems, when passing out of the river, took two Siamese vessels in tow and carried them off. And this same affront was taken so ill in Johor that some saletters (pirates) have been dispatched to Siam to avenge it. Whereupon, after they had taken some flat-bottomed boats the Siamese sent off prows but, before their arrival, the others had already departed again. Finding on the way instead of these a saletter come from Borneo, they took him down with them. Arrived at the mouth of the river, they persuaded each other that it was one of the saletter's boats and thereupon surrounded it with 37 frigates, against which the Bornean put itself on the defensive and overcame one of them and would have got away with it, but in crossing the bar grounded. Then, as it seems, despairing of escape, the Borneans, in order not to fall alive into the hands of the enemy, stabbed each other. How these occurrences between the two kings will turn out, time will show.

26
Dutch Accounts of the Court of Mataram

> *Rijklof van Goens, one of the highest officials in the Dutch East India Company and Governor-General of the Indies between 1678 and 1681, was one of the first prominent Dutchmen to observe the court of Mataram at close range. He was in charge of five successive missions to Amangkurat II,* Susuhunan *(emperor) of that realm between 1677 and 1703. The first excerpt printed below is taken from the diary of the first embassy and sheds light on its reception; the second is taken from a "travel account" written upon van Goens' return to Holland.*

[I]

On the 22nd [May, 1648], Monday, everything had been prepared early in order to appear before the *Susuhunan.* . . . [The] king awaited us on his south-square (. . . his most dignified place of audience); such [probably meaning *we,* tr.] immediately sat on our horses with all the honoring (gifts) carried before us, and arrived about half past nine before the court, where the command was given that all the gifts and our following should remain outside, thus going all together into the fenced-off square. The Tax Collector(?) was given a yellow ribbon around his neck and was ordered to carry the letter to about 18 to 20 steps from the king, where (we) all sat down on the sand with our legs crossed, when Angapraja produced the letter for the *Susuhunan,* which was immediately read by him and translated into Javanese. During the reading the *pangerans* [princes] Porbaja and Sarbaja advanced crawling to sit on the ground beside the *Susuhunan* at about five

H. J. De Graaf, ed., *De vijf gezantschapsreizen van Rijklof van Goens naar het hof van Mataram 1648–1654* (The Hague: Nijhoff, 1956), pp. 53–56, 248–250. English translation by Margaret W. Broekhuysen. By permission of H. I. De Graaf and Martinus Nijhoff.

feet distance; the *Susuhunan* commanded, after the reading of the letter, to bring the gifts before him, which was followed with unbelievable zeal; then the three horses, having been well fed on the road and not having been ridden for a long time, to our great pleasure entered very dapperly, merrily cutting a wide swath among the nobles who were seated there in large numbers; all the other gifts, wrapped in yellow, followed and were placed at the side of the *Susuhunan*. The king was sitting under a wooden summer-shelter, raised from the ground about three fathoms by a stone pedestal, on a square stool without backrest, at his right side three young women were seated on the ground, each holding a pike with the sharp end forward; behind him also six women each with a musket, without any male person being closer to him than ten steps. The *Susuhunan* asked the Tax Collector if he had any errand besides the letter, and what the [Dutch] Governor-General demanded from him; to which the aforesaid gentleman answered: nothing else but what was mentioned in the letter, and that the Governor-General did not demand anything but only the preservation and continuation of friendship and continued proofs of a sincere and pure heart, as would be always pursued by our [Governor-] General. To which the *Susuhunan* replied that Batavia and Mataram now were one country and that they would remain so forever; also that all that was in his land was open to the Governor-General and the latter would only have to demand what he desired, as he himself would also do on equal occasion; he said further: we should have no doubts about this; on which we assured him that we ourselves did not have any. . . . Finally the *Susuhunan* said that he was ready to go on a hunting trip but that, for our sakes, he would remain for three days and have each one [of us] appear before him, that we then would use his land as we pleased, since now Batavia and this country had become one; for this we thanked him, took our leave and departed for our residence, from which several persons were invited. In the afternoon the *Susuhunan* sent us a large quantity of fruits to refresh ourselves, and six cows. In the evening we went with the letter drawn up by the Governor-General and with gifts to the *tommagon* [high official of]

Mataram, who showed us friendship in an exceedingly large measure, coming to meet the Tax Collector at his inmost door and
embracing him; leading him further with his hand to sit down on a
rug, which was his own place to sleep, and that of all his women.
Angapraja read the letter to him which being understood by him
he assured us about the request . . . showing us further great signs
of friendship, wishing to [make] merry with us in the Dutch way.
The gifts from the [Governor-?] General were put aside wrapped
up, unopened, from which we judged that he wanted to show them
to the *Susuhunan,* as we learned the next day that the *Susuhunan*
sent everything back to the *tommagon* except the piece of cloth
and the piece of Persian velvet, which he kept for himself. When
it was well after midnight we took our leave and departed very
pleased about the reception by this man, who truly showed himself to be a good friend of the Dutch.

[II] MURDER OF PRIESTS

. . . Now in order to carry out his plan, he [the Emperor] calls
to him four of his favorite harem guests [eunuchs], who, . . . had
served him from early youth and were mostly of equal age; who
had already been placed by him in the most important service of
masters that had since been destroyed, and who had mighty warriors under them. His nephew [cousin?] Radin Maes, now called
Pangeran Aria . . . was the first; the second, *Tommagon* Natair
Nauwa, at present *Tommagon* Pâtij and our best friend; the third,
Tommagon Soura Nata, now *Tommagon* Demack, also our very
good friend; and the fourth, Quei Nebeij Wiera Patra, the King's
greatest minion, who had also stabbed Wiera Gouna. He commanded these four mighty lords to distribute themselves over four
places, that is in the south, in the north, in the east and in the west,
and to take care that not one of all those who bore the name of
priest should escape within all of the jurisdiction of Mataram; in-
structing them to this end, to inquire first from their people, under
pretext of a request, about their names, their race, their permanent
dwellings and more such as he judged to be conducive to kill them

all with one blow; forbidding to inform the inquirers themselves what was his aim. In the meantime the King, under pretext of his mourning, did not appear, but caused the weekly administration of justice in the courtyard to be continued (since they are very meticulous in purging the country of criminals). Now when the King had been informed of everything pertinent and had the names of both the guilty and the innocent, he commanded them to have their servants pay attention and everyone to take his *wis* (aim? tr.) without sparing man, woman or innocent children; giving them at the same time the signal that this should be done as soon as he had a gun fired from his courtyard. This having been arranged the King armed himself on the appropriate day with good guards, all distributed among his faithful friends, and scarcely had the gun been fired then no less than 5 to 6000 souls were miserably murdered inside of half an hour. The King, who had thus carried this out so skillfully without anyone knowing about it, appears the next day with a very disturbed and alarmed face, sitting for more than an hour without speaking; which caused such terrible dejection among all the *pangerans* and lords that no one ventured to give a sound or look up. Finally he spoke to his uncle, relating to him how these priests, who ought to give them an example in all virtues, were the cause of his brother's death; [the king then] having these four gentlemen who had carried out his will produce some of these priests, who confessed before the assembly that it was their intention to make the King's brother King. These were immediately taken outside and killed. The King now giving full rein to his anger had all the great lords, about whom he still had some suspicion, dragged away, to a number of 7 or 8, ordering them to be killed at once, which happened without delay, also to their wives and children; after which the King departed again, leaving all the old lords, who had been elevated during his father's reign, in great trouble and distress, such as was not without reason.

27
Philippine Social and Economic Problems in the Eighteenth Century

> *Don José Basco y Vargas, perhaps the most progressive of the Spanish governors-general, made great efforts during his administration (1778–1787) to improve the backward state of the Philippine economy. He ended Manila's dependence on Mexican silver by establishing a tobacco monopoly, and encouraged the development of native agriculture. Unfortunately, the proscriptions of the following decree (1784) were never put into effect.*

And since this chief executive, actuated by what he himself has observed in this province of Pampanga, in that of Bulacan, and in those of Tondo and Laguna de Bay (which he has visited personally), cannot any longer permit such extortions and injuries as are caused, among all classes of persons, to the farmers and poor Indians in the said provinces, and in the other districts to which this decree will also be made to extend: I command that in future the implements of labor—such as carabaos, plows, hemp-combs, and other field utensils belonging to the Indians, mestizos, creoles, Spaniards, or any other class of persons—shall not be seized for a civil debt, any more than their lands, since most of them have no ownership in these. Moreover, they shall not be arrested at the times when they must work in the fields, such as plowing, and gathering their harvests: and, at the times when they can be arrested, authority shall be given to the alcaldes-mayor so that they can grant them a respite of six months, without loading them with fees or other exactions.

And, as the backward state of agriculture in Filipinas proceeds

Emma Blair and James A. Robertson, eds., *The Philippine Islands* (Cleveland, Ohio: Clark, 1908), Vol. III, pp. 292–295.

also from the fact that, notwithstanding there are many industrious, laborious and charitable persons in the villages, there are also many others in whom sloth and idleness reign—for instance, many chiefs and their sons, and the heads of barangay; and generally those who have exercised the office of magistrate (who, on account of having served in these employments, afterward refuse through a sort of vanity and pride to go back to field work), all these caring only to subjugate the common people by compelling them to work without pay in their fields, and trying to exempt themselves from the common labor, and from the other burdens to which those who pay tribute are subject—likewise this chief executive has resolved to declare that such exemptions ought not to be understood for the classes of persons who are mentioned above, unless they possess at least eight cabalitas [approximately 2.2 hectares] of their own land cultivated and worked by their servants or day-laborers, expressly forbidding that they rent these lands to others—always provided that they are not prevented by age or infirmities from carrying on their farm-work in person, since in this case they are allowed to rent them.

And although, in regard to the contract of *casamajan* [tenancy] which they commonly practice, absolute prohibition ought to be made to them on account of the burden which ensues from it to the poor, and also to their own consciences, on account of the many usurious acts which are committed therein, (yet) considering, as has been already stated, that there will be many who, on account of age and sickness, cannot themselves attend to the cultivation of their land, this chief executive consents to grant such persons a contract of that sort, under the condition that whatever loan is made to the farmers by their partners [landlords], it shall be in the form of palay [rice], and they shall collect it in the same; that is, if they shall lend, for example, four cavans (of rice), they shall receive four others. And the same is ordained in regard to money, so that if they shall lend, for example, two pesos they shall receive only two pesos; and, if they shall lend cloth, if it is not returned they may only receive its just value at the time when the bargain was made—under the penalty that no judge shall admit any claim in contravention of this ordinance, and the complainants shall lose what they had lent.

Besides this, I have in the same manner heard of the unjust and vile bargains which the usurers make in regard to the cultivated lands, and even the trees which the farmers cultivate in their gardens, and their houses, binding them with the agreement of *retrovendendi*, as it is commonly called, exacting from him who is bound—sometimes for many years, and sometimes forever—the produce and the ownership (of those possessions), for a small amount which the lender has furnished. They also exact a premium for the money which they lend, sometimes in valuables, and sometimes besides these. This is done by a multitude of usurers who overrun the island, with great offense to God and injury to their neighbors. . . .

28
The First Nguyen Emperor Through European Eyes

After a long period of disunity between North and South Vietnam, the southern dynasty of the Nguyen succeeded in reuniting the realm, with French support, in 1802, bringing to a close the thirty-year Tay-son Movement of Annamese-led dissidents. The unifier of modern Vietnam, Nguyen-Anh (Caung-shung in the text), who adopted the reign name Gia-Long (1802–1819), was a man of unusual capacities. He is here described by Sir John Barrow, a much-traveled Britisher and comptroller of the British embassy in China in 1793.

. . . Before I proceed to give any account of our own transactions in this country, or of the manners and appearance of the people, I shall continue my narrative of the progress made by *Caung-shung* in the recovery of his kingdom; and select from my materials the leading features of the character of this extraordinary

John Barrow, *A Voyage to Cochinchina, in the Years 1792 and 1793* (London: Cadell and Davies, 1806), pp. 271, 273–279, 281.

man, who may justly be ranked among those few who are born with talents to rule in the world; who now and then appear, in all countries, with a splendour which outshines the rest of their fellow mortals. It may be right to apprize the reader that a considerable part of the sketch which I have here given, as well as that which follows, is the substance of a manuscript memoir drawn up by Monsieur Barissy, an intelligent French officer, who commanded a frigate in the service of this monarch. And as the former part agrees so well with what we learned in Turon bay, through our interpreter, from a Chinese secretary to the government at that place, and with the different relations of the missionaries who have resided there, I have no hesitation in giving to the sequel the most implicit belief. The material facts have, indeed, been corroborated by the testimony of two English gentlemen, who visited *Sai-gong* in the years 1799 and 1800. . . .

From the year 1790, in which *Caung-shung* returned to Cochinchina, to 1800, he was allowed to enjoy only two years of peace, 1797 and 1798: and these two years were, in all probability, the most important of his hitherto troublesome reign. Under the auspices of the Bishop Adran, who in every important undertaking was his oracle, he turned his attention to the improvement of his country. He established a manufactory of saltpetre in *Fen-tan* [Champa], . . . opened roads of communication between important posts and considerable towns, and planted them on each side with trees for shade. He encouraged the cultivation of the areca nut and the *betel* pepper, the plantations of which had been destroyed by the army of the usurper. He held out rewards for the propagation of the silk-worm; caused large tracts of land to be prepared for the culture of the sugar-cane; and established manufactories for the preparation of pitch, tar, and resin. He caused several thousand matchlocks to be fabricated; he opened a mine of iron ore, and constructed smelting furnaces. He distributed his land forces into regular regiments, established military schools, where officers were instructed in the doctrine of projectiles and gunnery by European masters. . . .

. . . He sent missions into the mountainous districts on the west of his kingdom, inhabited by the *Laos* and the *Miaotsé,* barbarous nations whom he wished to bring into a state of civilization and good government. These mountaineers are the people whom the Chinese designate by the degrading appellation of "Men with tails"; though, in all probability, they are the regular descendants of the true original inhabitants of this long civilized empire. In short, this Monarch, by his own indefatigable application to the arts and manufactures, like Peter of Russia, without his brutality, aroused by his individual example the energies of his people, and, like our immortal Alfred, spared no pains to regenerate his country. . . .

Caung-shung is represented to be, in the strictest sense of the word, a complete soldier. He is said to hold the name of General far more dear and estimable than that of Sovereign. He is described as being brave without rashness; and fertile in expedients, when difficulties are to be surmounted. His conceptions are generally just; his conduct firm; he is neither discouraged by difficulties, nor turned aside by obstacles. Cautious in deciding, when once resolved, he is prompt and vigorous to execute. In battle he is always eminently distinguishable. . . .

His conduct to foreigners is affable and condescending. To the French officers in his service he pays the most marked attention, and treats them with the greatest politeness, familiarity, and good humour. On all his hunting excursions, and other parties of pleasure, one of these officers is always invited to attend. He openly declares his great veneration for the doctrines of Christianity, and tolerates this religion and indeed all others in his dominions. He observes a most scrupulous regard to the maxims of filial piety, as laid down in the works of Confucius, and humbles himself in the presence of his mother (who is still living) as a child before its master. With the works of the most eminent Chinese authors he is well acquainted; and, through the translations into the Chinese character of the *Encyclopedie* by the Bishop Adran, he has acquired no inconsiderable knowledge of European arts and sciences, among which he is most attached to such as relate to navigation and ship-building. . . .

To enable him the better to attend to the concerns of his government, his mode of life is regulated by a fixed plan. At six in the morning he rises from his couch, and goes into the cold bath. At seven he has his levee of Mandarins: all letters are read which have been received in the course of the preceding day, on which his orders are minuted by the respective secretaries. He then proceeds to the naval arsenal, examines the works which have been performed in his absence, rows in his barge around the harbour, inspecting his ships of war. He pays particular attention to the ordinance department; and in the foundery, which is erected within the arsenal, cannon are cast of all dimensions. . . .

He neither makes use of Chinese wine, nor of any spirituous liquors, and contents himself with a very small portion of animal food. A little fish, rice, vegetables and fruit, with tea and light pastry, constitute the chief articles of his diet. Like a true Chinese descended, as he boasts to be, from the imperial family of *Ming,* he always eats alone, not permitting either his wife or any part of his family to sit down to the same table with him. . . .

In justice to the memory of (Bishop) Adran, who died in 1800, it ought to be observed, that the character of this Monarch, the recovery of his kingdom, his successes in war, the improvements of his country in the intervals of peace and, above all, the rapid progress made in various arts, manufactures and science, are greatly owing to the talents, the instruction and faithful attachment of this missionary. The King, on his part, loved him to adoration, distinguishing him by an epithet bestowed on Confucius alone, *the Illustrious Master.* And in testimony of his great veneration, after the remains of the Bishop had been interred by his brother missionaries according to the rites of the Romanish Church, he ordered the body to be taken up and again buried with all the funeral pomp and ceremonies prescribed by the Cochinchinese religion; nor could he be prevailed on to forego this signal mark of honour to his memory, notwithstanding the intreaties and expostulations of the French missionaries, who were not a little scandalized at such unhallowed proceedings. . . .

29

Letter from the Court of Ava to the Governor-General of India

> *Captain Michael Symes first went to Burma in 1795 on a mission from the Governor-General of India to King Bodawpaya (1781–1819), and later published the first full-scale account of that then little-known country. In 1802 Lord Wellesley sent Symes on a second mission to Ava. In reply to the governor-general's correspondence to the court delivered by Symes, the four chief ministers of the state (the* Wungyis) *sent the following letter back to Lord Wellesley.*

We, chief ministers of the Sovereign Prince of the golden city of Ummerapoora, to whom the sovereigns of all states and countries owe homage and respect, of him who is lord of the mines of gold, silver, rubies, and of the other seven sorts of precious things; Lord of the White Elephants . . . , Lord of the present life; We, the said chief ministers of the great God observer of the law, who, ever placing our heads under the golden soles of the royal feet, resembling a branch of Nymphaea [the water-lily], govern and decide all affairs of state, address this to you, Governor General of Calcutta. As the great princely angel resides in the delightful city of Ammerapoora, thus our Sovereign Prince, residing in the said great golden city, to which no Sovereign can boast a place equal in magnificence, beauty and delights, and willing to increase the welfare and advantage of all his subjects, great and little, of whatever rank and condition, having received the consecration of the pearl which all Princes through respect dread to receive, and being graced with all the virtues becoming to a King, and possessed of the eight prerogatives of an angel, the moon, the sun,

Michael Symes, *Journal of his Second Embassy to the Court of Ava in 1802,* D. G. E. Hall, ed., (London: Allen & Unwin, 1955), pp. 253–257. By permission of Allen & Unwin.

the wind, the sea, the Prince Rama, the Nat Pitzeen [the spirit who presides over the rain], and the Nat Ossoondri [the spirit who keeps the register of good works]; following the traces and laudable example of all ancient renowned princes . . . he exalts those who deserve to be exalted and humbles those who deserve to be humbled. . . .

. . . [One] morning, at the time of publick audience, the whole body of ministers represented to the King that Colonel Michael Symes, sent by the Governor General of Bengal, had arrived at the Port of Rangoon with letters and presents. His Majesty had already been informed that the Governor General after having, some years ago, paid homage under the golden soles of his royal feet, and requested to be received into his royal protection, had not only welcomed and refused to deliver up his Arracan subjects, who had taken refuge in the province of Bengal, but that he had even opposed an armed force to those sent to compel them to return. His Majesty had further received information that the Agents sent by him to purchase musquets had met with opposition from the Governor General, for which reason a Royal decision, dreadful as the fulminating arms of the Spirits above, thundered from his golden mouth that considering the conduct of the Governor General's, there was just reason to believe him a man of little faith, and that it was therefore, not expedient to receive his presents.

Colonel Michael Symes, on his arrival from Rangoon, having heard this Royal decision, represented that what he should say might be deemed the express words of the Governor General, Marquis Wellesley. That, as to the affair of the musquets and the subjects of complaint, be entreated that, forgiving the rusticity and ill humour of Captain Hiram Cox, to whom the whole was to be imputed, his Majesty would allow British subjects to trade in Rangoon and the other ports of his dominions according to the ancient custom, and that he would deign to accept the presents he had brought. Colonel Michael Symes having frequently made these representations and entreaties, his Majesty gave the following answer: "What other Princes would with difficulty suffer, I, being a sovereign who performs the ten good works and aspires to become

God [Buddha?], will submit to and patiently bear. Whatever has passed I regard as the sole act of Hiram Cox and not of the Governor General, who now sends to make this representation, nor of Colonel Symes: Be it allowed him to offer his presents, and to all the inhabitants of Bengal to come to the ports of this Kingdom to sell, purchase, and trade according to the ancient practice; let this order be communicated to Colonel Michael Symes." Previous to the execution of this sovereign mandate, and to the offering of the presents, two persons named Mushi and Bevan (means Monsieur Bevan), sent by the Governor of the Isle of France with a letter and presents, arrived under the golden soles of the royal feet. His Majesty has granted to the deputies of both countries on different days to offer their presents, and contemplate his royal face, and he has taken into his royal protection the English Nation both of Bengal and Europe in the same manner as he extends it to the countries of Assam, China, Ceylon and Kio Cassi [Vietnam], and letters having just now been received from the chief ministers of the great country of Kio Cassi, His Majesty has ordered that a copy of them be given to Colonel Symes. He therefore informs you that on the arrival of Colonel Symes in Bengal, with a peaceful heart and reciprocal friendly dispositions, and for the mutual advantage of both nations, he alows a free and open trade in all the ports of this Kingdom.

A true translation from the Italian.

(Signed)   J. Canning, Lieutenant
Ava Escort

30

Before Imperialism: The British in Malaya (1810)

In 1786 the Sultan of Kedah ceded the island of Penang and a narrow strip of territory on the mainland (subsequently known as Province Wellesley) to the East India Company. The transfer had been arranged by Sir Francis Light, who in vain endeavored to secure the British government's agreement to a guaranty for Kedah. The letter reprinted below (in abbreviated version), written by the Sultan's son, was presented to Lord Minto on December 24, 1810. Minto was then en route to Java which the British occupied until 1816. In 1821, the Siamese invaded Kedah without incurring British intervention.

In the year 1199 of the Hegira [A.D. 1786]*, in the time of my late father, Mr. Light bearing on the head of submission the commands of the King of England, and the orders of the Governor-General, with various splendid presents, appeared in the presence of my late father, the Râja, and requested in the name of the King of England and of the Governor-General, the island of Penang, for the purpose of repairing their ships-of-war, highly extolling the greatness, splendour, power, wisdom, beneficence, of His Majesty, the prosperity of the Honourable Company and all those connected in the ties of friendship with them; promising that the King and the Governor-General would assist my father in whatever might be required, and would prevent the enemies of Kĕdah engaging in proceedings detrimental to the country. Moreover, that they should pay rent for the island 30,000 dollars per annum, and entered into sundry other engagements. My father, consulting with the Ministers, considering that the neighbouring Burman and Siamese nations were more powerful than Kĕdah and having reflected that the King of Europe (i.e., England) was greater and more powerful than either of those nations, and that by means of the friendship of the English Company, these powers would be prevented from violence or molestation, perceived that it would be very desirable to enter into alliance with the Company, because the Europeans were just and regular in conducting all their affairs, and should the Burman or Siamese powers unjustly attempt violence, the powerful aid and protection of the Company would enable my father to repel the aggression. My father was,

Frank Swettenham, *British Malaya: An Account of the Origin and Progress of British Influence in Malaya,* new and rev. ed. (London: Allen & Unwin, 1955), pp. 47–52. By permission of Allen & Unwin.

* There appear to be discrepancies between the Hegira dates mentioned in the text and the conventional computation of the Hegira.

therefore extremely desirous of obtaining the friendship of the Company, under whose powerful shelter and protection, the country might be transmitted to his descendants increased in strength. ...My father accordingly granted permission to proceed to settle on the island of Penang, and sent his people to assist in the work, and his officers to protect them from the pirates in the commencement. My father having waited some time, at the expiration of the year, requested the writing from Mr. Light, who desired him to wait a little; at the end of six years no authentic writing could be obtained; he received 10,000 dollars per annum, but Mr. Light refused to fulfil the remainder of his engagements, and in consequence of my father insisting upon having a writing, agreeably to his former stipulation, a misunderstanding arose between Kĕdah and Penang, after which a new treaty of alliance was concluded. Since that time many Governors have been placed over Penang, but my father was unable to obtain a writing either from Europe, or from the Governor-General. ...

...So long as I have administered the government of Kĕdah, during the time of the late King of Siam, his proceedings were just and consistent with former established custom and usage. Since the decease of the King, and the accession of his son to the throne, in the year 1215 [A.D. 1802]*, violence and severity have been exercised by the Siamese against Kĕdah, in demands and requisitions exceeding all former custom and usage, and which I cannot support for a length of time. ... I have in vain endeavoured to avert the enmity of Siam, but without any appearance of success. I have made known to the Governor of Penang, every circumstance with relation to this country and Siam, and have requested his advice and the assistance of the Company, on which my father relied, because the countries of Kĕdah and Penang are as one country and as one interest. When, therefore, Kĕdah is distressed, it cannot be otherwise with Penang. The Governor advised me by all means to avoid coming to a rupture with Siam, alleging that it was not in his power to afford me assistance, for that the Supreme Government in Europe had forbidden all interference in the wars of the neighbouring powers. Perhaps this would be improper with respect to other countries, but Kĕdah and Penang are much distressed by the labours necessarily imposed to avert the resentment of Siam, and every exertion on my part has been made to prevent coming to a rupture with that power, but I was unable to submit to demands exceeding all former precedent, which induced me to apply to the Governor of Penang for the Company's aid to enable me to repel their demands, for my father having transmitted to me his friendship and alliance with the Company, it would be otherwise a reflection upon the power of the King of England, who is accounted a Prince greater and more powerful than any other. . . . In consequence, I request my friend to issue directions, and to forward a representation to the King and to the Honourable Company, of the matters contained in this letter. I request that the engagements contracted by Mr. Light with my late father, may be ratified, as my country and I are deficient in strength; . . . I desire to repose in safety from the attempts of all my enemies, and that the King may be disposed to kindness and favour towards me, as if I were his own subject, that he will be pleased to issue his commands to the Governor of Penang to afford me aid and assistance in my distresses and dangers, and cause a regulation to be made by which the two countries may have but one interest; in like manner I shall not refuse any aid to Penang, consistent with my ability. I further request a writing from the King, and from my friend, that it may remain as an assurance of the protection of the King, and descend to my successors in the government. I place a perfect reliance in the favour and aid of my friend in all these matters.

31

John Crawfurd's Mission to the Courts of Cochinchina and Siam

> *In addition to his service to the British government during its occupation of the Dutch East Indies (1811–1816), John Crawfurd served as emissary from the English East India Company to several kingdoms in Southeast Asia. Prior to his mission to Burma in 1827, Crawfurd set out for Cochinchina and Siam in the fall of 1821 in order to establish commercial relations with them. Reproduced below are excerpts, first, from his day by day account of Cochinchina, and, second, from his more contemplative and general assessment of conditions in Siam.*

[I]

We had by this time [August 30] found that our Cochin Chinese friends were extremely ceremonious, and partial to display and parade in little matters to the extent of ostentation. This humour was complied with, in exhibiting the letter of the [English] Governor-general. As soon as it was opened, the Mandarins proceeded to inspect it minutely, examining by turns the writing, the illuminated paper, and above all the seal of the Governor-general. This being done, we proceeded jointly, through the medium of a Portuguese translation which accompanied it, to render it sentence by sentence into Cochin Chinese. After this process had gone on a little time, the deputation considered it unsatisfactory, and begged that a written translation in the Chinese character

John Crawfurd, *Journal of an Embassy from the Governor-General of India to the Courts of Siam and Cochin China; Exhibiting a View of the Actual State of Those Kingdoms* (London: Colburn and Bentley, 1830), Vol. I, pp. 324–326, 375, 383; Vol. II, pp. 99–103.

might be effected. This was done accordingly. They now examined my credentials, and begged a Chinese translation of those also, and they farther required English and Portuguese copies of all the documents. This too was acceded to. On perusing the translation in the Chinese character, the Mandarins expressed entire satisfaction at the general purport of the letter; but advanced many objections to particular expressions, which they declared it was impossible to submit to his Majesty the King of Cochin China; the use of them, they said, however respectfully meant, being against the laws of the country. For example, towards the conclusion of the letter of the Governor-general, "His Excellency sends certain presents in token of his profound respect and esteem for his Majesty the Emperor of Cochin China." This was not to be endured, because, as the matter was explained to us, profound respect and esteem must be considered as matters of course from anyone that addressed His Majesty of Cochin China. At the suggestion of the Mandarins, the passage was rendered as follows: "I send your Majesty certain presents, because you are a great King." Strong objection was made to the expression in which His Excellency had disclaimed any wish for lands or fortresses; because it was not to be imagined for a moment that any one could desire lands or fortresses belonging to the King of Cochin China, and disclaiming the wish to obtain commercial factories alone was inserted. In the letter of the Governor-general, His Majesty was styled Emperor of Anam, a common term for Tonquin and Cochin China; and as it was well known that he had conquered a great part of Kamboja, and, as was asserted of Lao, Sovereign of these countries, also was added to his titles. This was much objected to, and the Mandarins informed me that it was no honour to the King of Cochin China to be styled "a king of slaves," for as such, it seems, the inhabitants of the conquered provinces are deemed by the governing race, that is, by the Anam nation, which includes both Cochin Chinese and Tonquinese. After the conference was over, I asked the Christian interpreter, in consequence of hearing this last observation, what opinion the Cochin Chinese entertained of the people of Kamboja. He had visited Bengal, and said without hesitation, "pretty much the same opinion that the English entertain of the black inhabitants of Hindoostan! !" The whole of this tedious conference lasted eight hours. The luckless interpreter, Antonio, was so overcome with the intricacy, not to say the danger of his part in the task, and the difficulty of pleasing every body, that he declared, that to have done it justice, would have required the head of an elephant! . . .

Sept. 28.—In our new residence we found ourselves treated with perfect respect, but we were close prisoners. Interpreters and Cochin Chinese servants were always at hand to do every office for us, but our Indian servants were not allowed to move beyond the doors without two or three persons to watch them, and this only once or twice in the course of the day. A singular exception was made in favour of our Chinese attendants. These were permitted to go abroad with entire freedom, and no suspicions entertained of them, any more than if they had been natural-born subjects of Cochin China itself. It is obvious from this, that all intercourse between European nations ought to be conducted through the instrumentality of the Chinese, and that the greater number of these people there are attached to an European mission, the fewer obstacles it will be likely to encounter. . . .

. . . We afterwards [Sept. 29] indeed learned, that, since his accession the Court etiquette had, in every way, become more ceremonious and uncomplying, and that it was the great ambition of the King to mimic the ceremonial of the Court of Pekin. I finally requested the Minister to represent to His Majesty our desire to have the honour of an audience. He endeavoured, for some time, to evade this demand; but at last consented to convey our request, promising that we should have an answer on the following day.

In the course of this last part of the conversation, the national vanity of the Cochin Chinese, and the exalted opinion they entertain of themselves and their Sovereign, were sufficiently conspicuous. "It is natural enough," said the Mandarin, with a smile, "that you should employ every expedient in your power to attain the honour of being presented to so great a King." . . .

[I I]

The Government of Siam, of which I am next to speak, is as
thoroughly despotical, as the absence of all legal restraint with
the aid of religion and superstition can well make it. We hear,
in other parts of the world, of pious individuals, who do not
pronounce the name of the Deity without pausing; but his subjects,
it is pretended, cannot pronounce the name of the King of Siam
at all. It is certainly never mentioned in writing, and is said to be
known only to a very few among his principal courtiers. I think
it doubtful, however, whether a King of Siam has in reality any
other name than the formidable epithets under which he is usually
mentioned. Neither must his health be inquired after, because,
however sick or wretched, it must be taken for granted that he is
free from bodily infirmities. No heir to the throne is appointed
during the lifetime of the King; for to imagine the death of the
King is not only in its legal, but in its popular acceptation, high
treason. In Siam, indeed, every thing connected with the Government is spoken of only in whispers. In common parlance, the King
of Siam is designated by various gentle epithets, among the most
frequent of which are, *Phra-penchao-yahuwa,* "the Sacred Lord
of Heads"; *Phra-pinchao-chuit,* "the Sacred Lord of Lives"; and
Kong-luang, "the Owner of All." The following epithets are also
in very general use in regard to him—"Most exalted Lord, infalli-
ble, and infinitely powerful." The language of adulation extends
to the members of his body. His feet, his hands, even his mouth,
nose, and ears, are never mentioned without the word *Phra,* meaning "Lord" or "Sacred Lord," being prefixed. Golden, is another
epithet appropriated to whatever belongs, or is attached to his
Majesty's person. Thus, to be admitted into the royal presence, is
to have reached the golden feet; and whatever comes to his Majesty's knowledge, is said to reach the golden ears. The following
was given to me as a literal translation of the ordinary prelude
to all addresses to his Majesty, either in speaking or writing: "Exalted Lord, Sovereign of many Princes, let the Lord of Lives

tread upon his slave's head, who here prostrate, receiving the dust of the golden feet upon the summit of his head, makes known, with all possible humility, that he has something to submit."

A large share of the veneration attached to the person of the King, is derived from the belief that his body is the vehicle of a soul in a highly advanced stage of migration towards a final state of beatitude, rest, or extinction. The bare fact of being a King is considered satisfactory evidence of religious merit and piety in former conditions of existence. In rank, there is no comparison between the Sovereign and the most exalted of his officers or courtiers, and the idiom of the language itself takes care to mark the immeasurable distance which exists between them. This gives rise to forms of expression which appear highly ludicrous to a stranger. The King, for example, will call a young prince, or a young nobleman, dog, or rat, with the incongruous epithets of Royal, Noble, Illustrious, etc., and these terms, far from being considered as opprobrious will be received by the young aspirants as expressions of kindness and condescension.

The manners of the Siamese Court, and the etiquette observed, seem to be nearly the same at the present day as they are described by the earliest European travellers. The King gives two audiences to his ministers daily, one in the morning and one late at night; asks each of them a few commonplace questions respecting his particular department, and decides on the spot on a few easy and trivial cases brought before him. His Majesty passes the rest of the day between the company of his women and that of the Talapoins [monks]. The latter pray to or for him; the former occasionally amuse him with reading romances.

With a few trifling exceptions in the provinces, there is no hereditary rank in Siam; no aristocracy of wealth or title; the despotism which reigns over all levelling before it every distinction, and rendering all subservient to its pleasure or caprice. The people seem to be considered as the mere slaves of the Government, and valued only in so far as they minister to the pride and consequence of the Sovereign, or of those to whom he delegates any share of his power. The most important feature of the Siamese

Government, is the universal conscription which prevails, and through which the labour and services of the adult male population, whether for ordinary labour, or for military or menial service, are placed at the disposal of the Government. Every male inhabitant of Siam, from the age of twenty-one upwards, is compelled to serve the state for four months in each year. The only exceptions are, the whole of the Talapoins; and the desire to escape from this servitude accounts for the universality of the practice of passing a portion of life in their order;—the whole Chinese population, because they pay a commutation in the form of a poll-tax;—slaves;—all public functionaries, great and small, and every father of a family who has three sons of a serviceable age. . . .

32

Siamese Kingship in the Nineteenth Century

> *Serving as English governess for the children of King Mongkut (1851–1868), Anna Leonowens not only helped shape the life of his successor Chulalongkorn (1868–1910), but also gave a vivid description of life in the Siamese Court. Part of her account of the character and administration of King Mongkut is presented below.*

One of the first public acts of the King P'hra Pooti-lootlah was to elevate to the highest honors of the state his eldest son (the Chowfa Mongkut), and proclaim him heir-apparent to the throne. He then selected twelve noblemen, distinguished for their attainments, prudence, and virtue,—most conspicuous among them the venerable but energetic Duke Somdetch Ong Yai,—to be tutors and guardians to the lad. By these he was carefully taught in all the learning of his time; Sanskrit and Pali formed his chief study, and from the first he aspired to proficiency in Latin and English,

Anna Harriette Leonowens, *The English Governess at the Siamese Court: Being Recollections of Six Years in the Royal Palace at Bangkok* (Boston: Fields and Osgood, 1870), pp. 237–243.

for the pursuit of which he soon found opportunities among the missionaries. His translations from the Sanskrit, Pali, and Magadthi, mark him as an authority among Oriental linguists; and his knowledge of English, though never perfect, became at least extensive and varied; so that he could correspond, with credit to himself, with Englishmen of distinction, such as the Earl of Clarendon and Lords Stanley and Russell.

In his eighteenth year he married a noble lady, descended from the Phya Tak Sinn, who bore him two sons.

Two years later the throne became vacant by the death of his father; but ... his elder half-brother, who, through the intrigues of his mother, had secured a footing in the favor of the Senabawdee, was inducted by that "Royal Council" into power. Unequal to the exploit of unseating the usurper, and fearing his unscrupulous jealousy, the Chowfa Mongkut took refuge in a monastery, and entered the priesthood, leaving his wife and two sons to mourn him as one dead to them. In this self-imposed celibacy he lived throughout the long reign of his half-brother, which lasted twenty-seven years.

In the calm retreat of his Buddhist cloister the contemplative tastes of the royal scholar found fresh entertainment, his intellectual aspirations a new incitement.

He labored with enthusiasm for the diffusion of religion and enlightenment, and above all, to promote a higher appreciation of the teachings of Buddha, to whose doctrines he devoted himself with exemplary zeal throughout his sacerdotal career. From the Buddhist scriptures he compiled with reverent care an impressive liturgy for his own use. His private charities amounted annually to ten thousand ticals. All the fortune he accumulated, from the time of his quitting the court until his return to it to accept the diadem offered by the Senabawdee, he expended either in charitable distributions or in the purchase of books, sacred manuscripts, and relics for his monastery.

It was during his retirement that he wrote that notable treatise in defence of the divinity of the revelations of Buddha, in which he essays to prove that it was the single aim of the great reformer to deliver man from all selfish and carnal passions, and in which he uses these words: "These are the only obstacles in the search for Truth. The most solid wisdom is to know this, and to apply one's self to the conquest of one's self. This it is to become the *enlightened,*—the Buddha!" And he concludes with the remark of Asoka, the Indian king: "That which has been delivered unto us by Buddha, that alone is well said, and worthy of our soul's profoundest homage."

In the pursuit of his appointed ends Maha Mongkut was active and pertinacious; no labors wearied him nor pains deterred him. Before the arrival of the Protestant missionaries, in 1820, he had acquired some knowledge of Latin and the sciences from the Jesuits; but when the Protestants came he manifested a positive preference for their methods of instruction, inviting one or another of them daily to his temple, to aid him in the study of English. Finally he placed himself under the permanent tutorship of the Rev. Mr. Caswell, an American missionary; and, in order to encourage his preceptor to visit him frequently, he fitted up a convenient resting-place for him on the route to the temple, where that excellent man might teach the poorer people who gathered to hear him. Under Mr. Caswell he made extraordinary progress in advanced and liberal ideas of government, commerce, even religion. He never hesitated to express his respect for the fundamental principles of Christianity; but once, when pressed too closely by his reverend moonshee with what he regarded as the more pretentious and apocryphal portions of the Bible, he checked that gentleman's advance with the remark that has ever been remembered against him, *"I hate the Bible mostly!"*

As High-Priest of Siam—the mystic and potential office to which he was in the end exalted—he became the head of a new school, professing strictly the pure philosophy inculcated by Buddha: "the law of Compensation, of Many Births, and of final Niphan [attainment of beatitude],"—but not Nihilism, as the word and the idea are commonly defined. It is only to the idea of God as an *ever-active* Creator that the new school of Buddhists is opposed, —not to the Deity as a primal source, from whose thought and pleasure sprang all forms of matter; nor can they be brought to admit the need of miraculous intervention in the order of nature. . . .

In the beginning of the year 1851 his supreme Majesty Prabat Somdetch P'hra Nang Klou, fell ill, and gradually declined until the 3d of April, when he expired, and the throne was again vacant. The dying sovereign, forgetting or disregarding his promise to his half-brother, the true heir, had urged with all his influence that the succession should fall to his eldest son; but in the assembly of the Senabawdee, Somdetch Ong Yai (father of the present prime minister of Siam), supported by Somdetch Ong Noi, vehemently declared himself in favor of the high-priest Chowfa Mongkut.

This struck terror to the "illegitimates," and mainly availed to quell the rising storm of partisan conflict. Moreover, Ong Yai had taken the precaution to surround the persons of the princes with a formidable guard, and to distribute an overwhelming force of militia in all quarters of the city, ready for instant action at a signal from him.

Thus the two royal brothers, with views more liberal, as to religion, education, foreign trade, and intercourse, than the most enlightened of their predecessors had entertained were firmly seated on the throne as "first" and "second" kings; and every citizen, native or foreign, began to look with confidence for the dawn of better times.

Nor did the newly crowned sovereign forget his friends and teachers, the American missionaries. He sent for them, and thanked them cordially for all that they had taught him, assuring them that it was his earnest desire to administer his government after the model of the limited monarchy of England; and to introduce schools, where the Siamese youth might be well taught in the English language and literature and the sciences of Europe.

There can be no just doubt that, at the time, it was his sincere purpose to carry these generous impulses into practical effect; for certainly he was, in every moral and intellectual respect, nobly superior to his predecessor, and to his dying hour he was conspicuous for his attachment to a sound philosophy and the purest maxims of Buddha. Yet we find in him a deplorable example of the degrading influence on the human mind of the greed of possessions and power, and of the infelicities that attend it; for though he promptly set about the reforming of abuses in the several departments of his government, and invited the ladies of the American mission to teach in his new harem, nevertheless he soon began to indulge his avaricious and sensual propensities, and cast a jealous eye upon the influence of the prime minister, the son of his stanch old friend, the Duke Ong Yai, to whom he owed almost the crown itself, and of his younger brother, the Second King, and of the neighboring princes of Chieng-mai and Cochin China. He presently offended those who, by their resolute display of loyalty in his hour of peril, had seated him safely on the throne of his ancestors.

From this time he was continually exposed to disappointment, mortification, slights, from abroad, and conspiracy at home. Had it not been for the steadfast adherence of the Second King and the prime minister, the sceptre would have been wrested from his grasp and bestowed upon his more popular brother.

Yet, notwithstanding all this, he appeared, to those who observed him only on the public stage of affairs, to rule with wisdom, to consult the welfare of his subjects, to be concerned for the integrity of justice and the purity of manners and conversation in his own court, and careful, by a prudent administration, to confirm his power at home and his prestige abroad. Considered apart from his domestic relations, he was, in many respects, an able and virtuous ruler. His foreign policy was liberal; he extended toleration to all religious sects; he expended a generous portion of his revenues in public improvements,—monasteries, temples, bazaars, canals, bridges, arose at his bidding on every side; and though he fell short of his early promise, he did much to improve the condition of his subjects.

33

Max Havelaar *and the Cultivation System*

> *E. Douwes Dekker has been aptly described as the Harriet
> Beecher Stowe of the East Indies, for it was* Max Havelaar
> *which served as much to bring about the demise of the
> Cultivation System in the Dutch East Indies as* Uncle Tom's
> Cabin *did to end the system of slavery in the United States.
> Published in 1860,* Max Havelaar *describes conditions under
> which the Indonesians labored. Fully acquainted with Indo-
> nesia, having been in Dutch governmental service in Sumatra
> and Java for seventeen years, Dekker challenged the Nether-
> lands to prove that the substance of his book was false. The
> debate which it provoked has not ceased to this day.*

. . . [A] native functionary is placed at the head of a district of
Java, who adds to the rank given him by the Government his
autochthonous influence, to facilitate the rule of the European
functionary representing the Dutch Government. Here, too, hereditary succession, without being established by law, has become a
custom. During the life of the Regent this is often arranged; and
it is regarded as a reward for zeal and trust, if they give him the
promise that he shall be succeeded by his son. There must be
very important reasons to cause a departure from that rule, and
where this is necessary, a successor is generally elected out of
the members of the same family. The relation between European
officials and such high-placed Javanese nobles is very delicate.
The Assistant Resident of a district is the responsible person; he
has his instructions, and is considered to be the chief of the district.
Still the Regent is much his superior—through local knowledge,
birth, influence on the population, pecuniary revenues, and man-

E. Douwes Dekker (Multatuli, pseud.), *Max Havelaar, or Coffee Auctions
of the Dutch Trading Company*, trans. Baron Alphonse Nahuÿs (Edinburgh:
Edmonston and Douglas, 1868), pp. 62–68.

ner of living. Moreover, a Regent, as representing the Javanese element, and being considered the mouthpiece of the hundred thousand or more inhabitants of his regency, is also in the eyes of the Government a much more important personage than the simple European officer, whose discontent need not be feared, because they can get many others in his place, whilst the displeasure of a Regent would become perhaps the germ of disturbance or revolt.

From all this arises the strange reality that the inferior actually commands the superior. The Assistant Resident orders the Regent to make statements to him; he orders him to send labourors to work at the bridges and roads; he orders him to gather the taxes; he summons him to the Council, of which he, the Assistant Resident, is President; he blames him where he is guilty of neglect of duty. This peculiar relation is made possible only by very polite forms, which need not exclude either cordiality, or where it is necessary, severity; and I believe that the demeanour to be maintained in this relation is very well described in the official instructions on the subject, as follows, "The European functionary has to treat the native functionary, who aids him, as his younger brother." But he must not forget that this younger brother is very much loved, or feared, by his parents, and in the event of any dispute, his own seniority would immediately be accounted as a motive for taking it amiss that he did not treat his younger brother with more indulgence.

The innate courteousness of the Javanese grandee,—even the common Javanese are much politer than Europeans in the same condition,—makes this apparently difficult relation more tolerable than it otherwise would be.

Let the European have a good education, with some refinement, let him behave himself with a friendly dignity, and he may be assured that the Regent on his part will do all in his power to facilitate his rule. The distasteful command put in an inviting form is punctually performed. The difference in position, birth, wealth, is effaced by the Regent himself, who raises the European, as Representative of the King of the Netherlands, to his own position; and the result of a relation which, viewed superciliously, would have brought about collision, is very often the source of an agreeable intercourse.

I said that such Regents had precedence over the European functionaries on account of their wealth; and this is a matter of course. The European, when he is summoned to govern a province which in surface is equal to many German duchies, is generally a person of middle or more advanced age, married and a father: he fills an office to gain his livelihood. His pay is only sufficient, and often insufficient, to procure what is necessary for his family. The Regent is "Tommongong," "Adhipatti," yes, even "Pangerang," that is, a "Javanese prince." The question for him is not that of getting his living; he must live according to his rank.

While the European lives in a house, *his* residence is often a *Kratoon* [palace], with many houses and villages therein. Where the European has a wife with three or four children, he supports a great number of women with their attendants. While the European rides out, followed by a few officers—as many as are necessary to draw up reports on his journey of inspection,—the Regent is followed by hundreds of retainers that belong to his suite, and in the eyes of the people these are inseparable from his high rank. The European lives citizen-like; the Regent lives—or is supposed to live—as a Prince.

But all this must be paid for. The Dutch Government which has founded itself on the influence of these Regents, knows this; and therefore nothing is more natural than that it has raised their incomes to a standard that must appear exaggerated to one unacquainted with Indian affairs, but which is in truth very seldom sufficient to meet the expenses that are necessarily incurred by the mode of life of such a native chief.

It is no uncommon thing to find Regents in pecuniary difficulties who have an income of two or three hundred thousand guilders. This is brought about by the princely indifference with which they lavish their money, and neglect to watch their inferiors, by their fondness for buying, and, above all things, the abuse often made of these qualities by Europeans. The revenue of the Javanese grandees may be divided into four parts. In the first place, their fixed monthly pay; secondly, a fixed sum as indemnification for their bought-up rights, which have passed to the Dutch Government; thirdly, a premium on the productions of their regency,— as coffee, sugar, indigo, cinnamon, etc.; and lastly, the arbitrary disposal of the labour and property of their subjects. The two last-mentioned sources of revenue need some explanation. The Javanese is by nature a husbandman; the ground whereon he is born, which gives much for little labour, allures him to it, and, above all things, he devotes his whole heart and soul to the cultivating of his rice-fields, in which he is very clever. He grows up in the midst of his *sawahs* [rice fields] . . . ; when still very young, he accompanies his father to the field, where he helps him in his labour with plough and spade, in constructing dams and drains to irrigate his fields; he counts his years by harvests; he estimates time by the colour of the blades in his field; he is at home amongst the companions who cut paddy with him; he chooses his wife amongst the girls of the *dessah* [village], who every evening tread the rice with joyous songs. The possession of a few buffaloes for ploughing is the ideal of his dreams. The cultivation of rice is in Java what the vintage is in the Rhine provinces and in the south of France. But there came foreigners from the West, who made themselves masters of the country. They wished to profit by the fertility of the soil, and ordered the native to devote a part of his time and labour to the cultivation of other things which should produce higher profits in the markets of Europe. To persuade the lower orders to do so, they had only to follow a very simple policy. The Javanese obeys his chiefs; to win the chiefs, it was only necessary to give them a part of the gain,—and success was complete.

To be convinced of the success of that policy we need only consider the immense quantity of Javanese products sold in Holland; and we shall also be convinced of its injustice, for, if anybody should ask if the husbandman himself gets a reward in proportion to that quantity, then I must give a negative answer. The Government compels him to cultivate certain products on his ground; it punishes him if he sells what he has produced to any purchaser but itself; and *it* fixes the price actually paid. The expenses of transport to Europe through a privileged trading company are high; the money paid to the chiefs for encouragement increases the prime cost; and because the entire trade *must* produce profit, that profit cannot be got in any other way than by paying the Javanese just enough to keep him from starving, which would lessen the producing power of the nation.

34
Early French Imperialism in Cochinchina

Francis Garnier, who under the pseudonym G. Francis, published several remarkable pamphlets on Cochinchina in the 1860's, was a precocious young man who had served as ensign in the French Imperial Navy in China and subsequently became an outstanding administrative official in Cholon. He strongly opposed the "retrocession" of the three eastern provinces of Cochinchina ceded to France, a subject seriously debated in Paris at that time. This attitude is clearly reflected in the excerpts taken from "La Cochinchine française en 1864" and "De la colonisation de la Cochinchine," written in 1864 and 1865, respectively.

FRENCH COCHINCHINA IN 1864

Communal organization remains the basis of Annamite society; this basis is so strong that, in spite of the war, in spite of efforts by the Annamite authorities of the French provinces, emigration outside of the French territory has taken place only to a very minor degree. We have here a powerful means of action of which we must carefully maintain (even) the least important cogs. Let us give the most complete liberty to the election of the mayors [chiefs]; let us increase (their) influence, (their) privileges, let us

Georges Taboulet, ed., *La geste française en Indochine* (Paris: Adrien-Maisonneuve, 1956), Vol. II, pp. 542–545. English translation by Margaret W. Broekhuysen. By permission of the author and Adrien-Maisonneuve.

make of them the born natural defenders of the population. . . . When this foundation of the structure is thus carefully preserved and respetced, the Annamites will accept very quickly . . . French administrators replacing the greedy mandarins at the head (of the state). At the same time, the arrival of European commerce, the opening up of markets will increase the general wealth a hundred-fold and will topple the latest prejudices. When the works have been executed, when the means of communication will have been established, the measures taken for the benefit of public hygiene will appear to them to be worthy of admiration and gratitude. . . .

It is scarcely three years ago that we definitely took possession of the shores of the "Donnai"; only a year has gone by since the last troubles. . . . Already taxes are coming in well, our orders are being carried out perfectly. The instigators of the insurrection who, eighteen months ago, ran through the country in all safety, strong through the secret sympathy of all, now have difficulty in finding a safe asylum; some have even been handed over by the villages where they had taken refuge. Unfortunately it is not so everywhere; in the most remote districts, where the insurrection for a time had the possibility to establish itself more completely, the rebel chiefs have preserved all their prestige. There an implacable repression is necessary. We must reassure the Annamites by unchallengeable proofs that our establishment is a stable one. . . .

If I have correctly evaluated the case with which the population could be made to submit promptly and completely, we can hope, after a very short lapse of time, to see the armed occupation reduced to more normal proportions and the military government replaced by a civil administration. Without ignoring all that the former has done for the conquest and the organization of the colony, one cannot deny that it has the drawback of constantly causing a certain uneasiness . . . (because of) the frequent and inevitable changes which it makes in the direction of (our) affairs. . . . (Also it is) too absolute in its way of seeing things, it often is wrong in wanting to have the country adjust to its ideas, instead of modifying the latter in accordance with the country. . . .

. . . It is indispensable that France follow with an attentive eye the progress and the vicissitudes of the battle of which China is the theater. . . . The present crisis constitutes a fatal blow to China's European markets. Already Shanghai, after having witnessed prodigious success, is standing still. If the Chinese Empire collapses, its debris will momentarily obstruct the avenues of its trade. Saigon, the only European port shielded from this perturbation and enjoying perfect tranquillity, is called upon to harvest the wreckage of this great calamity and grow to the extent of all that the others have lost. In continental communication with China it will for a moment be its almost exclusive outlet for trade, and Saigon's trade will attain proportions which cannot be measured in advance. . . .

. . . Cochinchina has cost a lot of money, I know. Will we recover the sums lost? Certainly not. Will it cost still more? I dare affirm that, if we want, our colony can go forward alone from now on. . . . Algeria was given thirty years before it was asked for an account of the blood and the gold spent on it. Shall we not give three years to Cochinchina, which I do not hesitate to compare with our African possession? As to commercial value, (Cochinchina) surpasses it [Algeria]; and as for its location, is its influence less considerable because it affects a more remote theater?. . .

. . . The manner in which England appreciates it is a sure indication of the value and the future of our Cochinchinese possession. No one has better insights in judging a conquest than a rival. In every one of the organs of the English press of the Chinese seas one can read diatribes without end on the occupation of Saigon by France and on the latter's unbridled ambition. Strange complaints coming from such mouths! (But) they should at least open our eyes. . . .

. . . Thus, having assumed an admirable position on the Asiatic continent through a fortunate and fruitful inspiration, having seen for a moment a more beautiful colonial future open up for us and a new empire of the East Indies rise up in the shadow of our flag, we are going to sacrifice everything to an hour of impatience, to a passing crisis, and we will have to resign ourselves without hope of return to seeing French influence and trade in the China seas vegetate in the stagnation of earlier times. ... Let a resounding denial go forth to reassure everyone, to give a new surge to our foundation which is just coming into existence, and to allow us to study the definitive proportions which it will be proper to assure them of.

ON THE COLONIZATION OF COCHINCHINA

... The possession of our three provinces remains insufficient and becomes dangerous if it is not supplemented, in a very short time, by the conquest of the rest of Cochinchina. The Annamites themselves have always considered the six provinces as forming an indivisible whole; the conquest by the Annamites of the Bienhoa territory on the Cambodians fatally involved them in that of the entire delta. ... The treaties obligate us to let the agents of Hué go through our territory; we cannot prevent their efforts to recruit, the annoying impression which the passing through and the view of their former mandarins produce on the Annamites. As long as this geographical situation exists we shall be subjected to the mute and permanent hostility of the upper classes, the defiant and ruinous hesitation of the masses. ... The occupation of the three other provinces would immediately reduce our frontiers by 70 miles ... which are very difficult to guard. This conquest, if skillfully conducted, would possibly cost us no more blood than a certain battle without tears in antiquity. ...

... For the purpose of a badly understood economy, the personnel of officers charged with the administration has been reduced to a bare minimum, or rather to an insufficient minimum; from this stems the impossibility to reorganize the country and more especially to collect the taxes, the continuation of a host of abuses which we have inherited from the Annamite regime, (and) the introduction of some others. We have to content ourselves with working from one day to the next; we cannot think of serious preparatory studies which are required by the reforms which everyone feels to be necessary yet powerless to undertake. The land tax for 1865 has been evaluated at 1,600,000 francs; no one doubts that the population pays much more. The levies taken by the native intermediaries attain a scarcely believable proportion, the triple amount, sometimes more. A land register would do a great deal for the country's moral well-being and for an increase of its financial resources. Establishing personal [tax] records would make it possible to do away with those fake and miserable revenues from opium and game leases which were deemed necessary at the beginning, and whose designation instinctive modesty has caused to disappear from the 1865 budget....

... In sum, taking possession of the six provinces, the organization, if not of a civil government, then at least of a local administration suited to the colony, the development of its agricultural resources and of (our) commercial influence ... in Indochina, seem to me to be realizable from this time on without increasing expenses by (reliance on) the resources of the colony only. By hastening to give it a definite stable position (now) we shall spare ourselves the long and costly groping for an obscure and undecided policy, for a government by an overly variable and overly unstable personnel.

35
The Birth of The Federated Malay States

On July 1, 1896 Perak, Selangor, Negri Sembilan and Pahang joined in the Federated Malay States. The federation had originated with Frank Swettenham, who was appointed its first Resident-General, residing at the federal capital of Kuala Lumpur (Selangor), and exercising executive control. In July, 1897, the first Conference of Malay Rulers was held at Kuala Kangsar (Perak). The document reproduces part of the Resident-General's Official Report of that meeting.

From every point of view the meeting has been an unqualified success, and it is difficult to estimate now the present and prospective value of this unprecedented gathering of Malay Sultans, Rajas, and chiefs. Never in the history of Malaya has any such assemblage been even imagined. I doubt whether anybody has ever heard of one Ruler of a State making a ceremonial visit to another; but to have been able to collect together, in one place, the Sultans of Pêrak, Sĕlângor, Păhang, and the Nĕgri Sambîlan is a feat that might well have been regarded as impossible. People who do not understand the Malay cannot appreciate the difficulties of such a task; and I confess that I myself never believed that we should be able to accomplish it. It was hardly to be expected that a man of the great age of the Sultan of Sĕlângor could be induced to make, for him, so long and difficult a journey, and to those who know the pride, the prejudices, and the sensitiveness of Malay Rajas, it was very unlikely that the Sultan of Păhang would join an assemblage where he could not himself dictate the exact part which he would play in it. It is not so many years since the Governor of the Straits Settlements found the utmost difficulty in getting speech with Malay Rajas in the States which are now federated; Sir Frederick Weld, even though accompanied by the present Sultan of Pêrak, by Sir Hugh Low, and the present Residents of Sĕlângor and Păhang, all officers accustomed to deal with Malays, had to wait several hours, on the bank of the Păhang River, before any one could persuade the Sultan of Păhang to leave a game of chance in which he was engaged with a Chinese, in order to grant an interview to His Excellency. It is difficult to imagine a greater difference than between then and now, and, though the Sultan of Pêrak has been far more nearly associated with British officers than any other of the Sultans, he has always been extremely jealous of his rights as a Ruler. I was, therefore, surprised to hear the frank way in which, at the Council, he spoke of British protection, which he did not hesitate to describe as control.

The deliberations of the Council were both interesting and useful, and there is no doubt that, in some respects, we could not have arrived at the same ends by any other means than the meet-

Frank Swettenham, *British Malaya: An Account of the Origin and Progress of British Influence in Malaya,* new and rev. ed. (London: Allen & Unwin, 1955), pp. 289–291. By permission of Allen & Unwin.

ing of the Rajas of the Federated States and their responsible advisers. All the proceedings of the Council were conducted in the Malay language, and I am convinced that, if ever it were necessary to introduce interpretation, no such successful meetings as those just concluded could ever be held. The Sultans and all their chiefs spoke on all the subjects which interested them, without either hesitation or difficulty, and on matters concerning the Mahammadan religion, Malay customs, and questions which specially touch the well-being of Malays, it would be impossible to find elsewhere such knowledge and experience as is possessed by those present at the recent meetings. Nothing can be decided at the Council, which is only one of advice, for no Raja has any voice in the affairs of any State but his own. This was carefully explained and is thoroughly understood. But it is of great value to get together the best native opinions and to hear those qualified to do so thoroughly discuss, from varying points of view, questions which are similar in all the Federated States. On several important subjects the members of the Council expressed unanimous views, and it now only remains to take action in the various State Councils to secure identical measures embodying the opinions expressed.

36
Dutch Colonial Policy in the Twentieth Century

The tenor of colonial administration is often best expressed in its reaction to perturbances among the governed. In late 1926, a rural rebellion, led by Communists, erupted in the province of Banten (Bantam) in West Java. This document is the conclusion of a report by the commission of inquiry set up by the colonial government in 1927; the commission consisted of one Indonesian and two Dutch officials.

In agreement with what has been mentioned above in outlining the basis for a new policy all these measures, generally speaking, arise from the principle that the population must first and foremost become accustomed to obeying and respecting the government, while the government on its part must constantly take into account the peculiarities of the population, which are not always agreeable. It is only in this way that law and order can become a possibility. The Commission realizes that the expense entailed by the proposed measures will be considerable, even very high. But it is convinced—and it believes itself to be supported in this by the opinion of all local administrative officials—that the high expenditure is justified. For not only the peaceful development of extensive regions which have been rather neglected by the authorities in the past is at stake but—and experience has unfortunately shown that this is no idle talk—also the lives of government officials.

Finally the Commission wishes to state emphatically that it is well aware that, however efficient all the proposed measures may be in themselves, however well the administrative system and organization visualized may function—quite apart from the fact that there will never be sufficient means or sufficiently trained persons available—the root of the evil will not be eradicated. A people such as the Bantamese, and the same applies to the population of many other parts of the Dutch East Indies, will always be greatly susceptible to propaganda which tempts them with the prospect of liberation from foreign rule. Therefore certainly no less important than the measures necessary locally to render the population less receptive to the activities of propagandists, which come from outside in the first instance, is the attempt to deprive such activities of their strength. Hence this must not only be effected by imbuing the object of these activities, the population, with more resistance to their influence, but also by attempting to guide the activities of their leaders into other channels.

The course of events has clearly indicated that the leaders of the movement could organize themselves in spite of police, administration, and the criminal investigation department with the reg-

Harry J. Benda and Ruth T. McVey, eds. and trans., *The Communist Uprisings of 1926–1927 in Indonesia: Key Documents* (Ithaca, N.Y.: Cornell Modern Indonesia Project, 1960), pp. 65–66. By permisson of the Cornell Modern Indonesia Project.

ulations which are at the disposal of these bodies, and that they could embrace thousands in the organization designed by them. The intellectuals who did not join that organization did not turn against it either.

This time it was so-called Communists, another time it will be extreme nationalists or others who attempt the same thing. The urge for freedom which stirs the best among these people—inferior elements need not be considered here—is not to be checked by any contrived system of preventive or repressive measures, but perhaps the excesses to which it gives rise in these regions may be prevented by always and unreservedly granting the population a voice in administrative affairs corresponding to its own development. As the population's share in the settlement of its own interests become larger, counter-forces may be developed which will turn against any organizations which jeopardize authority. At the moment, no substantial measures can be indicated for Bantam as to a solution of this extremely difficult problem. Nevertheless it is certain that attention must, in the future, remain focused on what may be achieved in this direction. It is also certain that in Bantam's case compulsion alone can never solve the problem.

In this report the considerations and conclusions are laid down to which the three members of the Commission have come after a partially joint but chiefly individual inquiry and after mutual discussions. The Commission visited almost the whole of the area which had been in rebellion, but particularly the districts of Pandeglang, Menes, and Labuan (Tjaringin) as well as Serang. They have not only tried to obtain the views of active or retired officials but also to learn the opinions of the native inhabitants of the region. To this end they have interviewed people from the *desas* [villages] in many places.

As complete unanimity was achieved concerning the fundamental items directly connected with the assignment, there was no reason for any of the members of the Commission to submit a minority report.

Finally the Commission wishes to thank all those within and

without Bantam who have, at its request, given their very willing assistance.

The Commission of Inquiry,
E. Gobée, Sumitro, Ranneft

37

In Defense of the Mission Civilisatrice *in Indochina*

> *This document consists of the introductory and concluding paragraphs from a long address surveying the state of the colony by Pierre Pasquier, Governor-General of French Indochina, on October 15, 1930. In February of that year, the Yen-Bay revolt had erupted in Tonkin, instigated by the Viet-Nam dan dang (Vietnamese Nationalist Party), which the colonial government suppressed with extreme severity (see Document 48, below). Pasquier, who knew Vietnam well, having written a valuable book on old Annam, was one of the ablest spokesmen of French colonial rule before the Second World War.*

Gentlemen,

Since the last session of the Great Council, Indochina has experienced grievous events. Before the highest representation of the colony I salute, with as yet unalloyed emotion, those Frenchmen and natives who have been the victims of these occurrences.

Gentlemen, it will soon be two years ago that, upon assuming my duties, I had indicated my desire to bring to conclusion the work of my predecessors, to apply myself with all my power to the realization of the loan, to the establishment of the banking organization of the colony, to endowing Indochina with a definitive

Grand Conseil des Interêts Économiques et Financiers de l'Indochine, Session ordinaire de 1930, *Discours prononcé le 15 octobre 1930 par M. P. Pasquier, Gouverneur général de l'Indochine* (Hanoi-Haiphong: Imprimerie d'Extrême-Orient, 1930), pp. 3–5, 117–119. English translation by Margaret W. Broekhuysen.

monetary system; at the same time I stated in detail my design to pursue a far-reaching inquiry, which had become necessary, into the very value of Indochina as well as its power and its future possibilities, without, however, interrupting the rhythm of [the colony's] life. The realization of this modest plan has not been dependent on my will alone, [and] delays have so far inhibited its completion, which, however, according to the assurances given us will be an accomplished fact in the very near future.

Despite dramatic incidents, despite the world crisis whose influence was felt here also, Indochina has nevertheless steadily progressed during these two years. No one's work has ever been slowed down. The efforts of the settler, the administrator, and the native have ensured the equilibrium of the present situation, which in no way justifies the crisis in confidence that has arisen in certain circles.

Here, where everyone is engaged in the jobs at hand, we can evaluate the difficulty of the tasks to be fulfilled, we can weigh the results obtained, here, where under the relentless criticism of our minds everyone recognizes nevertheless the grandeur of the structure erected by France in a joint and collective effort, it is easy to become inflamed against opinions which have been formulated far away from us on the progress of our evolution.

We find it difficult to understand the sudden interest in Indochina, the distant image of which appears to the metropolitan country [France] in the sudden light of striking incidents which for a moment hold the ever-changing interest of public opinion. We then see how, besides an impassioned but loyal investigation, solutions for Indochina's problems are arrived at, [including] hateful and perfidious campaigns which willfully ignore the facts, which are travesties of the realities, in order to represent the indigenous population as being bowed down under the yoke of I do not know what hard and pitiless law of haughty domination, misrepresenting the generous, just, and benevolent action which the Government has unceasingly exercised, and still exercises, in all moral and material aspects, for the development and vigor of the Indochinese Union.

These abominable indictments, this crafty or cynical publicity which interprets our most disinterested actions so as to distort them, all this is nothing but a maneuvering of the large methodically drawn-up and precisely executed program, which must necessarily lead to rebellion, to the destruction of our civilizing efforts.

Let no one misunderstand me; I am not protesting here against the noble and generous movements of opinion which derive their strength from the most unselfish and purest sentiments of the French soul. These force us at certain times to examine our conscience and thereby fortify all the more our reasons for persevering in the policies which men like Paul Bert have outlined for all times. But they also dictate to us the imperious duty to explain the attainments of this policy, to call attention to its errors, to the direction of its tendencies; to place before the French common sense the complete picture of our achievement, in order to have her [France] know it better, above all to have her understand it better. . . .

. . . I have tried to give a composite picture of our policies in Indochina, a sort of program of the goals to be attained. This program contains no ideology whatever, it is practical, social, realistic, completely stamped with that humane conception of things which is the mark of all that France does.

All of Indochina knows today the means which we have used to resolve the problems which present themselves to us.

We ask of the indigenous elite, which has always shown willingness to practice a highly successful, logical, reasonable association with us, to signify their adhesion to the policies we have just defined. We are prepared to pursue the realization of these policies with their active cooperation.

But let us be precise. If we ardently desired this cooperation—recognizing, as it has been so generously stated on the floor of the Chamber, no other imperialism than the imperialism of the heart; no other priority than the priority of the spirit—then we ask for it without reserve or reticence. This cooperation should be realized, if not on the same plane, then at least on planes on the same level, claiming no vassalage of gratitude, but demanding definite and real support from both sides. We want to exercise firmly, as the Head of the Department has stated it, "those rights which we claim to derive from a kind of paternal power the legitimacy of which cannot be prescribed."

But we want to exercise these rights with a view to a structure for the erection of which all the natives unite so that it may become a common structure, born of our concerted efforts, of the union of our cultures, of the agreement of the virtues of our races, of the reconciliation of our mutual interests. If this concurrence should fail us, which I cannot believe, since the natives have given us ample testimony of their intelligent approval, if those who have invoked our protection should repel our favors, considering them useless for their happiness and powerless to engender duties toward us, make no mistake [in believing that] France would not pursue any the less, on her own, her noble mission in accordance with her genius. Nothing could interrupt her generously beneficent action. I speak without subterfuge, without harshness, but I do not want to leave any room in your minds for ambiguities, for foolish and dangerous fancies.

Our generosity, or simply the accomplishment of our mission, should not be accepted as promises, as bills of exchange which we draw on the natives or which the natives draw on us.

We must not allow the detractors of our work to go on weaving a fallacious web which would hide the true face of Indochina from all those living here as well as those in France.

We must work towards ends which will satisfy our own altruism and our legitimate interests and which, precisely because of these, will make possible a future of better living, of a wider liberty within the framework of our civilization, for those peoples who live under the protection of the strong ramparts of our moral and material power; in the certainty that at some time, through the development of mutual feelings of respect and reasoned affection, France shall see on this Asian soil the flowering and the expansion of one of the most beautiful branches that has sprouted from her

genius and which in the harmony and the unity of all her sons
bears testimony to the enduring quality of her presence. . . .

38
An Official View of Rebellion in Burma

*In 1930–1931 Burma was shaken by a widespread, though
short-lived, uprising centered in the Tharawaddy district. It
was led by a former monk and Buddhist leader, Saya San.
The rebellion was easily suppressed and its originators executed by the colonial government. Excerpted below are parts
of the address given by the governor, Sir Charles Innes, to
the Legislative Council on February 12, 1931. It is a typical
example of the colonial government's approach to the political
upheavals of the times.*

I wish to say as little as may be about the rebellion. The news
came as a great shock to me when I was on my way out to Burma
and I am sure that it shocked equally all loyal persons in Burma.
We all sympathise with Sir Joseph Maung Gyi. It was indeed bad
luck that the rebellion broke out while he was acting as Governor
of Burma, but I am confident that every one in this Council will
agree with me when I say that we all regard it as his misfortune
and not his fault, and that no one attributes the rebellion to anything he did or left undone while he was in charge of Burma. On
the contrary, I am glad to have this opportunity of saying publicly
that since my return to Burma, and indeed while I was still in
England, I have heard many tributes from all sections of the community to Sir Joseph's popularity and to the skill with which he
discharged his high office.

I hope we may say that the rebellion is at an end. Things are
quiet in Pyapon and Yamethin and organised resistance to the

Yearbook of Compared Colonial Documentation, Year 1930 (Bruxelles:
Institut Colonial International, 1930), Vol. III, pp. 65–67.

Military and the Police has practically ceased in Tharrawaddy and Insein. But in these last districts law and order has not yet been restored, and armed bands of dacoits are still harrying the countryside, murdering village officers, burning villages and committing other outrages. Arrangements are being made to hunt down these bands but . . . it will not be an easy task, and I am afraid that our returns of violent crime will not make pleasant reading for some time to come. One of the consequences of the rebellion is that we are faced with the necessity of increasing our military police and also of strengthening the civil police in Tharrawaddy and Insein. Some part of the cost of this latter measure may be recovered from the disturbed areas, but in any event the greater part of the additional expenditure must fall on Provincial revenues at a time when they can ill afford to bear it. There is no help for it. But, as I see it, we must discharge our primary and most essential function of maintaining law and order. The inconvenience to Government however is a small matter compared with the loss of life and property and the general misery which have been caused in these unhappy districts by these deplorable risings. It is perhaps natural that in some quarters there has been a tendency to make excuses for the rebels, but there is no use in shutting our eyes to facts. All our enquiries go to show that the rebellion was carefully planned by those whose object it was to overthrow the Government. We have stated our conclusions in a recent communique, and have explained why we have had to take action against the Soe Thein G.C.B.A. [General Council of Buddhist Associations]. . . . There is no reasonable doubt that the rebellion was due to political rather than to economic causes, and that the main appeal of those who organized it was to the ignorance and credulity of the peasants. It is an unpleasant subject, and I do not wish to say more about it than I can help. Is it too much to hope that the more extreme sections of Burmese political thought will reconsider their position? For years past, their object has been to wreck the present constitution and to embarrass the Government. Now a new era is opening out for Burma. In future Burma will work out its own destiny, and it will depend on the Burmese people themselves how fast they will advance towards the declared constitutional goal of responsible Government within the Empire. Is there any reason why any section of the community should stand out and should devote itself to destructive rather than constructive activities? I merely put the question. It is not for me to answer it. Our duty is plain. It is to put down disorder of this kind by all means in our power, and I am confident that in that task we shall have the loyal support of this Council. We shall have to deal severely with those who have taken the lead in the rebellion, but no one need fear that we shall be harsh towards the misguided peasants who were deluded into joining it and who took no prominent part in it.

His Excellency the Governor-General [of British India] at our instance has recently promulgated an Ordinance arming us with powers to deal with the activities of the Bengal Revolutionary Party in Burma, and among the business which will come before the Council during this session is a bill to convert this Ordinance temporarily into the ordinary law of the land. The Hon'ble Home Member will explain in detail the necessity for this legislation. All I need say in this speech is that for years past we have been aware of the existence in Burma of a small section of the Bengal Revolutionary Party, and we have contented ourselves with keeping a careful watch upon them. Recently however they have increased in numbers, and some time ago we received warning that they were contemplating outrages in Burma. This warning was confirmed not long after by an attempt to wreck the train in which several high officials of Government were travelling. We have every reason to suppose that the outrage was the work of the Revolutionary Party, and we have also reason to believe that during the past few months, they have set themselves to the task of trying to corrupt the younger generation in Burma. It is for these reasons that we have thought it necessary to take action, and I commend the bill to the consideration of this Council. If the bill is passed into law, it will be used against no one who is not believed with good reason to be engaged in terrorist conspiracies. It is not directed against any other class or person in Burma, and there are ample safeguards against misuse. Every one will agree that it is entirely foreign to the nature of the Burman to commit outrages of this kind, and every one will also agree that not only must we protect the Police who are engaged in the dangerous task of checking the activities of these revolutionaries, but that we must also take measures to ensure that the younger generation in Burma is not infected with these sinister doctrines. . . .

PART IV

The Southeast Asian Response to the West

THE SOUTHEAST ASIAN response to the European in-
truders ranged from total disinterest to violent criticism. Therefore, the documents in this part have been
arranged by categories rather than chronologically. Although all the documents are "modern" in the sense that
they were written in the modern era, some of them are
examples of an ongoing tradition that is, or was until
recently, not or barely affected by change. They should
serve as a warning against the Europocentric view that
Western influence was all-pervasive in Southeast Asia. Not
everything of importance that happened during the century or so covered in the following pages was, directly or
indirectly, a response to the Western presence; and even
where such a response was involved, its form and content
matter quite often harked back to premodern times.

The first category, comprising only two documents, specifically dwells on developments that bear no relationship
to European dominance. The Malay author of the *Hikayat
Abdullah* (Document 39) portrays the strict education that
characterized Islamic upbringing from the early nineteenth century onward. The Vietnamese complaint about
Cambodian unruliness (Document 40) may serve as a
reminder that for many decades Southeast Asian politics

retained a momentum of its own, European power notwithstanding.

The four documents in the second category illustrate some of the timeless character of the Southeast Asian reactions to the steady Western encroachments upon Southeast Asian societies, especially the peasantry. These responses were variations on the perennial theme of utopian expectations in which the foreign overlord came to take the place of the unjust native ruler of former centuries. The examples for Java (Documents 41 and 42), Burma (Document 43), and the Philippines (Document 44) show how widespread these expectations were in colonial times and how little "modern" such movements really were.

Resistance to colonial rule was widespread, yet for many decades it remained anchored in the traditional patterns of restiveness and utopian expectations. Beginning in the late nineteenth century, an urban elite, with a modern education, gave this resistance a measure of ideological cohesion and organizational strength. The third category of this part provides a sampling of the varieties of these urban responses to the West. King Chulalongkorn, the Thai leaders of the 1930's, and Manuel Luis Quezon concern themselves with problems of internal improvement and stability rather than with colonialism since they spoke as the heads of independent and semi-independent states (Documents 45, 49, and 52). José Rizal, Pham Quynh, and Sutan Sjahrir, Western-trained intellectuals, envisaged some kind of rapprochement with the West so that their countries might benefit from Western achievements in science and government (Documents 46, 47, and 51). But, given the rigidities of most colonial governments, anticolonial nationalism very often took a far more radical turn, ultimately including demands for the expulsion of the West and immediate independence. This radical attack can be seen most clearly in the writings of Nguyen-Thai-Hoc and Sukarno (Documents 48 and 50). These few representatives of nationalism by no means exhaust the list of prominent leaders in colonial Southeast Asia; some others will be found in Part V.

The final category of documents sheds light on minority groups and problems in the area. The colonial governments were largely responsible for raising these groups to prominence, and Western neglect left the problem of their relations with the native majorities unsolved. Fear for the position of their groups in a Burman-governed state led Indian and Karen representatives to argue for special privileges for minorities (Documents 53 and 54). The last two selections illuminate Southeast Asian attitudes towards the Chinese. Document 55 captures the essence of native anti-Chinese prejudice, while in Document 56 a moderate Filipino serves as the rare and sensitive defender of the Chinese.

39

A Muslim Boyhood in Malaya

The Hikayat Abdullah *(The History of Abdullah) was written
by Abdullah bin Abdul Kadir (1797–1854) and published in
1849. Abdullah, born in Malacca of mixed Indian and Arab
extraction, had been employed by Sir Stamford Raffles. The*
Hikayat *provides many invaluable insights into life and
politics in early nineteenth-century Malaya. Abdullah's stern
religious upbringing, by no means typical of Malay boys at
that time, sheds light on the new Islamic orthodoxy that became fairly widespread, especially among urban Muslims, in
subsequent decades.*

ABDULLAH BEGINS HIS KORAN STUDIES

After practising in this way for some time my hand became accustomed to holding the pen and I could copy the form of written
letters, albeit roughly. One day when my grandmother saw that
my scribbling bore some resemblance to letters she wrote a few
lines of the Koran for me on a small tablet and told me to study
them. I did my lessons when I felt in the mood. When not I went
out and played. This continued until I was seven, at which age I
still could not read a single section of the Koran, for I was thoroughly spoilt by my grandmother who never scolded or struck me.
I did not care much for learning, preferring just to play about all
day. . . .

. . . Every day I used to go to school in the morning, and I was
taught by my father at night. Many times I was beaten and
slapped. Many writing tablets were smashed in pieces when they

A. H. Hill, trans., "The Hikayat Abdullah," *Journal of the Malayan
Branch of the Royal Asiatic Society,* Vol. XXVIII, pt. 3 (June, 1955),
pp. 41–44, 50–51. By permission of the Malaysian Branch, Royal Asiatic
Society.

were used to hit me on the head. Many canes were broken on my body. Time after time my mother used to weep because I suffered such frequent chastisement. Sometimes my fingers were beaten till they were swollen because I had made mistakes in writing. Mark well how difficult it is to aspire to knowledge, wisdom, skill and learning. Soon my heart was filled with hatred, anger and spite against my teacher. Many were the prayers I offered for his speedy demise, to release me from the pain of study so that I could go out and play wherever I liked. At that time I was very fond of flying kites. My father used to beat me frequently and hang the kite around my neck, ordering me back to my studies. I was highly delighted whenever my teacher was too ill to give me lessons for then I could go out and play; and if during a lesson he or any-one else ordered me to go anywhere, even to dangerous places, I was thankful to go just to get away from study. If I had the slight-est feeling of bodily discomfort I purposely made myself ill to avoid my lessons. I would rather look on the face of a tiger than on that of my teacher. For as everybody knows, if an orchard has fine trees but no fence to protect it, it is bound to be entered by animals and the like that will destroy it. . . .

Now when I remember how I was struck, beaten, slapped, and admonished, the many tablets broken over my head, the stern and angry looks, the nagging and scolding of all my teachers, I realize that each blow of the cane on my body has now become a lamp to guide me, each slap a pair of spectacles to my eyes. Had there been no lamp to my hand, no spectacles for me to use, doubtless many times I would have stumbled into the furrows and channels which lie thick on the highways and byways to knowledge, for without lamps to guide them many men before me have stumbled hither and thither, falling and jumping up covered in mud and filth, their limbs broken. I beseech Allah that it may please Him to grant a thousand mercies and the reward of peaceful repose to my teachers who have made me aware of these pitfalls, and who have provided a touchstone to my hand that I may avoid false imitations of gold and silver, and diamonds which are but gravel. . . .

I persevered in my studies, with the help of Allah and in fulfilment of my promise, until I could recite the Koran and also read and write; not like other children whose teachers used to write on their tablets for them. For indeed in those days nobody could write the Koran. But if people do not learn writing when they are young, when they are older and the desire to write arises what can they do? A human being is like a twig of wood. While it's still young, it yields whichever way we bend it, for it is pliable; when it has grown old, it has become dry and if we bend it, be it ever so slightly, it will snap. . . .

But I will not elaborate further the things that I suffered on account of my studies, like an *aur* stem rubbed the wrong way. My body became thin, my face sunken with the strain of thinking. I was worried because I did not succeed and because I was ashamed at giving cause for anger. But I realize now that however high the price I paid for my knowledge, at that price can I sell it. If I had picked up my knowledge as I went along, merely copying and listening, so far from people wishing to buy it I would be quite prepared to give it away free for the asking. It is well known to you, my readers, that anything cheap must be faulty: and anything expensive of superior value. Is not the precious diamond but a stone? Why is it held in such high regard by everyone? Is it not because of its brightness?

One day my father said to me: "You must no longer spend your time going about doing nothing. I have bought some paper. Sit down and write the Koran at home." And he showed me how to follow on paper the lines on a tablet. So I sat down and wrote. I did indeed receive presents and compliments, but the presents were blows with a rattan and the compliments abuse and sullen grumbling every day. This went on for six or seven months, my mistakes being pointed out to me. By the end I could correctly transcribe the Koran and Arabic manuscripts. When my father saw that I could write the Koran he said: "Here is a manuscript written in Malay and Arabic, a very fine one. Make a copy of it." So I copied it and after some time it was finished. Other people seeing my writing said it was good. Only my father poured unceasing discredit upon me saying: "Look at your writing, like a hen scratching, a sheer waste of paper. Even small children could write as well as that." He found fault with everything, nothing was right. But now at last I realize that my father in his wisdom did not wish to commend my skill or my work for fear it would make me arrogant and swollen-headed over my cleverness and erudition.

40
Nineteenth-Century Dynastic Rivalries in Mainland Southeast Asia

Although the French conquest of Vietnam had begun by the middle of the nineteenth century, dynastic rivalries continued to follow a traditional pattern for several decades to come, until European authority more or less put an end to it. This note on Cambodian-Vietnamese relations by the Vietnamese Minister of State, Phang-Thang-Giang, is taken from a volume of historical writings about Cochinchina, written by a Vietnamese mandarin in the middle of the nineteenth century.

NOTE from the Minister of State Phang-Thang-Giang [High Mandarin appointed by King Tu-duc as his plenipotentiary].

In the year Giap-ngo, the 15th year of Minh-mang [reigned 1820–1841], the Siamese army invaded Cambodia and its sailors spread over the province of An-giang; but this army was thrown back by Major General Truong-minh-giang. The Siamese sailors were forced to flee as far as Truc-bo, whereas the Siamese infantry, passing through Vua-sac, took refuge in the province of Battam-bong.

A citadel which was given the name of Trân-tay-thanh was constructed at Nam-vang by Truong-minh-giang. The latter assumed

Gia-Dinh-Thung-Chi, Histoire et description de la Basse Cochinchine, trans. G. Aubaret (Paris: Imprimerie Imperiale, 1863), pp. 129–132. English translation of the French version by Margaret W. Broekhuysen.

command of it and from then on was entrusted by the Annamite government with the protection and the supervision of Cambodia.

1835. In the year At-vi, the 16th year of Minh-mang, the King of Cambodia Neac-ong-chan died without issue. The mandarins of the kingdom then requested that the crown pass to the head of his daughter, Ngoc-van. This request was addressed to the Emperor of Annam through the intermediary of Truong-minh-giang, and since it was granted at the Hué court the investiture as Queen of Cambodia was accorded to Princess Ngoc-van. The three princesses Ngoc-bien, Ngoc-ty and Ngoc-nguyen were declared royal princesses of Cambodia.

1840. In the year Canh-ti, the 21st year of Minh-mang, the Cambodian mandarin Ki-to-tac levied troops to prepare a revolt, in agreement with the Siamese Chat-tri. The latter started out with peaceful propositions but it was not long before he threw off his mask and invaded the country, giving it over to looting.

Queen Ngoc-van, accepted by the Annam government, was installed at An-giang.

Later the governor general of An-giang and Ha-tien, Nguyen-tri-phuong, assisted by the governor of An-giang, completely defeated the Cambodian rebels and destroyed their fortress Thiet-thang. Then he blockaded the capital Udon by placing troops on three sides on land, thus intercepting any kind of communication for several years.

1847. However, in the year Dinh-vi, the 7th year of the Emperor Thiêu-tri [reigned 1841–1848], the Siamese Chat-tri asked by means of letters to enter into negotiations with the Annamite camp.

A conference house was then established in order to discuss there the Cambodian affairs, and when the day had arrived Neac-ong-duong (brother of Neac-ong-chan) was brought there; he avowed his submission and asked that his error might be forgiven him. The commanding Annamite general gave an account of these facts to the Hué court and the emperor, deigning to pardon the rebel, had an envoy give back to him the symbols of investiture which made him King of Cambodia.

Queen Ngoc-van and the royal princess Ngoc-tu could then re-turn to their country and to the bosom of their family. From this time on tribute was uninterruptedly offered by King Neac-duong up to the 12th year of the reign of Emperor Tu-duc [reigned 1859–1883].

Then when the Cambodians perceived that the empire of An-nam was in grave circumstances they hastened treacherously to take a bite (like dogs).

Heaven punished this ingratitude by causing King Neac-ong-duong to perish, and now his sons are devouring each other, al-though they are of the same flesh and blood; consequently their misery is extreme.

Cambodia has been a tributary of our empire for more than four hundred years. The Empire of Annam has always endeavored to deliver it from misery by restoring back peace and tranquillity to it. How many times we restored the country to this people! How many of its kings have we installed, supported, protected! . . .

In principle our intention is not at all to take possession of this country: we wish, taking heaven as an example, to let these peo-ple live and exist in peace; we do not wish the ruin of this little kingdom, as other people [Siam] plot against it with hearts full of malice.

The Cambodians are savages of a bad and vicious nature: now they submit, then they rebel, but they constantly forget rules and laws; it is as if they were stupid and devoid of reason.

The empire of Annam has always had the solicitude for Cam-bodia of a mother for the child she suckles, and to the present time Annam's feelings have not changed.

41

Messianic Currents in Java's "Little Tradition"

> *Messianic expectations have for centuries been prevalent in Java, sometimes cast in Hindu-Buddhist terminology, in the past few centuries as often as not with a more or less pronounced Islamic admixture. They usually center around the figure of a* ratu adil *(the righteous, just ruler), come to deliver the island from evil, especially from alien, i.e., non-Muslim, rule. The following brief excerpts come from two twentieth-century sources, collected, translated and analyzed by a Dutch scholar.*

This is a story originated by godly Arab sheikhs, and by the Prophet; to Thee, o Allah! They tell about His Highness the Prince who reveals the confession with which one is to answer the questions of him who regulates religion, whose rank is that of a sacred ruler, who is the pillar of the country of Java, (and) who reigns as sole sovereign in the country of Java. He is descended from the Prophet. For the latter begat Fatimah, who begat Hasan Husein, who begat sheikh Molana Maghribi, who begat Sultan Arip Mohammad, who begat Kyai Molana of Java, who went ashore at Sumenep, and whose wife came from (the) Sunda (region). They had one child, called Dewi Sribanon; she was taken by Sultan Arip Mohammad as his wife and had two children, both sons, the elder being named Sultan Muraidi(n), the younger Sultan Muradi(n). Their mother, Sribanon, came from Padjadjaran.

Subsequently the two princes fought for the crown of Arabia, but their father did not agree with this [their quarreling] because the elder prince ought to become ruler of Arabia. Their father

G. W. J. Drewes, *Drie Javaansche goeroe's, hun leven, onderricht en messiasprediking* (Leiden: Vros, 1925), pp. 168–169, 173–174. English translation by Margaret W. Broekhuysen.

said, "Muradi(n), if you want to become king I shall certainly pray that you may become king of the island of Java, but first you must have practised asceticism for thirty years on Mount Mandalagiri."

When he had lived as an ascetic for twenty-three years he subjugated all spirit rulers of the island of Java. They all paid their respects to Sultan Muradi(n), but he remained on Mount Surandil because his term as ascetic had not yet been completed.

(But) once the term is up, in the year *alip,* then there will be signs, (such as) eclipses of the sun and moon, a rain of ashes, the beginning of which will be that the sun rises in the wrong place [i.e., in the West], the water will be colored red, and the moon rises in the wrong place. Then watch out, people of the land of Java; a ruler of the unbelievers will come to the land of Java! Pay strict attention when the *ratu adil* has not yet come! And pay attention again when the *ratu adil* shall have come, (then) these are the questions he will ask and the answers that are to be given:

"Who am I?" "Yes, o Lord, Your Highness comes from *siti salam* (land of salvation)."

"What is my origin?" "Your origin is from Allah's omnipotence."

"Who is my wife?" "The wife of Your Highness is Ratu Agung, and the woman second to her is Ratu Agung Sengara."

"What do I bring?" "You bring, O Lord, the word *bismillah,* the perfect confession and the perfect faith." . . .

. . . Four rulers are subjects of the *ratu adil,* the ruler of Majapahit, called *ratu* Gumilang; that of Tjerbon, called *ratu* Tjahja Gumilang; that of Banten, called *ratu* Trus Gumilang; and that of Sunda, called *ratu* Sari Gumilang.

Moreover the *ratu pusaka,* who rules the island of Java as sole sovereign, will ask:

"From whence is your being?" "My origin is from God's light."

"What sort of person are you?" "I come from the land of justice."

"What road did you take to the world?" "My road leads from Egypt."

"Are you highly placed or a subordinate?" "I am a Muslim, a believer, inwardly and outwardly."

Then the *ratu adil* will say: "O Allah, O Allah's Prophet, this is a man who has been steadfastly looking for us."

Then the further question will be asked, "What is the meaning of all this?" To which the answer should be: "I agree, outwardly and inwardly, with all good works; I know good and bad behavior but I do not know the behavior of purity."

42
Prince Diponegoro as Islamic Deliverer

> *Prince Diponegoro of Jogjakarta led the most famous revolt against the Netherlands, the so-called Java War (1825–1830). After his capture by the Dutch, he wrote a long chronicle of that war, the* Babad Diponegoro *(not as yet published in toto in a Western language). The two excerpts point up the significance of both Javanese and Islamic religious concepts in rallying the population to Diponegoro's side.*

The thought of man's brief existence on earth never left him [Diponegoro] day or night. It was his heart's delight to think of the origin of his life; but his faith was still weak and he often succumbed to the temptations of the fair sex.

When he reminded himself of the end of all creation, he made his rounds and visited all the *misdjids* (temples), joining with the clerics. In so doing he imposed the strictest abstinence on himself and dressed very shabbily, so that he was rarely recognized; when this occurred, however, he moved on. He preferably consorted with undistinguished clerics and often changed his place of abode.

When the continued company of the clerics bored him he visited the woods, mountains, valleys and caves. Sometimes he travelled along the seaside. At the time of fasting (*puasa*) he most often

P. J. F. Louw, *De Java-Oorlog van 1825–30* (Batavia: Landsdrukkerij, The Hague: Nijhoff, 1894), Vol. I, pp. 91–93, 130–131. English translation of the Dutch translation by Margaret W. Broekhuysen. By permission of the author and Martinus Nijhoff.

stayed in a lonely cave. Thus he was in the cave of Sung-kamal, when the Lord visited him after midnight with all kinds of forms and appearances.... Then the visitation disappeared....

In the morning Diponegoro went on, his path leading along a mountain ridge. He did not mind dangers or difficulties, and had no thought for anything but the favor of the Lord that had fallen to his share. He walked through thick and thin, into ravines, up mountains, without definite aim, he was so absent-minded. When he became tired, he laid himself to rest wherever he might be. So he roamed and sometimes spent weeks in some cave or other, and held a prayer-meeting at Imagiri, the princely cemetery in the Southern Mountains, close to the confluence of the Opak and Oja rivers. In the cave of Langsé he stayed so long that the world of the senses disappeared for him and he was only conscious of an existence that, moreover, was not conscious of anything but itself.

Then the Ratu Kidul [Javanese deity of the Sea] appeared to him. It was light in the cave. But she, knowing that Diponegoro was just then absorbed in his imaginations and could not be disturbed, told him she would return when the right time should have come. Sech Ngabdulrachin [Muslim title and name for Diponegoro] heard what was being said but he did not look up and the Ratu Kidul disappeared again.

A few days later, at Parangkusuma, Diponegoro was sitting with his arms folded around his knees, leaning against a rock and slumbering. Then he heard a voice which spoke to him: "Well, Ngabdulrachin! Change your name and from now on call yourself Ngabdulkamid. I tell you, in three years' time the realm of Jogjakarta will have been brought to perdition, thus God wills it. You are destined to play an active part in these events. As a sign I give to you this arrowpoint called Sarutama. Verily I say unto you, Ngabdulkamid, be on your guard.... You may now set out on the way home."

Ngabdulkamid awoke from his slumber. He did no longer hear any human voice. But directing his glance toward the heavens he saw something like a flash of lightning shoot down before him, which got stuck in a rock. That was the arrowpoint Sarutama.

Ngabdulkamid pulled it from the rock and took it with him. . . .

Every *Puasa* month the Prince sat in the cave of Setjang and performed his prayers there. He sat there on a large, flat rock which was called Ambarmaja. The only objects which attracted his attention in that beautiful cave were a well in a cistern of masonry, like a deep lake in the shape of a well. Furthermore [he was attracted by] a fenced-in *widara*-tree, which was his audience hall as it were; also a large *gebang*-tree with steps that had been carved out for climbing it, representing the gate of his palace.

He had his eyes almost closed when suddenly someone came and stood before him, carried to him by a gust of wind. His apparel resembled that of a haji [a Mecca pilgrim]. The Prince was startled and asked, "I do not know you; who are you?"

The man answered respectfully, "I have no dwelling place and have come here with a mandate to call you."

The Prince replied, "What is the name of him who sent you and where does he live?"

"The one who sent me on this mission does not have a dwelling place either; the whole outer world serves him as an abode. His name is Ratu Adil [the Just Ruler]. He is just now on the top of a mountain situated to the southeast of here, called Rasamuni, but you are not allowed to take along any retinue."

Thereupon the Prince accompanied the man. Having arrived at the foot of the mountain, the messenger disappeared. Ratu Adil was standing on the top, vying with the sun as to splendor, so that the latter paled for a time. Because of this the Prince was unable to behold Ratu Adil's face, but he clearly saw his apparel. His turban was green, his shirt, outer garment and trousers were white, and his scarf was red. He said, "Hear me, Ngabdulkamid! I have summoned you to tell you that you must lead my whole army into battle. Conquer Java with it. When someone asks what your mandate is, tell him it is the Koran, let him search there." Ngabdulkamid answered, "I ask your forgiveness, but I can no longer go into battle for I cannot stand the sight of corpses; besides, I have formerly acted very badly towards my fellow men."

Ratu Adil replied, "No, this is not permitted. It is the will

of the Almighty, and it has been definitely decided that you and
no one else must execute this undertaking."

Then the Prince heard a loud noise as of something breaking,
as if a stone were thrown on an earthen vessel, and then both
disappeared in an indescribable (incomprehensible) manner.

43
A Nationalist Condemnation of British Rule in Burma

> *This document is taken from a nationalist attack on the
> governance of colonial Burma. It is cast in the form of a
> sharp rebuttal of the official explanation of the origin and
> causes of the Saya San rebellion of 1930–1931 (see Docu-
> ment 38). The author, a Rangoon-based editor, seeks to ex-
> plain how such a typically rural-traditional uprising could
> occur and attract a vast following. Written in 1935 or 1936,
> the essay was published for the first time in independent
> Burma.*

The excesses of the Burma Military Police only increased with
each year. . . . [T]hey were most rampant in Tharrawaddy District,
a place which was noted for its antipathy to pay taxes and its
contempt of authority . . . and they reached to such an extent
that the So Thein G.C.B.A. [Grand Council of Buddhist Associ-
ations] began to feel that something ought to be done. It could
no longer look on. It had to do something, and before determining on its line of action, it would be necessary to know to the
fullest extent where the people stood with a Government which
was taking from them more than it was prepared to give. Saya
San was accordingly chosen to go about the country on a fact-
finding commission. He went as Chairman and toured the whole

Cha Ne Cho-Ma Ma Lay, "The Real Origin and Causes of the Burma
Rebellion," *Thu lou lu* [That Kind of Person] (Rangoon: Lok kee Press,
1953), pp. 377–380, 387–389.

country, his heart hardening as he went on hearing tale after tale of the grossest excesses of the Burma Military Police. What second-hand information he formerly obtained of the real plight of the people starving and suffering so in their own home of plenty was now conclusively confirmed by the statements he had straight from the horse's mouth and by the heart-rending sights he personally saw, the unmistakable signs of woe and misery, dire want and destitution.

He was now quite firmly convinced that the people living in such conditions, and as long as they were to continue to live in such conditions, could never be able to afford to pay their taxes: that the laws of the land were oppressive to the sons of the soil, for they permitted, if at all, little or no scope for satisfaction of one's bare needs. He came back from the country with a report "in which he found it proved that illegal acts and excesses had been committed by the authorities; . . . it was necessary to protect villagers against a repetition of the aforesaid illegal acts and excesses by the formation of athins [groups] for the resistance of forcible collection of the aforesaid two taxes."

He pleaded strongly with the principal chiefs of the So Thein G.C.B.A. (i) to resist the forcible collection of the capitation and Thathameda [nonagricultural] taxes and (ii) to offer civil resistance against oppressive forest laws which deprived villagers of the free use of bamboo and timber for domestic purposes. That would mean open rebellion, and the G.C.B.A. was not prepared to go so far as that. A section was for supporting Saya San but it happened to be in such a minority that he thought it useless to press his points home. He saw now that he must act alone, all alone. He resigned from the G.C.B.A. and formed a Sandati Galon Association with the avowed purpose of carrying out the two proposals he had put forward. He could not run his party as a G.C.B.A. . . . there were too many of them already . . . and so he had to think of something original which would commend itself to the public and command a faithful and ardent following. He knew he would have to wage war against the British Government. He knew that it was no small affair. He must have as large a following in the country as possible. How could he raise it? Where and how soon?

The urban population was also badly hit but he doubted if it would rally to his cause. It formed the lower middle class and was living on crumbs which the British, the Indians, and the Chinese let fall. So long as there was bread and so long as there was that eating, there would always be crumbs for them however few they might be getting. He saw that h⌐ must go to the villages which were rueing already. And to go there as an ordinary leader would yield only ordinary results. His was going to be a very big fight and preparations had to be correspondingly big. And that in Burma meant one thing and only one. He must make himself a really Big person. And were not the people in their acute distress prayerfully hoping that a Burmese King would return and drive all these aliens away and restore the natural resources to where they belonged? He must bank everything on that hope of theirs. He decided to go to them in exactly the same way as they wanted their deliverer to come. So he came to the resolution of going as a King, no less, and accordingly went about making preparations to rise against the British in right royal fashion. That, as far as he could see, was the easiest, quickest and surest way and he fell on it without any qualms.

But it was not until 1929–30 that he proclaimed himself king with the title of Thupannaka Galuna Raja for the first time. It shows that Saya San was not eager to assume the title until it became absolutely necessary. At first he went about as merely President of the Galon Association collecting strength. Only on the 13th December 1930 did he openly declare to his delegates from various parts of the country his intention to rebel and outline his plan for the rebellion. Until then he did not speak of rebelling. He just went about his business. And had things improved, he would have abandoned the project but the callous neglect and the cold attitude of the Government only made matters worse. In 1929 things reached to such a peak that it was no longer possible to trust oneself to Fate. And to make matters far worse, still darker clouds were gathering on the horizon. . . .

Where, then, was help to come? What way was there to take

them out of the sea of distress whose hungry waves were already swallowing them up in their eternal fury?

Memories of the sad Past and the realisation of the utter helplessness and hopelessness of the Present forced their way in and haunted their troubled minds afresh. And the vision of an empty Future with its regular features of oppression in the name of law arose, in all its irony and melancholy, in their eyes which were getting dimmer and dimmer. What was left of them to do, ay, what?

There was a sound of approaching footsteps. A couple of men were coming up their way. Who was that man at the top who was coming on with light steps and a happy look as if the whole world had become his? Ah! Was he not the Headman of Seinza whom they had seen at the durbar [official audience] receiving awards from His Excellency? Now why did he get such rewards, why? Was it not because he had served the Government well? And did not serving the Government well mean exhorting us folks to bleed white until the last anna or pie was forcibly taken from us? Was it not he and his like who were directly oppressing us for the sake of those cursed rewards? Well, he would be a good riddance anyway, so let's finish him! Let us finish every damned agent of this accursed Government. . . .

If their fleeting thoughts were dark, as indeed they were, their hands raised in desperation were defter. A scuffle ensued, just a scuffle, and the man with the rewards went down like a dog, and Saya San's man collecting the arms and ammunition found in the possession of the fallen man and his party made quickly for the hills, where their Master was waiting impatiently for their return.

The Tharrawaddy Rebellion, father of several risings that were soon to spread all the country over in those troubled times, had started! . . .

The above is a tragic story. It is the story of a peasant revolt in ancient style à la Burmanie. But is that all? No, it is more than a peasants' revolt. It is an open rebellion against an open conspiracy, the conspiracy being that of the British to keep the Burmese as their own slaves of labour enjoying nothing of the country's riches which may be had in abundance and it has been the most adversely affected section of the population that has taken up arms against authority. And there is one other reason which has goaded the poor people into rising, and that is the forcible collection of taxes which have never been popular in the country under British rule. A student of politics will realise that the system of taxation which was finding favour with the Government of the day has been too ill adjusted to the ever varying and inequal incomes of the people. Nor has it been fair. People feel that they are wronged. And when the Government goes in for forcibly collecting them and for harshly treating the defaulters, well, it would, anywhere and in any case and at any time, mean trouble. In December of the year 1930 when the poverty-stricken peasants of Burma were asking the Governor for the reduction in and postponement of collection of taxes, they were asking not for more time to make effective preparations to rise against authority but for more time and opportunity to obtain a means of paying them. They were trying even at that moment to drive away the nightmare of the excesses of the Military Police who would certainly come if they could not pay. But none understood their harrowing experiences, none knew of their fluttering hearts and their feverish hopes.

44
Peasant Unrest in the Philippines

The Sakdal Movement began in 1930 as an effort to overturn Manuel Quezon's ruling Nacionalista Party. Drawing mainly upon the peasantry of Central Luzon for their strength, the Sakdals promised immediate independence and tax relief for the very poor. On May 2–3, 1935 the Sakdals, frustrated politically, sought by an armed uprising to forestall a plebiscite on the Tydings-McDuffie Act which promised the Philippines only gradual independence. The following interviews were taken from Sakdalistas captured during a skirmish with the Philippine Constabulary at Cabuyao, Laguna.

No. 1. Higino Javier (Sakdal)

Barrio Gulod, Cabuyao, Laguna. Age 22. Married, one child less than a year old. Never attended school. Cannot read or write. Takes care of forty ducks. Makes less than five pesos a month. Owns small hut worth P10.00. Owes P30.00. Paid cedula (poll tax certificate) last year. Not this year. Worse off than formerly because of the baguios (typhoons).

His story: "The Chief told me to come into town to help capture the municipality. When he captured it we would have independence. Juan de la Cruz, our leader, said we would capture it without trouble. I don't know anything about the [1935 Philippine] Constitution. I don't know what the Commonwealth is. They told me independence would be a good thing. No cedula to pay or a cedula for a peseta [penny]. I had no arms. I saw three guns in the hands of my companions. There were three hundred of us. They told us the Constabulary would not fight us. After the firing started, Juan de la Cruz put up his hands after about two shots. They did not stop shooting. I squatted down and put up my hands. A great many others put up their hands. We called out, 'We surrender; we surrender.' The Constabulary kept on firing. We fell on our faces. From the time Juan de la Cruz put up his hands no one inside the patio was shooting. I didn't read the 'Sakdal' because I can't read. I joined the Sakdals and paid them all together a half peso. Juan de la Cruz was the collector. He said the money was to be used to get independence and it is a good thing. Ramos is the only leader I know of. Juan de la Cruz told me of him." . . .

No. 3. Primitivo Algabre (Sakdal)

Barrio Banay, Cabuyao, Laguna. Age 25. Brother of Salud Algabre, woman leader who held up the trucks. Married, no

David R. Sturtevant, "Philippine Social Structure and Its Relation to Agrarian Unrest" (Ph.D. thesis, Stanford University, 1959), pp. 219–222, 226. By permission of the author.

children. Finished fourth grade in public school in Cabuyao. Raises 80 canvans of rice (P160.00) and P200.00 worth of sugar cane. Owns a solar (residential lot) worth P200.00 and a carabao worth P160.00. Owes P110.00 on mortgage on lot. Pays P1.20 property tax.

His story: "I don't know anything about the Constitution. I am opposed to the present administration because of the principles of our leaders. They are against it, so am I. I was denied the right of free speech and assembly on April 6th. Our leaders tell us foreign business kills the business of the Philippine Islands. I think it better to have our own government. When Almazan and Untevero (Sakdal representatives) had their meeting here we met in the house of Algabre. Untevero and Almazan told us not to be afraid. Ramos was in Japan making arrangements for assistance in arms and men to take over the government and get independence. They talked secretly. This was in March. On April 30th, Severo Generalia told me to go to their house in Banilio. Elpidio Santos was there. Jose Liage was there and someone was there who was introduced as a Captain of Scouts. They told us not to be afraid, but to take over the municipality on the evening of May 2nd. Ramos would come with a hundred airplanes and men and ammunition on the morning of the 3rd. They said the Scouts and Constabulary would assist in taking over the government. I am a Sakdal. I gave them about P2.00. Under independence I would pay no taxes. No cedula. Business would be in the hands of Filipinos. They know about things. I'm just a follower. They told me all municipalities were being seized and we would have independence."

No. 4. Salud Algabre (Sakdal)

Barrio Banlic, Cabuyao, Laguna. Woman leader. Age 42. Five children, one to sixteen years of age. Fifth grade in school. Sent some of her children to school in Tondo.

Her story: "We cannot send the children to school without money. Times are bad. What mother wouldn't send her children to school if she could. Two years ago we made a sugar crop for

Julia Lumpaco in Calamba. We were to take what they gave us after the sugar was sold. We harvested 122 tons of cane. We have received no pay as yet. We owe Julia P137.00. The account is mixed up. Sometimes when we got a peso she would put down P1.15 or P1.20. When we got P5.00 she would put down P5.75. We were dissatisfied. Couldn't stand the charges so we left. She said for every ton we harvested she would collect fifty centavos on the land. We were supposed to get a fourth of the harvest. They wouldn't let us raise chickens. We needed chickens to get spending money for the children, where we are now we get P1.20 a week for the chickens, have fruit trees and get odd jobs cutting cane. We had two carabaos, but both have been sold. We borrowed P400.00 on a mortgage when my child got sick. A surveyor agreed to survey our solar and get a title for P50.00. He did it in our absence and made mistakes in the boundary. Then he sued us for P130.00. We spent the P50.00 we had to pay for the title in the lawsuit. We haven't been able to pay the land tax for four or five years. My husband was put in jail because he had no cedula. We are against the Constitution. We are against the leaders because they promise us independence and never get it. We think there is no hope for us in our hardships without independence. We were told the same thing was being done in every municipality. They thought when they got the town they would have independence. Wednesday night I was at home putting the children to sleep. A man came saying he was sent by Jose Abueg. He said all trucks should be held up for confiscation of arms. About three hundred people came at 3 A.M., May 3rd. Said they had not been able to capture Calamba. An auto came very fast. A man in a bus had a revolver and acted as though he were going to use it. We took it away. We stopped other trucks and took away firearms. Our leaders were Benigno Ramos, Celerino Tiongco, Elpidio Santos and Simeon Ducena." . . .

No. 6. Isabelo P. Fuentes (Sakdal)

Barrio Mulini, Tayabas (examined at Calamba). Age ?. Second grade education. Tailor. Owns a solar worth P325.00 and partly constructed house worth P200.00. Owes P25.00. Some weeks makes nothing. Some weeks a little. No money. Paid P2.00 a year land tax.

His story: "I'm worse off than I used to be. I was able to raise a family but had to take my children out of school. I want immediate independence. I want our country to be free so we can show ourselves on equal terms with other countries. I am opposed to the present leaders because they put in the Commonwealth. I don't want it. It would be sweet to my heart to have independence even if I with my children must suffer every kind of hardship. I don't know why I was arrested. ["] ...

No. 14. Macario Aunsunurin (Sakdal)

Barrio Mamatid, Cabuyao, Laguna. Age 37. Married, two children, thirteen and seventeen. Has house worth 15 pesos and one old hen. Has second grade education. Fisherman. Makes 20 to 30 centavos a day. Borrowed P300.00 to buy ducks. They all died in the baguios. Has 50 centavos in money.

His story: "I heard the Sakdals had taken the Presidencia. I came out of curiosity to see what was going on. I was near the beach when I heard the shooting. I saw three guns among the Sakdals. The Chief of Police sent for me because someone told him I was in the fight. The Constabulary Lieutenant looked at the dobie itch on my back and said it was a wound." ...

No. 16. Gregorio Declaro

(Location of home not indicated.) Age 27. Married, one three year old child. Can read a little but can't write. Farmer. Makes P55.00 a year. Has a house worth P30.00 and a carabao. Owes ten pesos he borrowed when a child died. No money. Had a cedula two years ago. None since.

His story: "I'm not a Sakdal. I was coming to market. They

brought me in by force. I saw seven long guns. I was shot by the Sakdals with bird-shot when I tried to run away."

45

King Chulalongkorn on Slavery and Education

In large measure, Thailand's road to modernity was charted by one man, King Chulalongkorn (Rama V, 1868–1910). Not only did the King keep Thailand free from colonial status, but he initiated many reforms in government and society. The following passages reveal something of his attitude and approach to change within his country.

DISCOURSE OF PRABAT SOMDECH PRA CHULA CHOMKLAO CHAOYUHUA [CHULALONGKORN] ON SLAVERY AND AGE OF EMANCIPATION

On Wednesday, the ninth day of Waxing Moon, in the eighth month (corresponding to Wednesday, 12 July, B.E. 2417) [1874] the Advisers on State Affairs met in the Sommot Devaraj Upabat House in the evening, and the King brought up the question of reducing the age of emancipation for slaves and of allowing parents to sell them according to, and not at prices in excess of, the new scale. On this the King produced the following document outlining his view:

"I wish to see whatever is beneficial to the people accomplished gradually according to circumstances and unjust, though well-established, customs abolished. But, as it is impossible to change everything overnight, steady pruning is necessary to lighten the burden. If this practice is adopted, things will proceed smoothly and satisfactorily as time goes by. . . .

Prachoom Chomchai, trans. and ed., *Chulalongkorn the Great* (Tokyo: The Centre for East Asian Cultural Studies, 1965), pp. 51–52, 56–57, 87–89. By permission of Prachoom Chomchai and The Center for East Asian Cultural Studies.

... [P]ressure exists in the direction of making people want to become slaves despite our desire to see the contrary. Slaves do not have to pay high State dues and do not have to engage in any regular occupation, since they are maintained by their masters. They work when work comes to them; otherwise they are unoccupied. When there is nothing to do and they happen to come by a bit of money, they gamble, since there is no risk of losing their means of subsistence. To eradicate slavery it is necessary to go to its root causes; but whatever can be done in the circumstances should proceed step by step. Whenever time is ripe, the basic cause, namely, inequality in paying State dues, should be eliminated through levelling downwards and upwards so that, finally, no matter whether persons are free or not, the same payment is due from them. Moreover, sufficient public revenue must be found to make up for abolition of this important institution causing people a loss of time devoted to earning their living. For this to succeed buoyant times are required. Pending this state of affairs and pending an adequate increase in public revenue, there can be no complete abolition of slavery. But what is possible must be done to open floodgates to the reform which will ensue with a change of circumstances. If any one of you sees any inconsistency between my proposal on the one hand and the old law and customs on [the] other or any distress on the part of creditors and slaves now and in the future likely to be caused by my proposal, please say so, this business of slavery being connected with so many laws and so many other activities that it is unlikely for one man to have a whole view of it. If any one of you can think of snags likely to crop up now or in the future, kindly put the relevant considerations into writing for further discussion among us. If there are obstacles we can go as far as we can; if there are none, we shall see the whole thing through. If my proposal really succeeds, I can think of one other thing which can effectively liberate slaves' children from slavery. Slaves' children are compelled to serve their masters from an early age and know nothing other than what pleases their masters. Instead of getting vocational training, they spend their free time in gambling from early childhood so that this habit becomes ingrained, thereby preventing them from seeing any value in having a career. If they really have to quit slavery, they do not possess sufficient knowledge to improve their status and are compelled to return to slavery. It is because of this that there should be an institution for education similar to the old alms-house where, by royal command, education was given to children. There have been a good many men educated in this manner, and many available clerks at the moment came from such institution[s]. However, education was not thorough, since teachers were not interested in teaching and in enforcing discipline to ensure regular attendance. In addition to this, monastery schools have been founded for noblemen's children, and these have produced better results than alms-houses. Again, there is no regular attendance and it takes some time to educate these children. At the present time, there are not enough clerks to go round. Literate people are in great demand among the noblemen and will not readily remain slaves. This is why I feel that education can really free slaves. If slaves' children can be liberated in the manner I propose, then the establishment of schools can help them. . . ."

ROYAL PROCLAMATION ON SIAM'S EDUCATION

Prabat Somdech Prachaoyuhua Somdech Pra Poramen Maha Chulalongkorn, Lord of Siam, considers that, though the long-established practice in education in Siam has been to use the monastery as the seat of learning and the home as the centre of vocational training in the family, in modern times the increasing tempo of international communications by means of steamers at sea and railways on land and the increasing international contacts caused by the necessity of nations to exchange commodities, have dictated a reorientation of academic and technical training in a correct and useful manner and also a proper adjustment of outmoded disciplines and arts.

At a time when international contacts were not convenient,

international disparities in academic and technical advance could persist; but, now that such contacts have been rendered so close, international differences in levels of academic and technical achievements are bound to disappear.

As the times and the course of things in our country have changed, it is essential to promote the advancement of all our academic and technical knowledge and to prevent it from succumbing to competition from outside. In order to achieve this, it is imperative to make haste in education so that knowledge and ability will increase.

The Government has for some time maintained schools; but the original purpose of training people for the needs of the civil service has misled some into thinking that learning is meant exclusively for those destined for the civil service and that it is no part of the masses' duty to seek knowledge. However, as the network of schools is set up in the Kingdom, people are baffled with the proposition that it is the Government's duty to provide all the funds for popular education. All this misunderstanding has hampered national progress.

In actual fact, education leads to intelligence and proper behaviour and skill in earning one's living. No matter what a person's career is, whether it be in teaching, medicine, trade or mechanics, prior learning is essential for success in life. As every person has to have some career or other, there is nothing better than knowledge that parents can give to their children. It is a stepping-stone to higher attainments, and a genuine foundation-stone for proper behaviour, happiness and wealth. This is better than inheritance, which can be used up.

Having taken all this into consideration, His Majesty has graciously commanded his people in the following terms:

From now on it shall be the duty of parents and guardians to teach their children and afford them such opportunity for education as their status and financial means allow. The Government will, for its part, lay down the framework of national education as a guideline to be announced later by officials of the Ministry of Education. The purpose of such education and training shall be to inculcate the following qualities: inquisitiveness for knowledge to whet intelligence and capability, good and righteous behaviour, concern for family welfare, generosity to relatives, unity and harmony with spouses, faithfulness to friends, economy, kindness to others, regard for the public good, compliance with laws, willingness to serve the country with courage, loyalty to the throne in times of need, and gratefulness and loyalty to the throne at all times.

When all these elements of responsibility have become so deeply rooted in one's nature as to be manifested in all outward behaviour, then training and education may be said to have succeeded, and any one who has successfully undergone the process may be said to be an eminently worthy citizen of Siam.

46
A Filipino Critique of Spanish Colonialism

> *Reproduced below is Chapter 50 (slightly abbreviated) from* Noli Me Tangere, *the most famous Philippine literary work written in Spanish, by José Rizal (1861–1896), the hero of Filipino nationalism. It was published in 1887 in Berlin, while Rizal was studying in Europe. "Few novels," comments the book's most recent translator, ". . . have made a more shattering impact on the society in which they were conceived and read. . . . And surely no writer paid a higher penalty for self-expression." Shortly after the outbreak of the Philippine Revolution, Rizal was executed by the colonial government, on December 29, 1896. In the opinion of our translator, both characters who appear in this chapter, Ibarra and Elias, speak for Rizal.*

The sun had not yet set when Ibarra stepped into the boat of Elias along the lake shore. He looked annoyed.

José Rizal, *The Lost Eden (Noli Me Tangere),* trans. León Ma. Guerrero (Bloomington: Indiana University Press, 1961), pp. 306–314. By permission of Indiana University Press.

"I am sorry, sir," said Elias with a certain discouragement; "forgive me for daring to make this appointment with you. I wanted to speak to you freely and here we shall not be over-heard. We can be back in an hour."

"You are wrong, my friend," answered Ibarra, essaying a smile, "you must take me to that town; you can see its church steeple from here. Fate sends me there."

"Fate?"

"Yes. Fancy, on my way here I met the lieutenant, and he insisted on keeping me company. I thought of you: I am aware that he knows you; and so, to get rid of him, I told him I was going to that town. Now I shall have to spend the whole of tomorrow there because the fellow said he would look me up there tomorrow afternoon. He is really being much too friendly with me."

"I appreciate your thoughtfulness," answered Elias impassively, "but you should have simply let him come along."

"But what about you?"

"He would not have recognised me. The only time he saw me, he was not in a position to describe me for the military register."

"What rotten luck I have today," sighed Ibarra, thinking of Maria Clara. After a few seconds he asked: "What did you have to tell me?"

Elias looked round him. Already they were far from shore; the sun had set and since there is scarcely any twilight in the tropics, the darkness of the night was spreading, lending brightness to the full moon.

"Sir," began Elias in grave accents, "I am the bearer of the wishes of many unfortunates."

"Can I do anything for them?"

"A lot, sir, more than anybody else."

Elias told him in a few words the conversation he had had with the commander of the outlaws, omitting the doubts and threats expressed by the latter. Ibarra heard him attentively. When Elias had finished, a long silence fell which Ibarra was the first to break.

"So they ask for . . ."

"Radical reforms in the armed forces, in the clergy, in the administration of justice, that is to say, a more paternal approach from the Government."

"Reforms? In what sense?"

"For example, more respect for human dignity, greater security for the individual, less strength in the armed forces, less privileges for an organisation which so easily abuses them."

"Elias," replied the young man, "I do not know who you are, but I have the feeling that you are not an ordinary man. You do not think and act like the others. You will understand me if I tell you that, although the present state of things has its defects, it would have even more should it be changed. I could get the friends I have in Madrid to make speeches, by paying them; I myself could speak to the Governor General; but my friends would accomplish nothing, the Governor General has not enough power to introduce such innovations, and I myself would never take a step in that direction because I know very well that, while these institutions have their defects, they are necessary now; they are what is called a necessary evil."

Elias, astonished, raised his head and stared at Ibarra aghast.

"You too believe in necessary evils? You believe that to do good it is necessary to do evil?"

"No, I believe in the necessary evil as I believe in those drastic treatments we use when we want to cure a disease. Now then, the country is an organism which suffers from a chronic sickness, and to cure it the Government feels compelled to use means which, if you wish, are harsh and violent but useful and necessary."

"It's a bad doctor, sir, who only seeks to correct and suppress symptoms without trying to determine the cause of the illness, or, knowing it, fears to go after it. The Constabulary has only one purpose: to repress crime by force and terror, a purpose which is not achieved except by chance. Furthermore, you must consider, sir, that society can only be hard on individuals when it has first furnished them with the means necessary for their moral improvement. In our country there is no organised society as such since the people and the Government are not united; the latter therefore should be lenient, not only because it wants to be judged leniently, but also because the individual, neglected and abandoned by the Government, is less responsible precisely because he has received so little instruction in his duties. Moreover, using your own comparison, the treatment applied to the country's ills is so destructive that it makes itself felt only in those parts of the organism which are healthy, weakening their vitality and preparing the way for the spread of the disease. Would it not be more reasonable instead to strengthen those parts of the organism that are sick and to lessen the violence of the treatment?"

"To weaken the Constabulary would be to endanger the security of the towns."

"The security of the towns!" cried Elias bitterly. "It will soon be fifteen years that those towns have had the protection of the Constabulary, and look: we still have outlaws, we still hear that they sack towns and hold people up on the highways; robberies still take place and the robbers are not discovered; crime exists, and the real criminal goes about freely, but not the peaceful inhabitants of the town. Ask any honest citizen if he looks upon the Constabulary as a good thing, as a means of protection furnished by the Government and not as an imposition, a despotism whose excesses are more harmful than the depredations of the outlaws. . . ."

"I agree that there are evils," replied Ibarra, "but let us accept the evils for the sake of the good things that go with them. The Constabulary may not be perfect, but, believe me, the fear it inspires prevents an increase in the number of criminals."

"Say rather that this fear increases their number," Elias corrected him. "Before the creation of this organisation almost all criminals, with the exception of a very few, were driven to crime by hunger; they looted and robbed to stay alive, but when times were easier, the highways were once more safe. Outlaws could be scared away even by the municipal policemen and their primitive weapons—those poor brave policemen, so libelled by writers about our country, whose right is to die, whose duty is to fight, and whose reward is a sneer. Now outlaws are outlaws for life. One misdemeanour, one felony punished with inhumanity, one gesture of resistance against the excesses of authority, is enough, with the fear of atrocious tortures, to exile them forever from society, and condemn them to kill or be killed. The Constabulary's terrorism shuts the doors of repentance, and, since an outlaw fights and defends himself in the mountains better than the soldier whom he flouts, the result is that we cannot extinguish the evil we have created. . . ."

Elias was speaking with passion and enthusiasm; his eyes were flashing and his voice vibrant. An impressive pause followed. The boat, undisturbed by the paddle, seemed to float motionless on the water; the moon shone splendidly in the dark blue sky; on the distant shore a few lights gleamed.

"And what else do they ask?" Ibarra wanted to know.

"The reformation of the clergy," replied Elias with glum discouragement. "The unfortunate ask for greater protection from . . ."

"From the religious Orders?"

"From their oppressors."

"Has the Philippines forgotten what she owes to these Orders? Has she forgotten her immense debt of gratitude to those who redeemed her from error and gave her the True Faith, to those who shielded her from the tyranny of civil power? This is the evil result of not teaching the history of our country."

Elias, surprised, could scarcely believe what he heard.

"Sir," he answered gravely, "you accuse the people of ingratitude. Permit me, one of the suffering people, to defend them. If favours are to be acknowledged, they should be disinterested. We need not talk about such commonplaces as duty or Christian charity. . . . But you say that the religious Orders gave us the True Faith and redeemed us from error. Do you call external practices the True Faith, or the commerce in girdles and scapulars, religion; or the stories of miracles and other fairy tales that we hear every day, the truth? Is this the law of Jesus Christ?

God did not have to be crucified for this, nor we assume the obligation of eternal gratitude; superstition existed long before this, all that was needed was to organise it and raise the price of the merchandise. You will tell me that imperfect as our present religion may be, it is preferable to the one we had before; I believe you and I agree with you, but it is too expensive, for we have paid for it with our national identity, with our independence. For its sake we have given to its priests our best towns, our fields, and even our savings, which are spent on the purchase of religious trinkets. A product of foreign manufacture has been imported here; we have paid for it; and we are even.... But I admit that a genuine faith and a true love of humanity inspired those first missionaries who came to our shores; I recognise our debt of gratitude to those noble-hearted men; I know that the Spain of that age abounded in heroes of all kinds, religious, political, civil, and military. But because the forerunners were virtuous, are we to submit to the abuses of their degenerate descendants? Because we received great benefits, are we committing a crime in protecting ourselves against great injuries? The people do not ask for the abolition of the religious Orders, but only for the reforms required by new circumstances and necessities."

"I love our country, Elias, as you may love her; I understand somewhat of what is wanted; I have listened attentively to what you have said. Yet, my friend, for all that, I think we have been rather carried away by emotion. I see less need for reforms in this field than anywhere else." ...

Elias seemed to be listening still even when Ibarra had stopped; his face was grim, and his eyes had lost their brightness.

"It is true that the missionaries won this country for Spain," he answered. "But do you believe that Spain will keep it because of the friars?"

"Yes, and only because of them; all those who have written about the Philippines are of the same opinion."

"Oh," cried Elias, throwing down his paddle into the boat dejectedly. "I would not have believed you had such a poor opinion of the Government and of the people. Why don't you come out and say you despise them both? What would you say of a family that lives in peace because of the intervention of a stranger? A people that obey because they are deceived; a Government that rules by deceit, a Government that does not know how to make itself loved and respected for its own sake. Forgive me, sir, but I believe that your Government is stupid and suicidal when it is glad that such things are believed. I thank you for your kindness in listening to me. . . ."

47

Conservative Nationalism in Vietnam

In 1931, when French Minister of Colonies, Paul Reynaud, paid an official visit to the Indochinese states, he was presented with a letter from Pham Quynh, the most outspoken exponent of Franco-Vietnamese collaboration. The substance of that letter is reproduced below. Pham Quynh was then the publisher of a cultural magazine, Nam-phong. He later served in the cabinet of Emperor Bao Dai and was executed in 1945 by the Viet Minh.

Minister of the great and noble nation which has taken unto her to guide this country toward a better destiny, please allow me, a modest man of learning from Annam, respectfully to address you and inform you, in the most frank manner, what my compatriots desire from you during your visit to Indochina. . . .

I will not expound the program of such and such a party or the aspirations of such and such a group.

I will not place before you a detailed and extensive listing of liberties and freedoms of various kinds that the Vietnamese people are supposed to expect from the benevolence of the French government.

Pham Quynh, *Essais Franco-Annamites (1929–1932)* (Hué: Éditions Bui-Huy-Tin, 1937), pp. 463–464, 466–468, 471–472. English translation by T. B. Lam and J. A. Larkin.

You are, Excellency, broadly informed about all these complaints which, because they have been repeated time and again
for more than fifteen or twenty years, have ended by becoming
semi-ritualistic in character. But perhaps you would be interested
to learn what is hidden behind all the passive faces which you
saw bowed with respect while you travelled along the Mandarin
Route [the main highway of Indochina]. You might like to know
what was in their secret hearts . . . that began to beat a little
faster upon the announcement of your arrival. . . .

Envisioning with confidence the future and remembering with
pride a past which was not without glory, we are now ambitious
to partake of a national life, and to live it fully, intensely, under
the guidance of France. National sentiment, for a long time over-
shadowed, has begun to live again in our spirit, and increases
with every passing day. The fatherland that our ancestors have
nurtured with great pain and of which we have momentarily,
because of the difficult circumstances which surround us, cast
into oblivion, now is haunting our imagination with the secret
power and the strength of an obsession. . . .

We are suffering from a disease that does not seem to be
caused by anything, but which precisely stems from the progress
we have realised under the tutelage of France. Our moral and
intellectual evolution during the last quarter century has enabled
us to become conscious of ourselves and of our nationality. And
this consciousness does not fit into a regime which has not been
devised to give complete satisfaction.

From this discordance stems a disease which perhaps should
more properly be labelled a crisis of personality, an individual
as well as a national crisis.

From the national point of view, this crisis can be summed
up in the following terms: we belong to a people in search of a
fatherland and have not yet found it.

This fatherland, Mr. Minister, cannot be France. May my
thought not offend you. It does not convey any evil intention.
It is the simple expression of the truth. The Vietnamese cannot
consider France as their fatherland, for the simple reason that

they have one of their own. And this fatherland, France can give back to them by endowing them with a political regime suitable to the development of their personality as a nation, and by giving them a national life worthy of the name, within the French Empire.

In so doing, France would be even more than a fatherland to us. She would represent in our eyes a benefactor who helped us restore a fainting fatherland, under her protection.

It is not our duty to tell you how to achieve this goal. France who possesses the ultimate authority must solve this problem in the full exercise of her rights and powers. . . .

A Vietnamese kingdom with a modern constitution within an Indochinese state endowed with an appropriate federal charter, under the guidance of France—that, Excellency, is a reform . . . which fully answers our intimate national demands and our need for security under the careful protection of France. . . .

Thus, as far as the Vietnamese are concerned, they have only one wish to present to you, Excellency. This wish springs from the depths of their hearts, and . . . is much more important than all the others: they ask for a fatherland for them to serve.

This demand is not senseless. It is legitimate. It is a homage to French generosity. It is shining proof of our complete confidence in the protecting nation. It is not supplemented by any separatist intention. On the contrary, the fatherland which France will help us restore, we will offer to France with our two hands and ask her to integrate it forever into the French commonwealth.

But this fatherland, the Vietnamese do not yet have and they suffer from the lack of it. . . . France can give it to them through you, Excellency, by implementing the great reform which I have suggested above.

Your name will be honored in the memory of the Vietnamese people as the restorer of the Vietnamese nation.

48
Radical Nationalism in Vietnam

> *The Vietnamese Nationalist Party* [Vietnam Quoc dan dang *or VNQDD*] *was one of the most vehement anti-French organizations in the pre-World War II period. Following a VNQDD uprising in 1930, the French suppressed the party, incarcerating and ultimately executing its major leaders. The following letter was written from prison by the party's founder, Nguyen-Thai-Hoc, explaining to the members of the French National Assembly the aims and complaints of Vietnamese nationalists.*

Gentlemen:

I, the undersigned, Nguyen-Thai-Hoc, a Vietnamese citizen, twenty-six years old, chairman and founder of the Vietnamese Nationalist Party, at present arrested and imprisoned at the jail of Yen Bay, Tonkin, Indochina, have the great honor to inform you of the following facts:

According to the tenets of justice, everyone has the right to defend his own country when it is invaded by foreigners, and according to the principles of humanity, everyone has the duty to save his compatriots when they are in difficulty or in danger. As for myself, I have assessed the fact that my country has been annexed by you French for more than sixty years. I realize that under your dictatorial yoke, my compatriots have experienced a very hard life, and my people will without doubt be completely annihilated, by the naked principle of natural selection. Therefore, my right and my duty have compelled me to seek every way to defend my country which has been invaded and occupied, and to save my people who are in great danger.

At the beginning, I had thought to cooperate with the French

Nhuong-Tong, *Nguyen-Thai-Hoc, 1902–1930* (Saigon: Tan Viet, 1956), pp. 138–142. English translation by T. B. Lam.

in Indochina in order to serve my compatriots, my country and my people, particularly in the areas of cultural and economic development. As regards economic development, in 1925 I sent a memorandum to Governor General Varenne, describing to him all our aspirations concerning the protection of local industry and commerce in Indochina. I urged strongly in the same letter the creation of a Superior School of Industrial Development in Tonkin. In 1926 I again addressed another letter to the then Governor General of Indochina in which I included some explicit suggestions to relieve the hardships of our poor people. In 1927, for a third time, I sent a letter to the Résident Supérieur in Tonkin, requesting permission to publish a weekly magazine with the aim of safeguarding and encouraging local industry and commerce. With regard to the cultural domain, I sent a letter to the Governor General in 1927, requesting (1) the privilege of opening tuition-free schools for the children of the lower classes, particularly children of workers and peasants; (2) freedom to open popular publishing houses and libraries in industrial centers.

It is absolutely ridiculous that every suggestion has been rejected. My letters were without answer; my plans have not been considered; my requests have been ignored; even the articles that I sent to newspapers have been censored and rejected. From the experience of these rejections, I have come to the conclusion that the French have no sincere intention of helping my country or my people. I also concluded that we have to expel France. For this reason, in 1927, I began to organize a revolutionary party, which I named the Vietnamese Nationalist Party (VNQDD), with the aim of overthrowing the dictatorial and oppressive administration in our country. We aspire to create a Republic of Vietnam, composed of persons sincerely concerned with the happiness of the people. My party is a clandestine organization, and in February 1929, it was uncovered by the security police. Among the members of my party, a great number have been arrested. Fifty-two persons have been condemned to forced labor ranging from two to twenty years. Although many have been detained and many others unjustly condemned, my party has not ceased its activity. Under my guidance, the Party continues to operate and progress towards its aim.

During the Yen Bay uprising [1930] someone succeeded in killing some French officers. The authorities accused my party of having organized and perpetrated this revolt. They have accused me of having given the orders for the massacre. In truth, I have never given such orders, and I have presented before the Penal Court of Yen Bay all the evidence showing the inanity of this accusation. Even so, some of the members of my party completely ignorant of that event have been accused of participating in it. The French Indochinese government burned and destroyed their houses. They sent French troops to occupy their villages and stole their rice to divide it among the soldiers. Not just members of my party have been suffering from this injustice—we should rather call this cruelty than injustice—but also many simple peasants, interested only in their daily work in the rice fields, living miserable lives like buffaloes and horses, have been compromised in this reprisal. At the present time, in various areas there are tens of thousands of men, women and children, persons of all ages, who have been massacred. They died either of hunger or exposure because the French Indochinese government burned their homes. I therefore beseech you in tears to redress this injustice which otherwise will annihilate my people, which will stain French honor, and which will belittle all human values.

I have the honor to inform you that I am responsible for all events happening in my country under the leadership of my party from 1927 until the present. You only need to execute me. I beg your indulgence for all the others who at the present time are imprisoned in various jails. I am the only culprit, all the others are innocent. They are innocent because most of them are indeed members of my party, and have joined it only because I have succeeded in convincing them of their duties as citizens of this country, and of the humiliations of a slave with a lost country. Some of them are not even party members. They have been wrongly accused by their enemy or by the security police; or they simply are wrongly accused by their friends who have not been able to bear the tortures inflicted by the security police. I have the honor to repeat once again that you need execute only me. If you are not satisfied with killing one man, I advise you to kill also the members of my family, but I strongly beg your indulgence towards those who are innocent.

Finally, I would like to declare in conclusion: if France wants to stay in peace in Indochina, if France does not want to have increasing troubles with revolutionary movements, she should immediately modify the cruel and inhuman policy now practiced in Indochina. The French should behave like friends to the Vietnamese, instead of being cruel and oppressive masters. They should be attentive to the intellectual and material sufferings of the Vietnamese people, instead of being harsh and tough.

Please, Gentlemen, receive my gratitude.

49
The 1932 Revolution in Thailand

> *The year 1932 marked the end of absolute monarchy in Thailand and the establishment of constitutional monarchy. The following documents represent various stages in the "Thai Revolution." The first document is the ultimatum sent to King Prajadhipok on the afternoon of June 24 by the People's Party. The second document is the King's reply, dated June 25. The final document is the King's abdication announcement, written in England and dated March 2, 1935.*

[I]

The People's Party consisting of civil and military officials have now taken over the administration of the country and have taken members of the Royal Family such as H.R.H. Prince of Nagor Svarga as hostages. If members of the People's Party have

Reprinted from *Siam in Transition: A Brief Survey of Cultural Trends in the Five Years Since the Revolution of 1932* by Kenneth Perry Landon by permission of the author and The University of Chicago Press. Copyright © 1939 by Kenneth Perry Landon. Pp. 9–10, 257–259.

received any injuries the Princes held in pawn will suffer in consequence. The People's Party have no desire to make a seizure of the Royal possessions in any way. Their principal aim is to have a constitutional monarchy. We therefore enjoin Your Majesty to return to the Capital to reign again as king under the constitutional monarchy as established by the People's Party. If Your Majesty refuses to accept the offer or refrains from replying within one hour after the receipt of this message the People's Party will proclaim the constitutional monarchial government by appointing another Prince whom they consider to be efficient to act as King.

(Signed)   Col. Phya Bahol Balabayuha
Col. Phya Song Suratej
Col. Phya Riddhi Aganey

[II]

June 25th, 1932

To the Military in Defence of Bangkok:

I have received a letter in which you invite me to return to Bangkok as a constitutional monarch. For the sake of peace; and in order to save useless bloodshed; to avoid confusion and loss to the country; and, more, because I have already considered making this change myself, I am willing to co-operate in the establishment of a constitution under which I am willing to serve.

Furthermore, there is a possibility that, if I decline to continue in my office as king, the foreign powers will not recognize the new government. This might entail considerable difficulty for the government.

Physically I am not strong. I have no children to succeed me. My life-expectancy is not long, at least if I continue in this office. I have no desire for position or for personal aggrandisement. My ability to advance the progress of the race alone constrains me.

Accept this sincere expression of my feelings.

Prajadhipok

[III]

Noel, Cranleigh, England

When Phya Bahol with his party seized the powers of government by the use of arms on the 24th of June, B.E. 2475 [1932], they sent a letter inviting me to become their King under the constitution. I accepted the invitation because I understood that they would establish a government similar to that of other democratic nations, so that the citizenry would have the right to express their opinions on government, and so the people as a whole would be benefitted. I had already had great interest in that form of goverment and had planned to make a definite change to it in a quiet and orderly way. When unsettled conditions arose and when those who were leaders claimed that their intentions were to establish democratic rule, I saw that our hopes were identical. I accordingly felt that it was proper for me to fall in with their plans for the progress and peace of the nation. I did my best to maintain peace in the country but my best efforts were without avail because the new Government did not actually establish equality and freedom for all in matters of politics. They were unwilling to listen to the opinions of the people. In Section two of the Constitution actual power to carry on the Government is given to the People's Party who originated the movement and is not given to the representatives elected by the people. The temporary constitution shows that those not approved by the Government could not become members of the Assembly. The permanent constitution was an improvement. According to my request the people were allowed to elect one-half of the membership of the Assembly without interference. I was willing to allow both elective and appointive membership because I hoped to be able to appoint men experienced in government work without regard to their party affiliations. I expected those appointed to assist the elected membership with advice on matters of government. When the time came to appoint the members I had no voice in their selection at all. The Government selected only those who were members of their own party and without regard to their experience or ability. Furthermore, some members planned to change the economic policy of the country in a drastic manner. There thus grew up a division of opinion until the Assembly had to be prorogued for fear of violence. Several sections of the Constitution had to be made temporarily inactive. This was done by advice of the Government then in power. Later on Phya Bahol with his party again used the army to seize the powers of government. From that time there was little hope for favorable progress.

Because the People's Party did not give full democracy to the nation, the people had no opportunity to express opinions before important decisions were made. There was another rebellion of an independent party and much life was lost, Siamese killing Siamese.

When I pleaded that the Constitution be revised along true democratic lines so that it might be acceptable to all of the people the Government and its party was unwilling. I begged that the people be given a voice in important decisions that directly affected them. I had no favourable reply. Even the Assembly was not allowed to judicially consider my requests to the Government on behalf of the people. They were forced to come to a final decision in a single session without going into detail on any point. Furthermore, the Government set up a law to punish those who were suspected of having plans against the Government. They were treated in a manner contrary to the commonest principles of justice in a secret court, without aid of attorney, and so with no chance to fight. This is a method I never used, even in an Absolute Monarchy. I begged the Government to change this law and it refused.

I feel that the Government and its party uses methods contrary to the principles of a free people and common justice. I am unwilling to allow anyone or any party to carry on such a government in my name.

I am happy to turn over my power of rule to the people as a whole. I am not willing to give it over to any person or to any group to use in an absolute manner without heeding the voice of the people.

Now I see that my intention to allow everyone a voice in the government is without fulfillment. I feel that there is no longer any way to assist the people in my official capacity. I feel that it is necessary for me to resign my office as King dating from this present time. I wish to give over all of my kingly privileges but I desire to retain all of those privileges which were mine before becoming King.

I do not care to name anyone as my successor although it is my privilege according to law.

Furthermore, I do not care to have anyone rise up in rebellion in Siam against the Government in my behalf. If anyone names me as their instigator in rebellion kindly understand that I have no share in it and am not pleased.

I am exceedingly sorry that I am unable to serve my people and country according to my plans and hopes which I received from my royal ancestors. There remains only a sincere prayer that Siam will prosper and that the people will have peace and happiness.

Prajadhipok
March 2nd, 1935

50
Sukarno's Indonesia Accuses

Sukarno (1901–   ), a graduate in engineering of the Bandung Institute of Technology, became the most vociferous advocate of Indonesian independence from the Netherlands. A brilliant orator, he took a leading role in the nationalist movement from the late 1920's on, only to be removed from the political scene by the colonial authorities. Arrested in 1930, Sukarno delivered in his defense a long and passionate speech, entitled "Indonesia Accuses," which became a key document in the Indonesian struggle for independence. The brief excerpts reproduced below give an indication of the thought and style of the man who became President of the Indonesian Republic in 1945.

... And the word "Imperialism"? This too designates a concept.... It designates a tendency, a striving, to dominate or influence the affairs of another nation, of another country. It designates a system of economic control or domination of another nation or people. It is a social phenomenon that owes its origin to an economic necessity in the development of the affairs of a country or a nation. For as long as there has been a "social system," a "national economy," has the world beheld imperialism. We find it in the endeavor of the Roman Eagle to subjugate all countries on the Mediterranean and (even) those beyond its shores. We find it in the endeavor of the Spanish nation to conquer the Netherlands to enable it to vanquish England.

We find it in the endeavor of the Empire of Çrivijaya to bring under its rule the peninsula of Malacca as well as the Malay Realm, the endeavor to dominate the economy of Cambodia and Champa. We find it in the endeavor of the Empire of Majapahit to control and influence all the islands of Indonesia, from Bali to Borneo, from Sumatra to the Moluccas. We find it again in the endeavor of the Japanese Empire to occupy the peninsula of Korea, to obtain influence in Manchuria, to dominate the Pacific Islands. We find Imperialism again at all times and in all periods of (established) "social systems," we find it with all nations whose economy of necessity propels (them) to Imperialism. Imperialism is not a quality peculiar to the white races; it occurs among the yellow, the black, and among the brown races, as exemplified at the time of Çrivijaya and at the time of Majapahit. Imperialism is an "economically determined necessity."

... And, as we have already said, imperialism is not only a system or a tendency to subjugate other countries and peoples, but it can also find expression in the endeavor to dominate the economy of another country and people. It need not necessarily be carried out by means of the sword, the machine gun, the cannon

Indonesië klaagt aan! Pleitrede voor den Landraad te Bandoeng op 2 December 1930 door Ir. Soekarno (Amsterdam: De Arbeiderspers, 1931), pp. 8–9, 41, 42, 43, 64–65. English translation by Margaret W. Broekhuysen. (The English translation is rendered from the Dutch translation. The speech was originally given in Indonesian.)

or the "dreadnought"; ... it can also take place by means of a "pénétration pacifique." ...

Which roads must we follow? The Partai Nasional Indonesia [Sukarno's Indonesian Nationalist Party] answers to this question with full conviction: those roads that lead to Indonesia-Merdeka [Free Indonesia]! Behind Indonesia-Merdeka the P.N.I. sees the magnificence of the motherland of prosperity and the motherland of grandeur, behind Indonesia-Merdeka the P.N.I. sees the glowing brilliance of the future!

This is the essence of the conviction of the P.N.I. as it was written in the declaration of principle: "The Partai Nasional Indonesia has the conviction that the most important precondition for the reconstruction of Indonesian Society is National Freedom, and therefore the endeavor of the whole of the Indonesian nation must be directed first of all to National Freedom."

Deviating from the point of view of many other political parties which teach: "Reconstruct your economy, then freedom will come automatically"; deviating from the point of view of many other political parties which are of the opinion that freedom is the fruit of the [accomplished] reconstruction of the economy, the P.N.I. says: "Be zealous in the cause of national freedom, for only through national freedom can the Indonesian people bring about complete national reconstruction"; thus it says that complete national reconstruction is possible only after the return of national independence. ...

Almost every important measure in a colonial country is taken for the benefit of imperialism. This is why the measures taken by a country for its economy bear partially or completely the imprint of imperialism as long as it is still a colony, indeed as long as a country is a "protectorate" or a "mandated territory," in short, as long as a country cannot regulate its national economy completely on its own. That is to say: As long as a nation does not wield political power in its own country, part of its potential, economic, social or political, will be used for interests which are not *its* interests, but contrary to them. *It is bound hands and feet, prevented from combating the imperialism by which it is harmed;* it is not capable of preventing the use of its potential for the interests of others, not capable of applying its potential to its own economic, social, and political life. *In short, it is not capable of exerting itself in the struggle against, and the annihilating of, imperialism; it is not capable of helping itself.*

A colonial nation is a nation that cannot be itself, a nation that in almost all its branches, in all of its life, bears the mark of imperialism, a mark it owes to the great influence of imperialism. There is no community of interests between the subject and the object of imperialism. Between the two there is only a contrast of interests and a conflict of needs. All interests of imperialism, social, economic, political, or cultural, are opposed to the interests of the Indonesian people. The imperialists desire the continuation of colonization, the Indonesians desire its abolition. The regulations that came into being under the influence of imperialism are therefore contrary to the interests of the Indonesian people.

And yet it accepts the regulations without ado, you ask? Oh certainly, the people accept the regulations. The people respect those regulations. But they accept them and they respect them because they are forced to do so! . . .

. . . What are the roads to promote [Indonesian] nationalism? Those roads are of three kinds:

first: we point out to the people that they have had a great past;

second: we reinforce the consciousness of the people that the present is dark;

third: we show the people the pure and brightly-shining light of the future and the roads which lead to this future so full of promises.

In other words, the P.N.I. awakens and reinforces the people's consciousness of its "grandiose past," its "dark present" and the promises of a shining, beckoning future. . . .

Our grandiose past! Oh, much honored judges, what Indonesian does not feel his heart shrink with sorrow when he hears the stories about the beautiful past, who among us does not regret the disappearance of that departed glory! What Indonesian does not feel his national heart beat with joy when he hears about the greatness of the empires of Melayu and Çrivijaya, about the greatness of the first empire of Mataram, the greatness of the time of Zindok and Erlangga of Kediri and Singosari and Majapahit and Pajajaran— the greatness of Bintara, Banten and the second Mataram under Sultan Agung. What Indonesian does not feel his heart shrink with sorrow when he realizes that his flag was formerly seen even as far away as Madagascar, Persia and China. But on the other hand, in whom is hope not rekindled that a nation with such a grandiose past must *surely* have sufficient natural aptitude to have a beautiful future, must *surely* have in itself the possibilities to attain again that level of greatness in the future? Who of us is not imbued by new strength when he reads the history of those past times? And thus among the people, too, again conscious of their great past, national feeling is revived, and the fire of hope blazes in their hearts! Through this the people regain a new soul and new strength.

To be sure, that past is a feudal past, the present is a modern present. We do not wish to revive that feudal past; we are not at all in favor of a new feudal period. We know the bad aspects of the feudal system for the people. We only point out to the people that the feudalism of the past was a living, a healthy and not a sickly feudalism, a feudalism full of possibilities for development, (and one) that, had it not been disturbed by, for instance, foreign imperialism, would surely have achieved its evolution, *would in the end surely have brought forth an equally healthy modern society.* . . .

51
Sutan Sjahrir on the Dilemma of the Intellectual

> *Sutan Sjahrir (1909–1966), one of prominent leaders of the Indonesian nationalist movement and Prime Minister of Indonesia in the immediate postwar years, was born in the Minangkabau region of Sumatra and educated in Indonesia and Holland. The colonial authorities arrested him in 1934 and exiled him to Irian Barat (West New Guinea) and later to*

the Moluccas. A profoundly Western-oriented socialist, Sjahrir in his exile wrote many letters to his Dutch wife in Holland; the following, written on June 20, 1935, provides insights into his constant preoccupations concerning a proper political philosophy. In the 1950s, Sjahrir was excluded from active political life. He died in Switzerland where he had gone for medical treatment.

Am I perhaps estranged from my people? Why am I vexed by the things that fill their lives, and to which they are so attached? Why are the things that contain beauty for them and arouse their gentler emotions only senseless and displeasing for me? In reality, the spiritual gap between my people and me is certainly no greater than that between an intellectual in Holland and, for example, a Drents farmer, or even between the intellectual and the undeveloped people of Holland in general. The difference is rather, I think, that the intellectual in Holland does not feel this gap because there is a portion—even a fairly large portion—of his own people on approximately the same intellectual level as himself. And that portion is, moreover, precisely what constitutes the cultural life of Holland; namely, the intellectuals, the scientists, the artists, the writers.

That is what we lack here. Not only is the number of intellectuals in this country smaller in proportion to the total population —in fact, very much smaller—but in addition, the few who are here do not constitute any single entity in spiritual outlook, or in any spiritual life or single culture whatsoever. From the point of view of culture, they are still unconscious, and are only beginning to seek a form and a unity. It is for them so much more difficult than for the intellectuals in Holland. In Holland they build—both consciously and unconsciously—on what is already there. They stand on and push forward from their past and their tradition; and even if they oppose it, they do so as a method of application or as a starting point.

In our country this is not the case. Here there has been no spiritual or cultural life, and no intellectual progress for centuries. There are the much-praised Eastern art forms but what are these except bare rudiments from a feudal culture that cannot possibly provide a dynamic fulcrum for people of the twentieth century? What can the puppet and other simple and mystical symbols offer us in a broad and intellectual sense? They are only parallels of the out-dated allegories and wisdom of medieval Europe. Our spiritual needs are needs of the twentieth century; our problems and our views are of the twentieth century. Our inclination is no longer toward the mystical, but toward reality, clarity, and objectivity.

In substance, we can never accept the essential difference between the East and the West, because for our spiritual needs we are in general dependent on the West, not only scientifically but culturally.

We intellectuals here are much closer to Europe or America than we are to the Borobudur or Mahabharata or to the primitive Islamic culture of Java and Sumatra. Which is our basis: the West, or the rudiments of feudal culture that are still to be found in our Eastern society?

So, it seems, the problem stands in principle. It is seldom put forth by us in this light, and instead most of us search unconsciously for a synthesis that will leave us internally tranquil. We want to have both Western science and Eastern philosophy, the Eastern "spirit," in the culture. But what is this Eastern spirit? It is, they say, the sense of the higher, of spirituality, of the eternal and religious, as opposed to the materialism of the West. I have heard this countless times, but it has never convinced me. Did not Hitler also say that the Aryan *Geist* was the sense of the higher, the spiritual, the moral, the religious? And is this spirituality actually such a pre-eminently Eastern attribute and ideal? It seems to me definitely inaccurate. It is possible that climatic and racial factors have had an influence on the present differences in development between the East and the West. However, it is no longer possible to determine the direction or magnitude of that influence, because of the more direct and apparent expression of the influence of economic and sociological factors.

If one looks at world history as a whole and endeavors to understand its total gradual development, then the perennial so-called "essential" differences between the spiritualism of the East and the materialism of the West disappear; and instead the emphasis centers upon feudal culture with its spiritualism and universalism, on the one hand, and the bourgeois-capitalistic culture with its bourgeois ideology, its materialism, and its modern objectivity on the other. . . .

52
Manuel Luis Quezon's "New Deal for the Laboring Classes in the Philippines"

> *The guiding force of Philippine nationalism in the years before World War II was Manuel Luis Quezon, first President of the Philippine Commonwealth (1935–1944). He learned his politics under American aegis as majority floor leader in the Philippine Assembly (1907–1909), Resident Commissioner in Washington (1909–1916), and President of the Philippine Senate (1916–1935). The passage below is drawn from a speech made in 1939 to a group of discontented agricultural laborers of Pampanga province in Central Luzon.*

My countrymen: I know the situation of a laborer; I know that a man who is in a miserable condition thinks nothing and cannot think of anything except his way of getting some relief; and if nothing can help him out of his predicament, and he may die of hunger or of sacrifice, he cannot think anymore of his country; he cannot love anymore his countryman, because only his feelings

Manuel Luis Quezon, *Speech of His Excellency Manuel L. Quezon, President of the Philippines on New Deal for the Laboring Classes in the Philippines* (Delivered in San Fernando, Pampanga, February 14, 1939), pp. 10–12, 14–15.

and sufferings may dominate over his heart and mind. Hence, the paramount need in the Philippines today is a means whereby no person will be so miserable in life as not to be able to think of his duty to his native land. The Philippines is facing a very dangerous future. We shall be alone here. We will be duty-bound to defend the fate of our country in case a foreign nation comes to molest us. If our country is molested by any other nation, in order that every Filipino could feel, in the deepest core of his heart, true love for his native land, and that he may be prepared to readily offer his life in the defense of his country, it is necessary that he must have a decent living—a living, though not totally abundant, that at most must be sufficient as source of subsistence as long as he would want to work. It is not only a living enough for himself, his wife, and children—not only sufficient to provide food for himself and his family,—that is needed, but one that must also furnish them clothes even during Sundays only—clothes that are clean, and not those ragged and dirty ones worn throughout the year.

If we believe that the heart of the laborer throbs for the love of our country, we must exert our utmost to help every man in the Philippines to have a prosperous life. In order that we may expect a laborer to love and defend his country, it is necessary first to make him understand and feel that he is enjoying a prosperous life.

It is not because I am an enemy of the capitalists and landowners that I side with you now. No, indeed; I have no enemy. My responsibility to my position is a responsibility to all. I have a duty to defend the rights of the property owners, and likewise those of the poor. I favor the laboring class not because I desire to grab the property of the rich; I side with them owing to the fact that in order that the rich may enjoy peace and his legitimate share, he must give what rightfully belongs to his laborers.

I beseech you to have more patience; I ask you to desist from resorting to the worst—by burning the sugar-cane fields and harvesting the palay [rice] at your will and then seizing all, including that which does not belong to you. You must not do that! You should give the concerned his rightful share.

I know that in an incident here, the man who seized the palay was right. His landlord, the owner of the palay, was indebted to him. He wanted him to pay him first before giving his share of the crop. Since this is a civil case, it should be brought to the courts.

You should not violate the laws; it is not also proper that the landowners be given the opportunity to seek the intervention of the Government. The Government is duty-bound to give what help they ask for, and it can order the Constabulary to guard the palay.

I wish to call your attention to the fact that it takes time to help you improve your condition. Just be tolerant; have some more patience. If in the building of a shack you need to devote a few days or weeks, how much more when we are constructing a big and beautiful mansion, where we can reside peacefully and happily forever?

Now, with regard to strikes. Strikes are not always beneficial. They are a powerful weapon in claiming your rights; but, they should not be overused. If you have any complaints, present them to the Department of Labor or to the Court of Industrial Relations. It is true that it takes time for these government entities to decide the questions at issue, as my friend, Mr. Pedro Abad Santos [leading Philippine socialist], has indicated here, but we cannot do anything. You cannot expect other officials to do what I can, for I can even give orders to the Chief of Constabulary and make him comply with them at any time; but the other departments or offices which are devoid of the powers like mine cannot be employed immediately. But, what shall we do? Such being the case, we should be tolerant and wait for the appropriate time.

My friends: You can always hope for my help as long as you comply with the law. Your complaints and the alleged injustices done to you can be taken to the courts and to the proper authorities; once there, you can unravel everything that is in your heart. It is, therefore, not necessary that you use guns or any other weapon. No law officer or government official can abuse you because justice is dispensed to all alike. . . .

You can criticize anybody in the Government—that would not bother me a bit; what is important to me is your compliance with the laws. If you want to meet, go on, and hold your meetings. You can even say that you will spill blood but you must not insinuate that you will cut the neck of a man; you can also shout that you will kill, but kill only in words and not in deeds. You can lambast any official in the Government or even my administration; this would not matter to me. What I particularly desire is that you here will enjoy permanent peace and that you will give the Government sufficient time to be able to intervene in your behalf and to study thoroughly your situation.

Before I came, I learned that Secretary [of Justice] José Abad Santos requested his brother, my friend, Mr. Pedro Abad Santos, not to display red banners in welcoming us. To me that is not important. You can use any color for banner—red, blue, or whatever color you wish; you can also organize here any party association, be it a socialistic or communistic organization; you can even discuss matters with tight-fisted hands; such will not bother me as long as you do not create any disorder or violate the laws. I do not want to hear anybody say that this Government is weak; the Government will not let the people to be betrayed [sic]. . . .

53
The Indian Minority in Burma

Burma under British rule was until 1937 administered as a province of British India. One major result of Burma's provincial status was the flow of Indian immigrants allowed free entry into the country, where they came to play a key role in the economy. That role, in turn, formed one of the major and bitterest criticisms of Burmese nationalists. When the British proposed to separate Burma from India, the Indian community's apprehensions about their future in Burma was aroused. Addressing the Burma Round Table Conference in London, Mr. N. M. Cowasjee of the Burma delegation stated the Indians' case.

My Lord, Indians have settled in Burma for generations and have contributed very largely to the general progress and economic development of the Province. The population of Indians in Burma according to the last census is 1,340,000 odd. The financial and economic interests of Indians in Burma are considerable, and Indian capital, Indian enterprise and Indian labour have very largely contributed towards the development of the Province of Burma and Burmese agriculture, trade and industries. Had it not been for Indian enterprise, capital and labour, Burma would not have been what it is.

So far as local industries, the internal trade and agriculture are concerned, almost the whole of the finances have been advanced by Indians. Indians have also a very large share in the industrial activities of the Province, and in fact, those industrial concerns in Burma which are not purely British have been controlled by Indians. The share of Indians in the inter-provincial and the export and import trade of the Province is also very large.

Indian labour has played a very important part in the development of the Province. It has been admitted by Government over and over again that Indian labour has only supplemented, and not replaced, Burmese labour, which until recently was entirely unavailable except for certain agricultural purposes.

Indians have also invested their capital and their savings in the purchase of landed property in all parts of Burma and it is significant to note that most of the properties in the town of Rangoon, the capital of Burma, is owned by Indians, who contribute towards the municipal taxation of the Corporation of Rangoon more than sixty per cent of the total taxes collected. The banking business of Burma is mainly, if not entirely, Indian, and had it not been for the enterprise of the Nottu Kottai Chettiars of South India it would not have been possible for Burma to carry on its agricultural or industrial operations. The Indian Chettiars

Burma Round Table Conference, 27th November, 1931–12th January, 1932: Proceedings (London: His Majesty's Stationery Office, 1932), pp. 45–47.

have been carrying on business in the Province for over 70 years —almost a century. The present agricultural growth of Burma is due to a very great extent to the operations of these Chettiars, who have been lending money to the Burmese cultivators at all seasons of the year to facilitate agricultural operations at rates of interest recognised as reasonable and, according to the recent report of the Burma Banking Enquiry Committee, less than those charged by others. . . .

My Lord, the investments of the Chettiar community in the way of loans in Burma exceed 100 crores [1 crore = 10 million] of rupees annually, and the bulk of this capital is money belonging to the proprietors of the Chettiar firms residing in the southern part of India. From the point of view of general trade it must be borne in mind that it is not possible for the British firms to carry on their business in Burma without the assistance of Indian merchants and traders, to act as middlemen and large retail dealers between the British importing firms and the ultimate purchasers, firms or individuals to whom the British importing firms sell goods every year on credit to the extent of lakhs [hundreds of thousands] of rupees, relying solely on their integrity and business capabilities.

There is the further fact that large numbers of Indians have settled down in Burma; some of them are the issues of the third generation of the original settlers, and they have now made Burma their home, and have no link or connection with India in any shape or form.

The Indian community of Burma therefore asks that it shall have adequate and effective representation in the Legislative Council and the executive appointments; that it shall have adequate representation in the public services of the country, and that the constitution of Burma shall be such as to prevent any majority community from abusing their legislative power with a view to enacting laws which would create discrimination between one citizen and another.

The Indians in Burma are just as anxious as the Burmans themselves to see that Burma progresses to that goal which has already

been announced by His Majesty's Government, and we shall always feel it our duty to lend our support as far as possible so that
self-governing Burma may come into being. The basic principle of
self-government is that the government of a country both on the
executive and on the legislative side, must be truly representative
of the people of the country, and it must therefore follow that the
constitution we are called upon to frame will be truly representative of the various communities residing in the Province.

54
Minority Nationalism: The Karens in Burma

> *Speaking before the Burma Round Table Conference, held
> in London in 1931–1932 to discuss Burma's constitutional
> status, Sra Shwe Ba, a representative of the Karen elders,
> made a plea for a distinct Karen role in the future govern-
> ment of Burma. Karens, including both lowland and hill
> groupings, feared submersion within a Burman-dominated
> state.*

My Lord, ... I wish now to enlighten this Conference on the
position of the Karens and their contribution to the welfare of
Burma. It is true that others have some knowledge about us, but
it is a truism that we know the Karen people better.

I, therefore, take this opportunity to make the Conference understand the Karens better. We claim that the Karens are the
aborigines of Burma. Indeed, our history has maintained that we
were in the country before the Burmese people. Accordingly, the
Karens' claim to belong to Burma stands on a different and a much
higher plane than that which can be put forward by others. The
Karens have lived side by side with other races, but have not been
absorbed into any other races, as have some of the indigenous

*Burma Round Table Conference, 27th November, 1931–12th January,
1932: Proceedings* (London: His Majesty's Stationery Office, 1932), pp. 86–
87.

races of Burma. In the words of the Government of Burma, we are a distinct entity and are not likely to be assimilated. We consider ours a distinct nationality, and we do desire to evolve our nationality on our own lines. We may therefore claim that our position is unique and peculiar, and unlike that of any other community in Burma.

The Karens have always held together. We have no caste. We have absolutely no religious intolerance, and there is no conflict among us. Our women have always been treated on an equal footing with the men, and never as inferiors, even in theory. In point of literacy in English, the position of our Karen womenfolk, taking this matter on the basis of our proportion, is distinctly unique; never surpassed and not yet equalled.

The Karens have taken to education early and earnestly. Schools have been opened in the villages and in the large towns, with the result that tens and tens of thousands have been enabled to avail themselves of the benefits of education. The result is that literacy is quite high among us. We therefore repudiate any suggestion of being a backward race or a "hill tribe." If any race is ready for democratic institutions we claim ours is.

The Karens have contributed to the welfare of the country in various ways. Our schools, maintained and largely financed by us, open their doors to all alike, and have given education to Burmese and other races. The majority of Karens as agriculturists have also contributed to the prosperity of the country, but it is with deep regret that I have to say that many of their lands have fallen into the hands of the non-indigenous races.

For the defence of the country we have supplied men to the Army. . . . That we are law-abiding and peaceful citizens, the history of the Karens is a testimony. Karen villages are mostly free from crime. I do not say, nor do I want to be understood as meaning to say, that the Karens do not fight when offended. What part the Karens can play in the new Burma, with all the solid qualities that go to make law-abiding, peaceful and useful citizens, I leave it to the British Government to judge. In a self-governing Burma the Karens can assuredly be one of the main props of the new edifice.

I am happy to mention that in recent times there seems to be a better understanding and mutual respect between the Karens and the Burmans than in former times. But as the Karens are not yet well understood their needs are frequently overlooked and ignored. The Karens being naturally quiet and reserved are reluctant to raise their voice to others, except through representatives who are their own people. The Karens do feel that they have not had a due share of representation, consonant with their numerical strength and serviceability. We want to contribute our share to the building of the new self-governing Burma. We desire to do our part as a distinct entity, for only in that way can we bring our own contribution to the progress and the prosperity of our mother country, Burma. To do that we do need political training and experience and also more responsibility in the administration. We are in full sympathy with the desire for a full responsible government. We only ask that we may be able to take our share of the yoke in an effectual way.

No constitution would be satisfactory or would work successfully until and unless we have our rightful share in the Legislature and in the administration of the country.

55
The Jews of the East

> The Jews of the East, *published in Thailand in 1914, presents a view of the Chinese widely held in Southeast Asia. This small booklet caused a sensation at the time of publication since the pen name of the author, "Asavabahu," was sometimes used by King Rama VI (Wachirawut, 1910–1925), the reigning Thai monarch.*

The Anglo-Saxon peoples (that is England and America) are inclined to congratulate themselves on the lack of anti-Semitism in their countries. They parade their sympathy for the Jews, their resentment of the anti-Semitism in other European nations. Apparently they presume that this places them in a position to condemn the various countries in which the Jews have been the recipients of unjust treatment. They forget, however, that in territory under their own jurisdiction an analogous situation exists, differing only from anti-Semitism in that it happens to be called "The Yellow Peril."

When these nations speak of "The Yellow Peril" (by which they mean the danger of an attack by the yellow races upon the white), I must ask the privilege of objecting to the term, inasmuch as they use it generically to include all the races of Asia. As a matter of fact, the danger of which they speak has reference only to the Chinese. In Thailand we have quite as much to fear from the Chinese as the white races have; although at the present time we have not reached the place where we feel that we need to be unduly alarmed about it. That being the case, however, I protest any inclusion of the Thai in the term "The Yellow Peril," for the Thai are not even as much like the Chinese as Europeans are like Jews.

In what way are the Chinese like the Jews? The observing reader has probably already traced likenesses as he has compared those traits of the Jews which I have discussed with the characteristics of the Chinese. But in order that he need not refer to them, I shall recapitulate them as I draw my comparisons. I hope my readers will overlook a certain amount of repetitiousness.

The first point of likeness is "Racial Loyalty." No matter where they live, what nationality they assume, Chinese remain essentially Chinese. But they do not understand such a race loyalty as "patriotism," or "love of country," which is what such a term usually means. Thus we find Chinese registered as nationals of foreign

Kenneth Perry Landon, *The Chinese in Thailand* (New York: Oxford University Press, for the Institute of Pacific Relations, 1941), pp. 34–39. By permission of the author and W. L. Holland, American Institute of Pacific Relations, University of British Columbia.

countries, even within China itself. It is true that registration with a consulate other than one's own for convenience sake is understandable if a person has to live in a foreign country where his own nation maintains no consulate. But registration with the consulates of foreign nations in one's own country is a practice adopted only by Chinese. It serves to show how little national consciousness or love of the homeland Chinese have. But even though they register themselves as being under the sovereignty of a foreign nation, they do not by that act cease to be Chinese: they will be loyal to the new object of their unstable allegiance only so long as it serves their purposes as well as those of their rightful masters for them to be so.

It is their racial consciousness that makes Chinese undesirable immigrants, so far as possible usefulness to the country which they enter is concerned. The purpose of a country in permitting immigration is to swell, by that means, the number of its own citizens. But when immigrants regard their residence in a country as temporary and are unwilling to become citizens, they must be judged to have disappointed the purposes of the country which had admitted them.

There is not a farmer living who welcomes the insect pests which devour his crops and depart leaving his fields dry and bare of grain. In the same way, no country is glad to welcome aliens whose only purpose is to make as large a fortune as possible and then depart, without the slightest intention of returning favors received. It is true that not every Chinese is capable of amassing as much wealth as he desires in order to return to his homeland while he is still young. But it is also true that it is the purpose of each and every one of them so to do. And this attitude certainly does not contribute to their desirability.

As for the argument that Chinese intermarry with the people of other races, in this they are also like the Jews. To be specific, when a Chinese man marries a Thai woman, that woman becomes a Chinese and adopts Chinese customs in every detail. Their children become Chinese also. But, if a Thai man marries a Chinese woman, the woman continues to be Chinese, while the man finds himself adopting Chinese ways and performing such acts as fit into the accepted Chinese pattern of life. As for the children, even though they are Thai in name, they are psychologically Chinese. That is, their ways of thought are Chinese; and they recognize this fact by the circumstance that they feel most at home in a Chinese group. There are exceptions, of course; but it is our misfortune that there are fewer of these exceptions than we could wish. In conclusion, then, marriage between a Chinese and a Siamese, regardless of whether the Chinese partner is male or female, works out to the advantage of the Chinese. It was our hope in this matter of intermarriage that the Chinese would put down roots in our country. The opposite has occurred. Nations which have admitted Chinese have invariably been out of pocket as a result of the return to China of such immigrants, with wives and children, whenever opportunity arose. Some immigrants have even gone so far as to send wife and children back ahead of themselves.

Chinese are unwilling to recognize any obligation to the countries in which they reside, or to become citizens of such countries. In this characteristic they are nowise different from the Jews, as I have already described them. If there are privileges to which the native inhabitants of a country are entitled, Chinese immigrants demand them; since they consider it their inalienable right to receive the same preferential treatment accorded citizens. But if an occasion arises on which they are required to fulfill the duties of citizens, they evade such obligations so far as possible.

No doubt you can all remember the time four or five years ago when the Chinese suspended work. Their purpose on that occasion was to protest having to pay THE SAME POLL TAX THAT ALL THAI PAY! Their action corroborates what I have decided to say quite explicitly: the Chinese expect to enjoy all the privileges of citizens without assuming any of the obligations.

Their racial loyalty, which is one of the strongest of Chinese characteristics, is the primary cause, then, of most of their difficulties; as a similar attitude is in the case of the Jews. Such an attitude arouses a sense of apprehension in the citizens of countries in which they reside, and definitely inhibits intercourse on equal terms between two races. Their feeling of superiority to their neighbors is the essential reason why they have to endure persecutions as often as they do.

The second characteristic of the Jews is found fully developed in the Chinese also. That is: the Chinese, like the Jews, are an ancient race whose high civilization was developed at a time when our ancestors had not emerged from savagery. Through the ages Chinese have been taught to divide mankind into two classes: Chinese and Huan (Barbarians), so called according to their way of thinking. Europeans are as much Huan (Barbarians) to them as other Asiatics or blacks. Since they regard us so, I need not tell you that they have no slightest intention of dealing with us either honestly or honorably. They are likely to think that we exist only to be robbed and cheated. In all their contacts with Huan, Chinese recognize no right or wrong; nor do the Jews in their dealings with Gentiles.

In manners and address they are unfailingly gentle and courteous, but, believe me when I say, their courtesy is a means of deception, and their soft words are a trap, intended to divert attention that people may be by so much the more easily ensnared. If they see that there is an advantage to be gained or a profit to be made, they are eager to ingratiate themselves, and even, on occasion, to seek ways of being useful to us. But when our vision has been somewhat obscured they spit on our heads. Perhaps it is a good thing that we do not understand their language, since we are thus not aware of the way in which we are being execrated, sometimes even to our faces, in the vilest of language. . . .

The methods and practices of the Chinese in matters of making money are without doubt quite as sharp as those of the Jews. If we speak in the usually accepted way, we are wrong to blame the Chinese for their money-making ability. But the Chinese are like the Jews. If they start with the same amount of capital and the same opportunity as people of other races, they get rich much sooner.

There are many reasons why the Chinese are able to make money more rapidly than other people, most of them no different from those that apply to the Jews (for the Jews are able to do the same thing). According to Chinese thought, money is the beginning and end of all good. There is nothing greater.

Chinese appear to be willing to do anything and everything for money. Only Chinese will exchange even life itself for money. A condemned Chinese criminal who is rich enough can usually hire a poor man to be executed in his stead, for a consideration; something that could happen no place else but China. Chinese are willing to endure every sort of privation for money. Anyone who has watched Chinese coolies eat cannot help but feel a sense of revulsion, since it seems that the food they eat would hardly attract the curs which roam the streets. And if one speaks of the places where they live, it is amazing that so many persons can squeeze themselves into a space so small that the people of no other race on earth could manage to breathe in it. This being the case, it is not surprising that the Chinese can manage to corner most of the available work for themselves. No matter how small the wages, they are ready and glad to accept them, since they know how to sustain life on an incredibly small amount of food. . . .

There is no kind of work that they will not do, provided that they are paid for it. Let it be ever so vile, but recompense them for it, and they will do it. In matters of money the Chinese are entirely devoid of morals and mercy. They will cheat you with a smile of satisfaction at their own perspicacity. And they are quite capable of robbing and killing in the most brutal fashion for two or three dollars. They have the most devious ideas imaginable for accomplishing embezzlement or dacoity, by land or by sea.

Is it necessary for me to offer examples to illustrate this shameless attitude toward crime of the Chinese in matters pertaining to money? I am sure that the employees of insurance companies could tell many a tale that would illustrate my point well. Who has not heard of some of the dishonest practices used by the Chinese in matters of bankruptcy? Whenever a company has debts that have become uncomfortably large, it goes into bankruptcy. A little later a new company appears on another street. The owner of the new company is the same as the owner of the former company. According to commonly accepted ethics, bankruptcy is an unsavory process and reason enough for loss of reputation. But the Chinese (or the Jews) approve of it as a smart practice to be used by the clever and the knowing.

Maybe there are those who will object to this indictment on the grounds that the Chinese are Buddhists. But, Chinese are Buddhists to no greater extent than Jews are Christians. Just as the Jews have never been able to swallow the teachings of Jesus Christ about covetousness, the Chinese are unable to act according to the precept of the Buddha, which likewise forbids covetousness. . . .

Another point relative to my claim that the Chinese are no more Buddhists than the Jews are Christians: it is true that in China there are religious observances and temples, but in Palestine there are churches and Catholic priests also.

In a play called "The War God" of which Israel Zangwill is the author, there is a character called "Karl Blum," who is confidential secretary to the Chancellor, Count Torgrim. Karl Blum has changed his religion and become a Christian. As a result of this action he has secured the position of confidential secretary and right-hand man to the chancellor. Further, through his position he has had the opportunity of securing gifts from people seeking government positions, who have been only too glad to oblige. Blum remains a Christian so long as the chancellor remains in power. When, in due time, the chancellor loses his post, Blum discards his Christianity immediately as one would throw off a cloak which one has donned as a temporary convenience, and returns to the observance of the religion of his ancestors. This play is a strange one in that it was written by a Jew, himself, without a doubt, like Karl Blum in character. Zangwill wrote it to show the typical Jew as he is.

At this very time there are many Chinese Karl Blums. Only there has not yet been a Chinese to write such a play about them. Adherence to a religion, which most of us regard as important because it forms our sense of right and wrong, Chinese regard as merely a matter of convenience. If it is to their advantage to do so,

Chinese are glad to adopt Buddhism or Christianity or Mohammedanism or Hinduism. They will worship any god or any madness at all if only in so doing they derive a profit. To sum up: the Chinese have only one god, more precious to them than all other gods together, and that is the GOD MONEY. Chinese hold that the external observances of any religion are unimportant. Only let them hold fast to the GOD MONEY, who is the one lord. . . .

56
In Defense of the Chinese

> *Few statements better answer the attacks against the Chinese in Southeast Asia than the following piece written in 1962 by Teodoro M. Locsin, for the* Philippine Free Press. *The article predates by less than two years the enforcement of a law which "nationalized" the retail trade. By insisting that retail outlets be Filipino-owned, the government essentially excluded the Chinese community from its major source of income.*

Today, a Chinese may not be a farmer. He may not engage in certain professions. The law nationalizing the retail trade would eventually keep him out of that business. To stay in business, Chinese merchants have paid out millions of pesos in bribes to Filipino officials, the Mayor of Manila has disclosed. For a while, every crook in the police or in the army could make money by accusing a Chinese of subversive activities if he did not come across. We do not know whether the practice is still going on; perhaps not. Chinese businessmen are continually threatened with cuts in their import allocations. The Chinese may go into industry, for not enough Filipinos are doing that yet; there is an economic vacuum to be filled. But if Filipinos follow the Chinese into industry, Congress may be expected to pass a law throwing the Chinese

Shubert S. C. Liao, ed., *Chinese Participation in Philippine Culture and Economy* (Philippines: n.p., 1964), pp. 385–388.

out of it. The Chinese may not do this, may not do that—what are the Chinese, finally, to do?

Not that they are not doing pretty well, in spite of restrictions. Everything has been tried to put the Chinese down; he keeps getting up. The Chinese community is richer than ever and can therefore afford to bribe more Filipino officials. . . . The Chinese response to every nationalistic challenge has always been adequate. Practice in overcoming difficulties makes perfect; the tougher the Filipinos get, the keener the Chinese become. Nationalistic laws are creating a group that keeps getting smarter and smarter. Eventually, there would be no alternative left but to resort to massacre. But that has been tried many times before and has always failed.

Laws are futile; bloodshed won't work. What are Filipinos to do with the Chinese? Repression has not only failed; increase of it may produce domestic and international complications. There are perhaps 500,000 Chinese nationals in this country. Some of them are Communists, others Nationalists; all are trying to make a living. They are here to stay; it is impossible to throw them out of the country.

What is to be done? More repressive legislation, perhaps, may finally ruin the Chinese, but what would be the consequences of that ruin? There would be 500,000 Chinese unable to leave the Philippines and prevented from making a living in it at the same time. The situation can only be described as explosive.

If the Chinese are pressed hard enough, they may be expected to cry for help—either from Nationalist China, or, if it proves impotent to help them, from Communist China; with its more than half a billion people and an increasingly modern army, Red China may be expected to do something about the plight of the Chinese in the Philippines; it could justify intervention in Philippine affairs before mankind. No nation could very well tell Red China to do nothing for 500,000 human beings for whom life is slowly made impossible; not even the United States, so hostile to the Communists and all their works, could tell Red China not to intervene. As a matter of fact, to forestall such intervention in the Philippines, the United States itself may be forced to make representations with the Republic—to let 500,000 human beings live.

Repression means trouble. Massacre won't work. It is time, surely, to try something other than discrimination or force. Perhaps, Christianity is the answer to the question that this Christian nation has found so vexing for centuries.

We propose a Christian solution to the problem with a certain hesitation. Once, we wrote advising the Catholics of a certain province not to throw stones at a Protestant gathering no matter how ill-mannered the Protestants were—no matter what the provocation. It did not seem Christian to us. The Catholic paper, "The Sentinel," promptly attacked us for being anti-Catholic. We do not know what we shall be called for proposing a Christian solution to the Chinese problem, but we have no alternative; it is the only way to avoid chaos. We hate to think of what would happen if the 500,000 Chinese in the Philippines should become desperate. So here goes . . .

What is a Christian solution?

Well, to put it as simply as possible, we should not do to the Chinese what we would not have the Chinese do to us. If the Chinese violate our laws, jail them. Do not drive them into breaking the law through repressive legislation; then they would have no alternative but to break it.

The Enigma of Shylock

If a Chinese cannot be a farmer, a professional, a merchant, a miner, what is he going to do? Beg? That, or go berserk. There is industry, into which he is being invited to enter, but if he prospers there, should he not expect to be driven out of it? What is a Chinese to do?

It is said that he puts Filipinos out of business by unfair trade practices, by combinations, through monopolies, etc. The thing to do, in such a case, is to go after him for breaking the law on trade practices; thus the U. S. government goes after American trusts. Nationalization only forces the Chinese to use Filipino dummies—there is always a plentiful supply of this commodity. The cut the dummy gets means an increase in price. In the end, it is the people who pay.

The Jews were the Chinese of medieval England; they made money and suffered the same fate. Religious scruples prevented Englishmen from making money with money; the bankers had to be Jews. They performed a service; they became prosperous; they were persecuted. . . .

Shylock is an enigmatic figure. Is he the hero or villain of Shakespeare's play? The villain? But who had made him villainous? The beastly conduct of Christians drove him mad. . . .

. . . Here is an indictment of Christian practice unparalleled in literature. The villain is human nature; the only thing that can keep it in check is Christian charity, and who should show it more appropriately than Christians?

In the Philippines, Christian Filipinos have made the Chinese what they are, the object of Christian complaints, the object of Christian acts of repression. If Chinese businessmen hurt Filipino businessmen, that is not right—but who hurt whom first? Who is the villain? The reconciliation of the two peoples should be the aim of legislation, not their further alienation.

A Christian solution to the Chinese problem may well prove the greatest national experience since independence.

PART V

The Era of Decolonization

IN THIS PART the documentary record moves into the most recent past, or rather, into the beginning of the present. It embraces barely more than two decades, those in which the process of decolonization started on its uneven course. The main concern is not with the often kaleidoscopic state of accelerated change, nor with the coming and going of political leaders and governmental systems, but rather with some of the unfolding patterns, in historical perspective.

The first group of documents is devoted to selected aspects of the Japanese occupation, the catalyst and cataclysm which terminated European hegemony in Southeast Asia and set decolonization—albeit still under the auspices of a foreign overlord—in motion. The first of these documents speaks with the voice of Imperial Japan, giving an over-all policy guideline to be followed in the occupied territories (Document 57). The subsequent documents present a far from complete spectrum of events under and reactions to Japanese rule. The interesting reminiscences of an Indonesian aristocratic official, the texts pertaining to the Burmese declaration of independence of 1943 (as far as we know, here published for the first time), and the two Filipino views of wartime collaboration all explore the issue of cooperation between conqueror and conquered

215

(Documents 58, 59, and 60). The unique situation whereby Indochina remained under French supervision is described in Governor-General Jean Decoux's panegyric to the French wartime role in her colony (Document 61). The remaining documents are grouped together by country, to present significant factors, mainly ideological, of the decolonization era in their appropriate national settings. Three Indonesian spokesmen show us the profound social and ideological cleavages that have rent the island republic ever since President Sukarno first developed what became the official state philosophy. That philosophy, the *Pantja Sila,* stressed the theme of Indonesian unity (Document 62), but large segments of the population have continued to adhere to diametrically opposed belief systems, most notably Islam and Communism (Documents 63 and 64). A seemingly similar polarity is represented in the two Philippine documents in which a president, Roman Magsaysay, and a Communist leader, Luis Taruc, express opposite opinions on Filipino-American relations (Documents 65 and 66). Though quite uneven in strength and numbers, both Indonesian and Philippine Communists unsuccessfully used armed force against the newly independent nation states. Only in Vietnam did Communism, for some decades already deeply intertwined and identified with nationalist agitation, emerge victorious at war's end. Though the country has been divided since 1954, no clear and authoritative statements have as yet emanated from South Vietnam that could be placed side-by-side with those of Ho Chi Minh, president of the Democratic Republic of Vietnam (Document 68). Independent Burma's first prime minister, Aung San, a student organizer of the *Thakin* group turned war-time military leader, is here represented in a sober speech, a fine if relatively rare example of confrontation with the very serious problems of decolonization and nation building (Document 69). The independence day sentiments expressed in

Tengku Abdul Rahman's speech (Document 70) appear in sharp contrast to the thoughts of the Vietnamese declaration of 1945 (Document 67). A policy statement by the Thai premier is important in underlining the prominent place occupied by the military in modern Thailand, and also the even more deeply rooted Thai ability to adjust to a changing international enviromnent (Document 71).

57

The Japanese Blueprint for Southeast Asia

The Japanese Empire's basic aims and policies in the occupied territories of Southeast Asia, as often as not arrived at after thorough discussions among various governmental and military agencies, were spelled out in a long series of documents. The extracts presented below are from a rather comprehensive set of instructions, modeled on some of the basic papers issued in Tokyo; they were issued in Singapore, which during the war acted as the center for the various military and naval commands in Malaya and Indonesia, in the confident phase of the early occupation years.

INSTRUCTIONS OF THE SUPERINTENDENT-
GENERAL OF MILITARY ADMINISTRATION
(Gunsei sōkan shiji)

Military Administration General
Headquarters [Singapore]

August 7, 1942

Although the present Sacred War originated in the self-preservation and self-defense of the Empire, its essence is to rally the various peoples of East Asia and plan the construction of a new world order. In planning and implementing military administration, the long-term objectives should definitely not be lost sight of and care should always be taken in the policies toward the various peoples so that such will be neither too lenient nor too harsh. Appropriate guidance shall be furnished to secure the resources of

Harry J. Benda, James K. Irikura, and Kōichi Kishi, eds., *Japanese Military Administration in Indonesia: Selected Documents* (New Haven, Conn.: Yale University, Southeast Asia Studies, Translation Series No. 6, 1965), pp. 187–192. By permission of Southeast Asia Studies, Yale University.

the Southern areas and rapidly strengthen the war potential of the Empire. Special resources having international trade value shall be actively fostered and developed, and industrial and land development plans based on geographic surveys shall be devised with a view to increasing the national power. Japanese subjects shall be afforded opportunities for development everywhere, and after establishing firm footholds they shall exalt their temperament as the leading race with the basic doctrine of planning the long-term expansion of the Yamato [Japanese] race.

Following are details on matters confronting us.

1. On the future status of occupied territories

The national policy is to defer final decisions on the eventual status of the occupied areas. As a matter of course, local military authorities should not prematurely reveal the Empire's intentions or make commitments to the local inhabitants. Care should be taken to avoid military administration policies which may complicate the question of the future status of these areas.

As a matter of reference, the intentions of the Central authorities are as follows:

As made clear in repeated Imperial declarations, the Philippines and Burma are links in the Greater East Asia Co-Prosperity Sphere and their independence shall be sanctioned at an appropriate time in the future after they have evidenced their cooperation with the Empire.

However, particular heed should be taken of the fact that this independence is such that military affairs, foreign affairs, economics, and other affairs shall be placed under the firm control of the Empire. Moreover, since the Empire has not yet made commitments concerning the degree of independence, extreme prudence should be exercised on this matter in guiding the peoples concerned. . . .

4. On policies governing the various peoples

Because the present war was begun for the preservation and the self-defense of the Empire, there are some who, in their haste to acquire resources, have overlooked the tremendous capacities of the peoples of Greater East Asia in the Empire's planning. The acquisition of resources vital to national defense is obvious, but the various peoples must be guided so as to accept the Empire's policies and push forward toward the construction of Greater East Asia in harmonious unity. The said peoples of the occupied areas should be treated as follows:

(1) Overseas Chinese

Although it is essential that political and economic pressures be applied where necessary, it is vital that they be utilized henceforth under strict supervision and thereby contribute to the execution of our policies.

(2) Natives

Although it is anticipated that the livelihood of the natives will be difficult temporarily, particular care should be taken in their guidance in order that they endure this patiently and never lose hope for the future.

(3) Enemy nationals

The total capacities of persons with special skills among enemy nationals, as well as others who can be utilized, should be fully and cooperatively employed in our construction. Care should be taken so that any local administrative abuses be corrected by separate measures.

(4) Axis nationals

The existing rights and interests of Axis nationals shall be recognized, but the future expansion of these should be restricted.

The policy toward transfers of rights and interests of enemy nationals to third-power nationals undertaken even prior to December 8th—not to mention since that date—which were executed with ulterior motives, shall be one of absolute nonrecognition.

5.   On the employment of natives

Although the policy is to dispatch personnel necessary for the implementation of military government from the homeland wherever possible, since it is difficult to dispatch the large number of personnel required for each military unit particularly in the realm of military government because of the manpower mobilization situation in the homeland, some inconveniences should be tolerated and efforts made to employ natives. In particular, since this is a significant period when the male youth, who are the nucleus of the future State, should be invested with the capacities which will enable them to take charge of the construction of the Greater East Asia Co-Prosperity Sphere, the youth who are dispatched should not be utilized simply for odd jobs but care should be taken so as to afford them leadership training at every opportunity. . . .

9. On respecting mores and customs in administering the occupied areas

Matters relative to respecting the existing organizational structure and ethnic mores in administering occupied areas shall be as previously stated, but great care should be taken in matters such as the hasty institution of public holidays, the casual changing of names, or the enforcement of Japanese morality and customs. In particular, religious customs should be especially respected and extreme circumspection must be used in exerting coercive pressures upon Buddhism or other religions.

It has been decided to coordinate the revision of geographic names through a geographic name revision conference which has been created in Japan and which will be constituted from the Cabinet and the three ministries of the Army, Navy, and Foreign Affairs. Items of consideration shall include national designations, major regional names, major municipal names, and leading seas, mountains, lakes, rivers, and islands. Since these names should take cognizance of local opinions as much as possible, especially of the invasion forces, the revision of major place names should not be conducted solely on the local level but should always be communicated to the entire Army. Further, those names which have already been conceived should be reported promptly.

10. On education

The emphasis of native education shall be upon industrial technological instruction adapted to practical lifet and the vigorous cultivation of an atmosphere respectful of labor. At the same time an education conforming to the special character of each region and to local circumstances shall be implemented, but policies such as compulsory or universal education should not be devised.

Schools beyond the existing precollege level shall be universally closed and, following an examination of the educational system and content, the reopening of those which are considered especially necessary shall be subject to the approval of the Supreme Commander.

As to the propagation of the Japanese language among the natives, plans should be made for its prompt and thorough cultivation from a beginning which must tolerate some disadvantages and inconveniences until its complete utilization and acquisition.

An idea for consideration at this time is to utilize the musical talents of the natives and teach them the Japanese language through songs.

Since the improvement of the character of the people who are the guiding race is extremely essential to the establishment of Greater East Asia, special consideration should be given to the education of Japanese residing in the Southern sphere. Their understanding of the Southern sphere should be increasingly deepened together with the cultivation of their character and the strengthening of their solidarity, and they should be instructed so as to take the initiative as exemplary embodiments of self-sacrificing service.

Where those going to the Southern area for the first time are concerned, although the establishment of a coherent training and educational system through the central and local levels is anticipated, it is desirable that special efforts also be made by all military units because of the importance of the education of the Japanese.

58

Java Under Japanese Occupation

The following excerpts are taken from the memoirs of a Javanese aristocratic official who served as Regent (Bupati) of Banjumas in Java under both the Dutch and Japanese regimes. His observations on the occupation era were apparently written after the war, and thus do not represent on-the-spot reporting; nor are they entirely free from either personal bias or a certain caution.

Through its slogans of friendship and its encouragement to the people of all classes to learn Japanese, Japan had succeeded in obtaining the complete confidence of a portion of the Indonesian people. During the Dutch colonial period, not everyone could learn Dutch. It was only the upper class which was permitted to learn Dutch and of the lower class one may say only those who were allowed to enter the Dutch-Native Schools. This type of distinction was not to be found in the treatment of the Indonesians by the Japanese. If in the Dutch period the people felt prevented from making progress, under the Japanese government, they were given the widest possible opportunities to increase their knowledge. School teachers who had followed courses in Japanese had to take part in competitions in the language, in writing and reading, singing, speaking, etc. Various prizes were presented to the winners. The winners in the Under-Districts were sent to competitions in the Districts, and those who passed these examinations were sent in turn to the Regencies, Residencies, and finally to the last competition in Jakarta. In this way the Indonesian people were able easily to accept Japa-

S. M. Gandasubrata, *An Account of the Japanese Occupation of Banjumas Residency, Java, March 1942 to August 1945*, trans. Leslie H. Palmier (Ithaca, N.Y.: Cornell University Southeast Asia Program, Data Paper No. 10, 1953), pp. 12–13, 15. By permission of Southeast Asia Program, Cornell University.

nese habits and customs, Japanese influence, Japanese understanding so that among Japanese leaders there were those who
said outright that the Indonesian people who were so "excellent"
were to be made Japanese.

Confidence in Japan was not limited to the poor only. Some
intellectuals, also, had their hearts stolen. In Purwokerto, for
instance, there was a headmaster's wife who spoke to her children in Japanese every day, swallowing whole Japanese customs
and habits. There was also an Indonesian legal expert (Master
in Laws) holding the office of President of the Court. He was
already proficient in Japanese and according to his own statements he was already so far advanced that he was able to read
Japanese legal works, etc. It was not surprising that the Japanese
were delighted and placed great hopes on being able to change
the Indonesians to "Nipponjin." . . .

We said above that the Indonesian people were an "excellent"
people. The Japanese were happy to possess pupils who were
clever, industrious, and cultured, but they also understood that
for the Indonesians to progress as quickly as possible Javanese
customs such as the "homage," "squatting," had to be abolished.
With the training which I have described above the character of
the Indonesians began to change. The lower class began to acquire self-respect. Added to the shortage of textiles, it became
usual to wear practical clothes, that is the man used shoes and
shorts for daily wear, whilst the women, especially the young
women, wore frocks. Eventually this simple type of Western
clothing became popular even in the villages, only the more conservative people remaining attached to the original Javanese
costume.

As a Regent I certainly held the opinion that some of the
Javanese customs of their nature could hinder the development
of our people. Furthermore, they made those of little education
feel inferior to those in high positions. I myself could therefore
approve the changes in the spirit of our people. It was to be
hoped that a belief in oneself would become the property of the
whole of the Indonesian people. This was the only condition to

stand alone. As long as the Indonesian people were kept down by the disease of "inferiority complex," so long would it be difficult for us to free ourselves from the prison of foreign colonisation.

Even though I realized that among Indonesians it was certain that there would be some who would lose their heads because of these sudden changes, I felt it was necessary to set an example so that the general public should favour the wearing of practical clothes. I never wore shorts, but I ceased wearing the "belangkon" (Javanese head-cover, formed by folding a batik kerchief). In the Dutch period though I wore trousers I still used a head-kerchief. I myself also felt that the "sembah" [sign of obeisance with folded hands], and so on, in these times was out of place. Some officials usually performed this salutation to me. I did not allow them to do so any more. . . .

Japan was a country which dared to take risks. Holland for centuries had held the opinion that the Javanese could not become satisfactory soldiers. Japan, in a little while only, felt and was able to see the desire of the people to defend their fatherland against the Allied powers. Japan was willing to invite the Javanese people to oppose the Allied attack together with her. Even though at that time the hatred of the Indonesians, who learnt industriously and trained themselves in the Japanese fashion, had already arisen and was clearly seen, because the behaviour of the Japanese was in general extremely coarse, nevertheless Japan continued to be concerned to build up an army made up of Indonesians.

Propaganda to receive officer candidates for the FDA (Fatherland Defense Army) was conducted actively, especially among the teachers and police, because there the Japanese spirit had entered most deeply, even though there also was felt a feeling of hatred towards Japan. At that time in order to tempt the Indonesian people, who in general like high positions, Japan declared that the rank of Major in the FDA was the same as that of a Regent. . . . Japan truly understood that in the eyes of the people of Indonesia there is no rank other than of Regent which is recognised as the peak of respect and greatness. To live in a Regency, facing the alun-alun [open, grassy square] with a pair of "walled banyans" was an honour which bore no comparison. So, seen from the point of view of psychology, Japan was not wrong in using propaganda which gave Indonesians a hope of obtaining a rank equivalent to that of a Regent by following the road of the FDA. The results of Japanese propaganda were satisfactory. FDA officer candidates mostly originated from the teachers. Local Government officials, the Police and other officers did not feel drawn by the Japanese inducements.

59

The Burmese Declaration of Independence (1943)

Although many parts of Southeast Asia were retained by Japan under the control of the Imperial Army or Navy after the conquest of the area in 1942, selected countries were granted nominal independence during the war years. The following documents indicate the nature of the process by which Burma received her independence from Japan in 1943. The first document, dated March 22, is the unilateral declaration by the Imperial Government which outlined the new Japanese policy toward Burma, signed by Premier Hideki Tōjō. The second document, dated August 1, is the Burmese Declaration of Independence from Great Britain and the Empire of Japan, signed by the President of the Burma Constitutent Assembly, Dr. U Ba Maw.

[I]

STRICTLY CONFIDENTIAL
(Translation)

To enable all nations each to find its proper place and all peoples to pursue their lives in peace is the immutable national policy of the Empire of Nippon.

Unpublished manuscripts, U Ba Maw Collection, Yale University Library, New Haven, Conn. By permission of Yale University.

On the basis of this national policy, Nippon is now prepared to enable the Burmese people to attain the independence of the new Burma which has so long been their cherished desire. It is, therefore, my very great pleasure to express to you the intentions of Nippon on this matter.

1. The spirit of national foundation

In connection with the establishment of the new Burma, it is her spirit of national foundation in which Nippon entertains the greatest interest. Since the new Burma is to become a fully independent state, it is needless to say that the spirit of her national foundation is a matter to be decided by Burma herself. It is the firm belief of Nippon, however, that the new Burma will be established upon the basis of ethical principles as a member of the Greater East Asian Sphere of Co-prosperity in order to contribute to the creation of a new world order.

2. The composition of the state

It was previously announced that the territory of the new Burma would comprise the areas under the jurisdiction of the existing Administrative Council, but I hereby declare that it is further to include the whole territory of Burma with the exception of the Shan and Karenni areas.

It is desired that the composition of the new nation be determined in accordance with the aim of harmoniously embracing the various peoples within the territory with the Burmese people as its base.

It is also desired that the political organization be so formed as to render the administration of the state simple and forceful.

3. Basic relations between Nippon and Burma

Nippon earnestly hopes that, through her own incentive and responsibility, the new Burma will speedily substantiate her status as an independent state and, in this regard, Nippon is ready to afford all possible assistance. She further hopes that the new Burma, as a member of the Greater East Asian Sphere of Co-prosperity, will, on her part, long maintain with Nippon the closest relations of co-operation in all such matters as politics, military affairs, diplomacy and economics.

4. Declaration of war against the United States and Britain and firm establishment of the wartime structure

It is sincerely desired that the new Burma will, following her independence, declare war against the United States and Britain and that she will speedily complete a national structure consonant with wartime requirements and, in inseparable union with Nippon, bend her fullest efforts for the successful prosecution of the war.

5. Military affairs

In view of the requirements of military operations, it is desired that the new Burma will fully co-operate with Nippon in perfect unity and extend every facility to the Imperial Forces and that, at the same time, the Burmese Forces will, in regard to their wartime operations, serve under the command of the commanders-in-chief of the Imperial Army and the Imperial Navy.

6. Economic affairs

The new Burma is expected to promote her economic development by just and unhampered activities under her own authority as a unit in the general economic construction of Greater East Asia; and in this regard Nippon is prepared to extend the necessary assistance.

In this connection, it is desired that, with respect to matters necessary for the prosecution of the war, measures be taken to secure full co-ordination with the steps to be taken by Nippon.

7. Preparations for independence

Nippon desires, Dr. Ba Maw, that you who are to stand at the helm of the new state of Burma will, with due understanding of the foregoing several points, soon set up a preparatory commission for independence and push forward all preparations necessary for independence.

The independence of the new Burma is expected to be effected around August and it is hoped that the necessary preparations will be completed by about the end of June.

You are requested to obtain the details thereof from the Commander-in-Chief of Nippon's Forces in Burma.

Although the creation of a state is no easy task, the ardent desire of the over ten million people of Burma will surely bring the efforts to a glorious consummation; and I presume that in carrying out this grand task there is no greater satisfaction to you, gentlemen, upon whose shoulders rest the heavy responsibilities.

It is my fervent hope, that you will bear in mind the intentions of Nippon and, by surmounting all difficulties, will successfully perform the great task of founding a new state, and that, in co-operation with Nippon, you will proceed with courage and determination with the successful prosecution of the war as well as with the construction of the new order in Greater East Asia.

The 22nd Day of the Third Month,
the 18th Year of Showa.

(Signed)   Hideki Tōjō
Prime Minister of the Imperial
Government of Nippon

[II]

DECLARATION OF THE INDEPENDENCE OF BURMA

Today, after more than fifty years of British occupation, Burma resumes her rightful place among the free and sovereign nations of the world. She proudly occupied that place throughout a very long stretch of unbroken history during which her glory shone like the sun and the moon in the heavens. Her empire once extended far beyond the hills to the North, South, East and West; many among her people were famous and mighty; the strength of her arms also was acknowledged to be great; and she contributed in her time worthily to the progress of mankind. Pagan and its architecture still mark a peak in that progress.

Throughout all their long history before British aggression the

Burmese people maintained their independence unbrokenly after subduing every enemy sooner or later in incessant wars.

Fifty years or so ago Burma lost her independence for the first time as a result of three Anglo-Burmese wars. Britain waged these wars in pursuance of her predatory designs upon Asia at a time when Asia was divided and unprepared and the whole weight of sea-power, superior war equipment, and the vast newly-discovered resources of the industrial revolution was on the British side. To these she further added her traditional weapons of intrigue, bribery, and every conceivable fraud and device. The result of this unequal contest was that most of the small Asiatic nations were destroyed by British cunning and material superiority. It was Burma's tragedy to be among those small nations which were overpowered by this material superiority.

The years of British occupation were indeed sorrowful for Burma. She entered into a long bondage, and dishonour and disruption ate deeply into her flesh. The Burmese people were slowly expropriated, losing, as time went on, most of their national substance, their vast material resources and opportunities, their culture, their language and even their own way of living, while Britain, according to whose plans these [things] were happening, derived the evil gains.

However, the Burmese national spirit remained uncorrupted by the darkness of these years. The struggle against the aggressor continued in one form or another as opportunity allowed or weapons were available while British greed and tyranny kept the fire in every Burmese heart raging. Periodically the people broke loose in their desperation, there were mass risings, slaughter, destruction, and then the most violent British reprisals followed; whole Burmese villages went up in flames, the men were taken away for ever and their homes left desolate. But still the struggle went on, gaps were slowly filled, new patriots came forward to suffer, in a spirit of utter dedication, the same repressions, imprisonment, exile, torture and often death itself. These heroes suffered and even died so that Burma might live. Their names and deeds shall be remembered always.

While the fortunes of this desperate unequal struggle rose and fell the Asiatic consciousness appeared for the first time in Burma. The Burmese people began to look around and abroad and then at themselves, and found that they were Asiatics and that Asiatics must stand together if Asia is to rise again. Looking for the leadership which would unite and save Asia the Burmese found it in the great Nippon Empire. Thereafter Burma began to turn her face towards the East.

With the outbreak of the present war for the liberation of East Asia the Burmese struggle came at last to a turning-point. The irresistible forces of Nippon, after utterly breaking the enemy everywhere, swept through all East Asia and finally reached Burma where the entire people, who had long waited for this hour, rose unitedly to march side by side with Nippon's great army of liberation against the Anglo-American enemies. East Asia had at last come together, her enemies were swiftly expelled from Burma and elsewhere, and the joy of the Burmese people was unbounded. From that day onwards they have given themselves completely to the cause of East Asia. Their gratitude to Nippon as the leader of East Asia is profound. They bow too in gratitude and homage to the war heroes, both Burmese and Nipponese, who have died in this war so that East Asia may conquer and live, so that Burma also may be free.

Today the Burmese people will at last reap the harvest which was sown for many years with ceaseless struggle and sacrifice. They will come once more into their own rights. They will solemnly proclaim their independence and sovereignty and enter into all the rights and obligations of a free people. Nippon's strength and heroism, Nippon's nobility of purpose, have made this possible. With an entire nobility which is in keeping with the spirit of her national foundation, Nippon, who conquered Burma from the British, has promised to recognize Burma's Independence. Burma desires to place on perpetual record her gratitude to Nippon for this act of supreme service to her.

The Burmese people therefore, by this solemn declaration now made in their name and in accordance with their national will by a Constituent Assembly representing them, publicly proclaim that from this day for ever Burma is a fully independent and sovereign State and that she has severed herself completely from Britain and the British Empire. Burma, as an independent State, is further declared to be established upon true ethical principles which will always represent the spirit of her national foundation. The Burmese people are convinced that such principles alone will preserve them and make them great and prosperous.

Burma also declares herself to be a member of the Great East Asia Co-prosperity Sphere. She enters into this free and equal partnership so that, by the united resources, will and work of East Asia as a whole, a new Asiatic order and economy may be established as a part of the new world order which will ensure justice, peace and prosperity to all peoples. Burma pledges herself with her entire will to the fulfilment of this great task.

The New State of Burma is also established upon the principle of Burmese unity in one blood, one voice, one leader. It was national disintegration which destroyed the Burmese people in the past and they are determined that this shall never happen again.

Burma is now not only Burmese but East Asiatic as well and she must bear her part of the burden in accordance with this new conception and order while at the same time the rest of East Asia bear their part of the burden towards Burma in the same spirit. Burma must construct the new order in her territories in accordance with a plan which will ensure strong administration, stability, justice, self-sufficiency and strength in all directions. A strong, stable, and self-sufficient Burma is the greatest contribution that Burma can make to the East Asiatic order and economy, and Burma, owing to her geographical position, must be strong if East Asia is to be strong. The New State of Burma will pursue this policy resolutely.

Burma, in her foreign policy, will also promote peace, justice and the establishment of a new world order. She will endeavour constantly to maintain the closest relations with all friendly powers on the basis of justice and reciprocity.

Regarding the present Great East Asiatic War which is being waged against the Anglo-American enemies and their allies the Burmese people solemnly declare that it is also their war, a war which will decide the issues of their own independence, their prosperity, their very survival as a people. It concerns them as Burmese and also as East Asiatics, for it is further a war which will definitely settle the fate and fortunes of the East Asiatic peoples for a very long time. The Burmese people further declare their strongest resolution to support this war together with the other East Asiatic powers under Nippon leadership till the enemy is reduced to utter submission. They will support this war with all their resources, both material and moral, whatever may happen and however long the war may last. The great heroes whose sacrifices have redeemed Burma and made Burmese Independence possible have passed away but their work still remains unfinished; the work of Burmese Independence also still remains unfinished; the work of making East Asia safe for East Asiatics also remains unfinished. All these tasks, which are so vital to the Burmese people, can only be finished by winning the present war. The Burmese people therefore dedicate themselves completely to the cause of winning the present war.

Finally, it is declared that the New State of Burma will be governed in strict accordance with the laws and constitution which are in force for this purpose. All peoples in Burma are in this manner assured of good government, justice, and of all their just and lawful rights.

The Burmese people, acting through a Constituent Assembly representing them for this purpose, have here made a solemn declaration of Burmese Independence and of the principles upon which the New State of Burma is founded and will be governed. This declaration represents the whole national will of the Burmese people and it shall be faithfully maintained. The Burmese people pledge themselves to the utmost to this end before all devas [gods] and men who are witnesses to this solemn act and declaration.

(Signed)   U Ba Maw
President,
Burma Constituent Assembly.

Rangoon, the 1st August 1943.

60

The Philippines During the War Years

The continuing large-scale guerilla activities during the Japanese occupation of the Philippines caused a deep cleavage in the native leadership of the Islands. One group, accepting the Japanese presence, supported the conqueror's plan for an independent government within the Greater East Asia Co-Prosperity Sphere, while the other remained loyal to the American-oriented Commonwealth of the prewar years. The following documents explore the nature of the split. Part I is an excerpt from José P. Laurel's inaugural address (October 14, 1943) as president of the Japanese-sponsored Philippine Republic. Part II contains part of a letter from Tomas Confesor, resistance governor of Panay, to Dr. Fermin Caram of Iloilo City.

[I]

Fellow Countrymen:

. . . The Republic which we are consecrating here today was born in the midst of a total war. Our countryside was transformed into a gory battlefield to become a historic landmark of that titanic conflict. From the crucible of a world in turmoil was unleashed the mighty forces that were to spell the liberation of Asiatic peoples from foreign domination. Today, as we witness the triumphal realization of our national ideal, we would be sadly wanting in those magnanimous qualities which distinguished a noble and valiant race, if we forget the wounds and havoc inflicted by that war, the immolation of our youth with their golden promise of the future, the untold sufferings and privations undergone by our innocent population. This is no time for indulging

Teodoro A. Agoncillo, *The Fateful Years* (Quezon City: R. P. Garcia, 1965), Vol. II, pp. 968–972, 974–976, 1000–1003. By permission of the author and R. P. Garcia.

in unseemly recriminations or for the ventilating of our grievances. In all dignity and out of the fullness of our hearts we could
do no debt of honor to the August Virtue of His Majesty, the
Emperor of Nippon, for ordaining the holy war and hastening
the day of our national deliverance.

The presence here of high diplomatic and official representatives of the Nipponese Empire and other nations of Greater East
Asia testifies to the traditional friendship and mutual understanding among all Oriental peoples. In the name of the Filipino people, I wish to convey to the honored guests our sincere assurances of good-will and to express the fervent hope that the fraternal ties which unite our people with theirs will grow ever
stronger and firmer in the years to come.

I wish to take advantage of this opportunity also to make public
our grateful appreciation of all the acts of kindness showered
upon the Filipino people by the Commanders of the Imperial
Japanese Army and Navy in the Philippines, past and present.
I make special reference to General Sigenori Kuroda, Highest
Commander of the Imperial Japanese Army in the Philippines,
and to General Takazi Wati, Director-General of the Japanese
Military Administration, without whose sympathetic assistance
and encouragement, the Preparatory Commission for Philippine
Independence would not have been able to accomplish its work
promptly and expeditiously.

Our first and foremost duty as a free and independent nation
is to maintain peace and order within our borders. No government worthy of the name will countenance public disorder or
tolerate open defiance of its authority. Unless we enjoy domestic
tranquility, we cannot prosecute to a successful conclusion those
labors essential to our daily existence and our national resources
will remain undeveloped, our fields uncultivated, our industry and
commerce paralyzed; instead of progress and prosperity, we shall
wallow in misery and poverty and face starvation.

In the ultimate analysis, all government is physical power and
that government is doomed which is impotent to suppress anarchy and terrorism. The Constitution vests in the President full authority to exercise the coercive powers of the State for its preserva-

tion. In order to make those powers effective, my administration shall be committed to the training, equipment and support of an enlarged Constabulary force strong enough to cope with any untoward situation which might arise. Certainly, everything must be done to forestall the indignity and humiliation of being obliged to invoke outside intervention to quell purely internal disturbances.

With the attainment of independence and the consequent abolition of the military administration, those of our citizens who have heretofore been engaged in guerilla activities would prove untrue to the ideal for which they have forsaken their families, sacrificed the comforts of home and risked their lives, if they did not lay down their arms and henceforth tread the pathways of peace. I cannot believe that their sense of duty would dictate to them otherwise than to come down from the mountains and other hiding places and participate in the common enterprise of nation-building. If perchance recalcitrant elements would still persit in the sabotage of our program of reconstruction and threaten the very existence of the Republic, I shall have no other alternative than to consider them public enemies of our government and people and to deal with them accordingly.

Even during the artificially prosperous years of the Commonwealth regime, we had to import heavy quantities of rice and other foodstuffs; with the outbreak of the present war, and worse, in the brief phase of its incursion into our country, our agricultural and industrial activities were thrown out of gear, our trade with other countries was disrupted, and the shortage of our food supply became more acute than ever. With our vast tracts of fertile and arable land it would be indulging in mere platitude to assert that we can produce two times, not to say three times, what we actually need to feed our population. Whether the problem is expansion or intensification of our agriculture, the common denominator is hard work.

We must till our idle lands, improve and diversify our crops, develop our fisheries, multiply our livestock, dairy and poultry farms. Next we must produce other necessities such as clothing, fuel, building materials, medicinal preparations, articles of daily use; in short, the minimum requirements of civilized life. Then, we must turn our attention to the demands of heavy industry, explore the possibilities of our exporting to other members of the Sphere those raw materials which we have in abundance in exchange for goods which we cannot locally produce, adjust our internal economic structure in coordination with the regional economy of the Asiatic bloc, and thus contribute our share to the realization of the noble purpose of common prosperity. This means that we have to rehabilitate and plan out our national economy; adopt a sound and stable currency; overhaul our credit and exchange systems to insure the steady flow of capital; foster private initiative and research; create new industries; establish industries; establish factories and manufacturing plants; improve our existing transportation and communication facilities; construct more roads in accordance with a well devised general plan to promote mutual intercourse; build bottoms to accommodate our overseas and coastwise trade; and finally, adopt a more efficient machinery of price control to prevent hoarding and profiteering and insure a more equitable distribution of prime commodities consistent with our war-time economy. All these cannot be undertaken haphazardly but must be accomplished in accordance with a well conceived economic planning if we expect to rise to the full stature of independent nationhood. Our political emancipation would be vain and illusory if we did not at the same time work out our economic salvation. . . .

[I I]

UNITED STATES OF AMERICA
COMMONWEALTH OF THE PHILIPPINES
Office of the Governor
Panay

February 20, 1943

My Dear Doctor:

. . . I feel flattered, indeed, by your statement that should I return to the city I would bring relief, peace and tranquility to our people in Panay. In this regard, I wish to state with all frankness that peace and tranquility in our country, especially in Panay, do not in the slightest degree depend upon me nor upon the Filipino people, for as long as America and Japan and their respective allies are at war with one another, peace and tranquility will never obtain in our country nor in Panay. This is a total war in which the issues between the warring parties are less concerned with territorial questions but more with forms of government, ways of life, and those that affect even the very thoughts, feelings and sentiments of every man. In other words, the question at stake with respect to the Philippines is not whether Japan or the United States should possess it but more fundamentally it is what system of government should stand here and what ways of life, systems of social organizations and code of morals should govern our existence. As long, therefore, as America and Japan remain at war, these fundamental questions will remain unsettled. Consequently, peace and tranquility will not reign in Panay, much less in the whole Philippines.

Despite this fact, however, there is a means to bring about peace even under the present circumstances if Japan is really sincere in her desire to see peace and tranquility here. To this effect, she should declare the Philippines free and independent proclaiming at the same time our neutrality. To further demonstrate her sincerity of purpose to this end, she should evacuate all her forces, military establishments and other governmental organizations from the Islands with the guarantee that she would not land forces therein nor within her territorial waters. I am sure that should Japan declare this proposition and formally present the same to the United States, the latter would be compelled to accept it. Her sense of honor would give her no other alternative but to back up Japan in this regard. . . .

The burden of your so-called message to me consists of the entreaty that further bloodshed and destruction of property in Panay should stop and that our people be saved from further sufferings and miseries resulting from warfare and hostilities now obtaining between Japan and ourselves. The responsibility, however, of accomplishing this end does not rest upon us but entirely upon your friends who have sworn allegiance to Japan. For it was Japan that projected and created these conditions. Japan is the sole author of this holocaust in the Far East.

I agree with you when you say that our people are "experiencing unspeakable hardships and sufferings" because of these hostilities, but you should realize that our people are bearing these burdens cheerfully because they know that they are doing it for a good and noble cause. They know why we are resisting Japan. They are aware that Japan is trying to force us to accept her system of government and ways of life which are unacceptable to us to say the least. You may not agree with me but the truth is that the present war is a blessing in disguise to our people and that the burden it imposes, and the hardships it has brought upon us are a test to our character to determine the sincerity of our convictions and the integrity of our souls. In other words, this has placed us in the crucible to assay the metal in our being. For as a people, we have been living during the last forty years under a regime of justice and liberty regulated only by universally accepted principles of constitutional governments. We have come to enjoy personal privileges and civil liberties without much struggle, without undergoing any pain to attain them. They were practically a gift from a generous and magnanimous people— the people of the United States of America. Now, that Japan is attempting to destroy these liberties, should we not exert any effort to defend them? Should we not be willing to suffer for their defense? If our people are undergoing hardships now, and are doing it gladly, it is because we are willing to pay the price for those constitutional liberties and privileges. You cannot become wealthy by honest means without sweating heavily. You very well know that the principles of democracy and democratic institutions were brought to life through bloodshed and fire. If we sincerely believe in those principles and institutions, as we who are resisting Japan do, we should contribute to the utmost of our capacity to the cost of its maintenance to save them from destruction and annihilation, and such contribution should be in terms of painful sacrifices, the same currency that other people paid for those principles.

You were a member of the Constitutional Convention that adopted the Constitution of the Philippine Commonwealth. You did not only subscribe to it but you became a Filipino citizen by virtue thereof. Now that the hour of test has come, how dare you advise the people, as you do now, to forsake that sacred document and accept anything for peace and tranquility which at all events will be only temporary? Should I hearken to you, I would be conspiring with you and the Japanese military authorities to destroy the Constitution, that you and I signed with all solemnity, and everything for which that Constitution stands. Do you not realize, therefore, that what you are doing now is a repudiation of your Filipino citizenship and all the sacred privileges attendant thereto, things which I am sure you hold dear and precious? . . .

It pains me to read your letter saying that you and I at one time nursed devotedly identical convictions on democracy and liberty but that you have to revise your own for the sake of "peace and tranquility." How can you honestly and truthfully say that you may enjoy peace and tranquility when you are unfaithful to your own convictions? Do you mean to tell me that you have revised your convictions because you believed that they were not righteous or because you considered your personal convenience over and above that of the Filipino people? . . .

. . . For your information and guidance, let me tell you that Japan is digging her grave deeper and deeper everyday in New Guinea. In China and in Burma she is on the run and is losing extensive territories which she formerly conquered. In Europe, Germany is in flight pursued by the Russians. In Africa, Tripoli and Tunisia have fallen into the hands of the Allies. Everyday the cities of Italy are being bombed and smashed to pieces. The Italians will soon demand for separate peace. By June, next, the Philippines will be redeemed from Japan, definitely. What are you going to do next, revise your conviction again? . . .

I hope I have made myself clear enough to make you under-

stand my position. I will not surrender as long as I can stand
on my feet. . . .

Sincerely yours,
Tomas Confesor
Governor

61
French Indochina in the Co-Prosperity Sphere

*The fall of France in June, 1940 marked a turning point
in the history of the French colonies as well. In this respect,
Indochina was no exception. Under heavy pressures from
the Japanese, the French administration in Indochina was
forced to yield to most of Japan's demands during the war
years. The French Governor-General during this critical
period was Admiral Jean Decoux, who served in this capacity from 1940, after the fall of Metropolitan France to
the German forces, until the collapse of nominal French
suzerainty in Indochina in the spring of 1945. His memoirs,
À la barre de l'Indochine, an excerpt from which is reproduced below, give some indication of the spirit which moti-
vated this wartime administrator.*

Before bringing my memoirs to an end, it is my duty to draw
a few conclusions from the events which have been related in the
body of this work.

What I should like to stress in the first place is, that in spite
of the beginning of the new worldwide conflict, in spite of the
reverses in our fortunes in 1940, French Indochina has never
suspended its efforts, and has never ceased for a moment to
progress during the five years which followed the armistice.

The pages which France wrote in Indochina from 1940 to

Jean Decoux, *À la barre de l'Indochine* (Paris: Librairie Plon, 1949),
pp. 482–483, 486–487. English translation by Margaret W. Broekhuysen.
By permission of Librairie Plon.

1945 are worthy of her past and her best traditions. I state this forcefully here because this was actually the case, and moreover I report on the merit of those achievements of which I am proud, and on all our compatriots in Indochina who, from the beginning to the end of this dramatic period, helped me with their energy and their intelligence, so that a great French achievement might be safeguarded. This handful of Frenchmen, cut off from the motherland, at the other end of the world, has done its duty in a magnificent way under the hardest and most thankless conditions.

They deserve some credit for this. To the rigors of that isolation was added, in fact, the presence of Nipponese troops on Indochina's soil. And if we cannot properly speak of occupation, as I have shown, yet almost every day incidents occurred which often provoked dangerous tension. To overcome these difficulties for close to five years it was necessary to display vigilance and firmness all the time.

The result of this at times desperate policy of resistance, of this intensive interior activity, of this unshakeable confidence in the restoration of the country, was remarkably efficacious.

Until March 9, 1945, the political, administrative, military, and economic apparatus of Indochina had remained intact. Under unexpected conditions, French sovereignty survived all these trials. Order and safety had been maintained uninterruptedly, and nothing, apart from the American bombings, had occurred to disturb the daily life of the masses of the natives.

Amidst dangers of many kinds, internal as well as external, and in spite of the disintegrating effect of Japanese propaganda, Indochina's loyalty to France was never for a moment belied. One does not keep the loyalty of three sovereigns [i.e., the kings of Laos and Cambodia and the Emperor of Annam] and of 25 million inhabitants by force, compulsion, or fear—indeed, I had neither the means nor the desire to do so—but through prestige, through confidence, and through a wise administration. . . .

The errors which I have just enumerated are at the root of the chaos in Indochina. At the moment when these lines are being written the situation is still, from a political as well as military point of view, precarious. Disorderliness continues, losses are heavy on both sides, frightful destruction has accumulated. A still graver fact is that an enormous bloody trench has been dug which we must attempt to fill without delay.

It is fitting first of all to keep constantly in mind that the Indochinese problem is only one of the aspects of a vaster problem, a problem of international ramifications.

We have to know [ask ourselves] whether Communism is going to rule Eastern Asia, a part of the world which is among the richest in men and in raw materials.

From now on we shall witness a general offensive which has the same origin and identical goals. It is being directed from Kharbin, the seat of the Asian Cominform. This offensive is being developed in Malaysia, Burma, Indonesia, Siam, the Philippines, Korea, Vietnam, and as far as Japan.

The problem is to ascertain whether this offensive will be strangled in time or whether, on the contrary, it will triumph. In the latter eventuality the whole of Asia will become a fief of Moscow; and Stalin, having made Ghengis Khan's dream his own, and on an even larger scale, will not be far from ruling the world. Once again it will be only the United States which is strong enough to bar the way to this colossus with clay feet.

62

The Oratory of President Sukarno

Apart from his being the national hero of the Revolution and President of the Republic of Indonesia from 1945 until 1967, Sukarno may be justly considered one of the great political orators of the twentieth century. In his blending of Western intellectual arguments with traditional Javanese folklore and mythology Sukarno has no peer. Presented here are typical examples of his oratory. The first document is an excerpt from his speech of June 1, 1945, in which he outlined the

five cardinal principles of the new Indonesian nation, the
Pantja Sila. *The second document is part of his address of*
August 17, 1959, subsequently known as the "Political Mani-
festo," in which Sukarno restated the principles and history
of the Indonesian Revolution.

THE "PANTJA SILA"

Indonesian State: All for All

As I said a while ago, we are establishing an Indonesian state
which *all of us* must support. *All for all.* Not the Christians for
Indonesia, not the Islamic group for Indonesia, not Hadikusumo
for Indonesia, not Van Eck for Indonesia, not rich Nitisemito for
Indonesia, but the Indonesians for Indonesia—all for all! If I
compress what was five into three, and what was three into one,
then I have a genuine Indonesian term, *gotong-rojong,* mutual
co-operation. The State of Indonesia which we are to establish
must be a gotong-rojong state. How wonderful that is: *a Gotong-*
Rojong State!

Gotong-rojong is a dynamic concept, more dynamic than the
family principle, friends. The family principle is a static concept,
but gotong-rojong portrays one endeavour, one act of service,
one task, what was called by Mr. Sukardjo one *karyo* [work],
one *gawé* [task]. Let us complete this "karyo," this "gawé," this
task, this act of service, together. Gotong-rojong means toiling
hard together, sweating hard together, joint struggle to help one
another. Acts of service by all for the interest of all. *Ho-lopis-*
kuntul-baris—One, two, three, heave! for the common interest.
That is gotong-rojong! (Loud applause on all sides.)

The principle of gotong-rojong between the rich and the poor,
between the Moslem and the Christian, between the non-Indo-
nesians and those of foreign descent who became Indonesians.
This, Brothers and Sisters, is what I propose to you. . . .

Pantjasila becomes *Trisila* [three principles], *Trisila* becomes

Sukarno, *Toward Freedom and the Dignity of Man* (Djakarta: Republic
of Indonesia, Department of Foreign Affairs, 1961), pp. 19–21, 59–62.

Ekasila, one principle. But it is up to you, gentlemen, which you choose: trisila, ekasila or pantjasila? I have explained the content to you all.

Pantja Sila: Enduring and Age-Long Foundation

Principles such as I have proposed to you are the principles for an Indonesia Merdeka [Free Indonesia] which will endure. For decades my heart has burned fiercely with these principles.

But do not forget that we live in a time of war, friends. It is during this time of war that we are going to establish the state of Indonesia—in the midst of war's thunder. I even utter thanks to God that we are going to establish an Indonesian state not under a clear sky, but with the sound of the drums of war and in the fire of warfare. Indonesia Merdeka shall emerge a tempered Indonesia, an Indonesia Merdeka tempered in the fire of war. Such an Indonesia Merdeka is an Indonesian state which is strong, not an Indonesian state which would gradually collapse. It is because of that I thank God Almighty.

In this connection, it is perhaps necessary to make emergency regulations, as proposed by several speakers, regulations which are temporary in character. But its principles, the content of an Indonesia Merdeka which is enduring and age-long, must, in my opinion be Pantja Sila.

As I said a while ago, this is what must be our *Weltanschauung.* I do not know whether you agree with me or not, but I have struggled since 1918 up to this present 1945 for that *Weltanschauung,* for the setting up of a nationalistic Indonesia, for Indonesian nationalism, for the Indonesian nationalism which lives within *perikemanusiaan* [humanity], for the system of *mufakat* [consensus], for social justice, for belief in God. Pantja Sila! That is what has always burned in my heart for decades past. But friends, it is up to you whether it is accepted or not.

Condition for Realization of Pantja Sila: Struggle!

However, I myself fully understand that there is not one *Weltanschauung* which can materialise by itself, become a reality automatically. There is not one *Weltanschauung* which can become a fact, can become a reality, if not through struggle! Let alone the *Weltanschauung* made by men, let alone that made by Hitler, or by Stalin, or by Lenin, or by Sun Yat Sen. *De Mensch,* mankind, must fight for it; without that struggle it can never become reality.

Leninism could never have become a reality without the struggle of the whole Russian people. San Min Chu I could never have become a fact without the struggle of the Chinese people, friends, never! I will even say more than that: without the struggle of human beings, there is not one matter of religion, not one religious ideal, which can become a reality. Let alone the deeds of men, not even the commands of God, written down, black on white, in the Qur'an, can be translated into reality without the struggle of those who are called followers of Islam. The same applies to the words written in the Bible, the ideals contained therein can not come into being without the struggle of the followers of Christianity.

Hence, if the people of Indonesia desire that the Pantja Sila I propose become a reality, that is, if we wish to live as one nation, one independent nationality, if we wish to live as a member of a free world imbued with *perikemanusiaan,* humanity, desire to live upon the basis of *permusjawaratan,* unanimity arising out of deliberation, desire to live a life perfected by social justice, desire to live in comfort and peace, in the widest and most perfect belief in God—do not forget the condition for the realization of this, and that is struggle, struggle and once again struggle!

Do not imagine that with the setting up of the state of Indonesia Merdeka, our struggle is at an end. No! I even say: *within* that Indonesia Merdeka *our struggle must continue,* only its character will be different to that of the present struggle, its characteristics will be different. Together, as a united people, we shall continue our struggle to realize our ideals contained in Pantja Sila.

And, primarily in this time of war, be sure, realise, implant it in your hearts, that Indonesia Merdeka can not come if the people of Indonesia do not dare take a risk, do not dare dive for pearls into the depths of the ocean. If the people of Indonesia are not united, and are not determined to death to win independence, the independence of Indonesia will never be the possession of the Indonesian people, never, until the end of time! Independence can only be achieved and owned by a people whose soul is aflame with the determination of *Merdeka, Independence— or death!*

THE "POLITICAL MANIFESTO"

The Rails of the Revolution

Indeed that political-economic-social ordering is at bottom the *essence* of our Revolution, the *soul* of our Revolution. It constitutes the main pillar that supports our Revolution. Without this main pillar, our Revolution cannot possibly achieve its objective, and more than that: Our Revolution will collapse in the middle of the road. "A Revolution is an outburst of the *collective* will of a people," as was said by a scholar. And how would our Revolution be able to continue and attain its purpose, if that *collective* will has been made faint by liberalism, individualism, "suku"-ism [familism], group-ism, and others of the like?

Thus the political-economic-social ordering is actually the main power—*the highest holder of power*—of our national life. Every person, every citizen, every group, yes, everything that lives on the soil of Indonesia, should be subordinated to the authority of this highest power. The highest authority in our National life, the Tjakrawati authority in our Revolution, is the collective ordering I spoke about. This is because that authority *determines* whether or not we will be able to continue to live as a Nation desirous of realizing a just and prosperous society. This authority *determines* whether our Revolution will achieve its objective, or whether our Revolution will fail midway.

It is clear that the highest authority is not a person, not the President, not the Government, not a council, but a *concept of life* which animates our Revolution. In brief, and to put it simply everything that is the ideal of the 1945 Revolution, that is the highest authority, that is the highest power, that is the Tjakrawati. That is what we must put into practice, that is what we must be loyal to, and that is what we must serve. We must direct and subordinate all the layers of our national life to the realization of the ideals of the Revolution. And whoever refuses to be directed there, or whoever does not want to be subordinated, is an obstructor of the Revolution.

That is what I meant with "ordering," "re-ordering," "retooling," and the like. And this is the good of the 1945 Constitution: ordering and retooling are made possible and can be executed through the channels of the 1945 Constitution. It also because of that, that we return to the 1945 Constitution. . . .

A Strong Structural Basis

. . . I call this year "The year of the Rediscovery of the Revolution."

Yes, with our return to the 1945 Constitution, we have already "rediscovered the Revolution." We, thanks be to God, have "rediscovered our Revolution." We now feel ourselves to be a wanderer, who after ten years of roving around all over the world to find a place to live outside of his country, at last has returned to the home of his birth—has come home to his own house, as the buffalo comes home to his pen. . . .

The devil of liberalism, the devil of federalism, the devil of individualism, the devil of suku-ism, the devil of groupism, the devil of deviation, the devil of adventurism, the devil of the four kinds of dualisms, the devil of corruption, the devil of scraping up wealth at one blow, the devil of the multiparty system, the devil of rebellion—all kinds of devils have jumped on us in the realm of the Inferno, and now we are undergoing purgatory in all fields. Re-orientation, re-ordering, re-tooling, re-shaping, re-making—all of that is necessary, so that we will be able to continue our journey on the rails of the Revolution, proceeding towards the objective of the Revolution.

Let the imperialists abroad be in an uproar! They accuse us

that the 1945 Constitution is "Japanese-made." They also impute that the authority of the President within the framework of the present 1945 Constitution starts from the base of military dictatorship.

Once again, let them be in an uproar! The 1945 Constitution is not "Japanese-made." The 1945 Constitution is the genuine reflection of the identity of the Indonesian nation, who since ancient times based their system of Government on *musjawarah* [deliberation] and *mufakat* [consensus] with the leadership of one central authority in the hands of a "sesepuh"—an elder—who did not dictate, but led, and protected. Indonesian democracy since ancient times has been Guided Democracy, and this is characteristic of all original democracies in Asia.

Yes, indeed, without concealing anything we have made a complete divorce from western democracy, which is free-fight-liberalism, but on the other hand since ancient times we have flatly rejected dictatorships. Guided Democracy is the democracy of the family system, without the anarchy of liberalism, without the autocracy of a dictatorship. . . .

63

Islam Versus the Secular State in Indonesia

The cleavage between "secular" nationalism and Islam in Indonesia has deep cultural and political roots. It erupted forcefully in the Constituent Assembly, elected in 1955 and dissolved five years later without having accomplished its task. Presented below are segments from a marathon speech by Islam's fiercest spokesman, K. H. Muhammad Isa Anshari, during the Assembly's first general session in 1957. It is entitled "We are Moving towards a Republic of Indonesia Based on Islam."

Our bloody revolution that broke out on August 17, 1945 has been the realization of the determined will and the solid conviction of the heroic forces who, on November 10, 1945 [date of battle against the British for Surabaya], stood up and marched with the sacred and Holy phrase, "God is great!" [That] phrase echoed and reverberated throughout Indonesia, from Sabang to Merauke, from Anjer to Banjuwangi.

Koranic injunctions . . . resounded loud and far. They were the dynamic voice of the Indonesian Holy War fighters who never retreated.

They had only one battlecry: To win or to perish.

Mr. Chairman, what was the aspiration, the divine will that inspired those Holy War fighters?

What was the inspiration, the divine inspiration whose bright rays of light warmed the breasts and hearts of those Holy War fighters?

What was the idea that possessed the minds of those Holy War fighters, coming out of the dark trenches, hurtling themselves in the heat of the struggle on the battlegrounds, covered in blood and staking their lives?

At the opening session of this Constituent Assembly, President Sukarno made the following statement:

"It is clear that all the sacrifices offered by our heroes in the revolution were brought to defend the idea of the National state, what we call the Unitary Republic which we proclaimed on August 17, 1945. They died for the idea of that state, for the idea of the National state, the Republic of the Proclamation of August 17, 1945, and not for the idea of a different state!"

President Sukarno's statement contains only half the truth. Mr. Chairman, according to my opinion and conviction, those heroes and patriotic sons of Indonesia willingly sacrificed themselves, not only for the idea referred to by President Sukarno, not only for defending the freedom of the fatherland, not only for

K. H. M. Isa Anshari, "Kami menudju Republik Indonesia berdasarkan Islam," *Tentang Dasar Negara Republik Indonesia dalam Konstituante* (n.p., n.d.), Vol. II, pp. 181–182, 189–191, 218–221. English translation by Soebagio Sastrowardjojo. The citation from the Koran is taken from Arthur J. Arberry, *The Koran Interpreted* (London: Allen & Unwin, New York: Macmillan, 1955), Vol. II, p. 272, by permission of Allen & Unwin.

liberating the Indonesian soil and seas from foreign domination, not only for the Unitary State of the Republic of Indonesia, not only for defending the Proclamation of Indonesian Independence, but for something more profound and more all-embracing than all of these.

They fought and sacrificed themselves—those who died to become Martyrs no less than those who still live and stand upright, the Holy War fighters of our time—for one idealism, for one ideal inspired by the goal and purpose of their lives: to devote themselves to God, praise be to Him the Most High, by upholding His Word and by expecting merely His grace.

They fought to place Islam in the life of our society and state. They fought to establish the Sovereignty and the Law of Islam. . . .

Mr. Chairman, if we study Bung Karno's [President Sukarno's] address before the meeting of the "Exploratory Body for the Preparation of Independence," which was held on June 1, 1945 —the speech that was subsequently published in book form under the title "The Birth of *Pantja Sila*"—it is quite obvious, Mr. Chairman, that that *Pantja Sila* had died in its womb. Why do I say so?

Mr. Chairman, read page 37 of "The Birth of *Pantja Sila*" brochure! We shall find there Bung Karno's following statement: "If I compress the five (principles) to become three, and the three to become one, I shall then get one original Indonesian word, that is the word *gotong rojong* [co-operation, mutual help!"]

You see, Mr. Chairman, as a result of Bung Karno's compressing and squeezing, the Belief in One God [i.e., the first of the Five Principles in *Pantja Sila*] has been completely obliterated. God Almighty has been dissolved . . . in the phrase *"gotong-rojong."* . . .

Mr. Chairman, I have arrived at the specific task placed upon me by my faction in this General Session, that is, to respond to the Communist ideology and atheistic teachings. I shall fulfill my task to the best of my ability, [and] in my own words and in my own manner.

In my own words and in my own manner, Mr. Chairman, for

perhaps you may already have heard that this very speaker has been ordered by God Almighty to be the man in the forefront of the fight and struggle against Communism in Indonesia. I feel it necessary to make known to you, Mr. Chairman, that the motivation that presses me to come forward with this speech, to challenge and oppose the Communist ideology and teachings, does not at all stem from a feeling of hatred towards the members and leaders of the Indonesian Communist Party, whether they are here in this building or outside.

The nature and character of the Holy War of Islam has, praise be to God, educated and tempered me, so as not to face the ideological opponent on the basis of hatred or the feeling of enmity. . . .

Above all, Mr. Chairman, many of the young men at present on the Central Committee of the Indonesian Communist Party have been old friends of mine, in the Dutch colonial period as well as in the era of Japanese fascism. Many of them at one time worked with me in the illegal movement when fascist Japan held sway here. [But] . . . Mr. Chairman, the Communist ideology has separated them from me, and the teachings of Islam have separated me from them. . . .

Mr. Chairman, before I present the motivation and the reasoning that underlie the argumentation employed by the *ulama* to anathematize Communism, permit me first . . . to express my regrets and the regrets of the entire Islamic community in Indonesia with respect to President Sukarno's speech at the first annual celebration of the Youth Pledge, held at the State Palace on October 27. Using his well-known style and manner of speech he declared that if there ever existed a Muslim group that disliked and opposed Communism, he would ask them to go and leave Indonesia.

Mr. Chairman, the Islamic community considers President Sukarno's agitation and demagogy a challenge. . . . It regards [the speech] as an ultimatum and a threat to itself. President Sukarno's speech has already led to disturbance and consternation and to spontaneous reactions among Indonesian Muslims. . . .

Mr. Chairman, as for us Muslims . . . Islam itself makes quite clear what attitude a Muslim should adopt towards individuals or groups of people who wish to drive Muslims out of their own country, towards people who oppose and fight the enforcement of Islamic law in society and the state.

Throughout the Koran are Allah's injunctions, advising and directing Muslims how to act and behave towards such people. Among the hundreds of relevant Koranic verses, I have found one in [the following passage]:

"God only forbids you as to those who have fought you in religion's cause, and expelled you from your habitations, and have supported in your expulsion, that you should take them for friends. And whosoever takes them for friends, those—they are the evildoers" [The Koran, Sura LX, Verse 9].

Mr. Chairman, obviously this Koranic precept and command has so far not been acted upon, thanks [only] to the tolerance and good will on the part of the *ulama* and the Muslim authorities in Indonesia.

Don't [let anyone, however,] abuse the Muslim Community's tolerance and benevolence too long. Don't force the Muslims to adopt radical . . . measures. It is certainly not the Muslims who will lose and bear the responsibility, but those, on the contrary, who force them to act that way.

64

A Communist Interpretation of the Indonesian Revolution

> *Reproduced below are excerpts from the concluding pages of a long essay, "Indonesian Society and the Indonesian Revolution," by the late D. N. Aidit, Secretary-General of the Communist Party of Indonesia (PKI in Indonesian, CPI in this translation). The essay, written in 1957, was used as a manual in training courses in party schools. Under President Sukarno's "Guided Democracy," the party enjoyed consider-*

*able freedom of movement and organizational latitude until
the fall of 1965.*

*On the Driving Force or the Force Pushing the Indonesian
revolution forward,* the General Program of the Consitution of
the CPI states that "the driving force of the Indonesian revolution is the working class, the peasants, the petty bourgeoisie and
other democratic elements whose interests are harmed by imperialism." All these make up the progressive forces in Indonesian society. The question of the forces pushing the revolution
forward or the driving forces of the revolution is the question of
which classes and sectors in Indonesian society consistently fight
against imperialism and feudalism. The problem of the basic tactics of the Indonesian revolution can only be correctly solved
if this is clearly understood. . . .

There is in Indonesian society today a landlord class and a
bourgeois class: the upper strata of the landlord class and the
upper strata of the bourgeois class are the classes that govern.
The governed are the proletarian class, the peasants and all types
of petty bourgeoisie besides the peasants; all these make up by
far the largest group in society. Thus, it can also be said that
the way out of the semi-colonial and semi-feudal conditions in
Indonesia is by changing the balances of forces between the classes
that govern on the one hand and the classes that are governed
on the other.

The attitudes and position of all classes, both those that govern
and those that are governed are completely determined by their
social and economic position. Thus the character of Indonesian
society not only determines the targets and tasks of the revolution but also determines the forces pushing the revolution forward. Which classes can be included within the forces pushing
the Indonesian revolution forward? In order to know this, we need
to make an analysis of the classes within Indonesian society.

The Selected Works of D. N. Aidit (Washington, D.C.: U.S. Joint Publi-
cations Research Service, 1961), Vol. II, pp. 200–205.

The landlord class[es] which exploit and suppress the peasants and which do more to oppose the political, economic and cultural development of Indonesian society than to play a progressive role, are not forces pushing the revolution forward but are a target of the revolution.

The bourgeois class is composed of the compradores and the national bourgeoisie. The big bourgeoisie that are compradore in character directly serve the interests of the big foreign capitalists and they are thus fattened up by them. In the Indonesian revolution, the compradore bourgeoisie are not a driving force but are an obstacle in the way of the revolution, and this is why they are a target of the revolution. However, the national bourgeoisie displays two features; as a class that is also suppressed by imperialism and whose development is also stifled by feudalism, this class is anti-imperialist and anti-feudal, and in this respect it is one of the revolutionary forces. But on the other hand, this class does not have the courage fundamentally to fight imperialism and feudalism because economically and politically it is weak and it has class ties with imperialism and feudalism. The dual character of the national bourgeoisie is the reason why we have two sets of experiences with them, that is, at certain [times], this class can take part in the revolution against imperialism, against the compradores and against the landlords . . . but at other periods they trail behind the compradore bourgeoisie and become their ally in the counter-revolutionary camp. . . .

In facing the wavering characteristics of the Indonesian national bourgeoisie attention should be paid to the fact that it is precisely because . . . it is politically and economically weak that it is not very difficult to pull this class to the left to make it stand firmly on the side of the revolution so long as the progressive forces are large and the tactics of the Communist Party correct. This means that the wavering nature of this class is not fatal, it is not insurmountable. But on the other hand, if the progressive forces are not large and the tactics of the Communist Party not correct, then this economically and politically weak national bourgeoisie can easily run to the right and become hostile to the revolution.

The petty bourgeoisie besides the peasants, that is, the urban poor, the intellectuals, the small traders, the handicraft workers, the fishermen, the independent workers and so on, have a status which is almost the same as that of the middle peasants. They also suffer from the oppression of imperialism, feudalism and the big bourgeoisie and are every day pressed further and further towards bankruptcy and ruination. This is why they are one of the forces pushing the revolution forward and are a reliable ally of the proletariat. They can only attain their freedom under the leadership of the proletariat. The intellectuals and the student youth are not a class in society but their class position is determined by family origin, by their conditions of living and by their political outlook. The small traders in general have stalls and small shops and either employ just a few assistants or none at all; they live under the constant threat of bankruptcy because of the exploitation of imperialists, the big bourgeoisie and the money-lenders. The handicraftsmen and fishermen possess their own means of production, they do not employ any workers or perhaps employ only one or two. The independent workers are persons in various spheres of work, such as private doctors and lawyers, they work on their own, they do not exploit others or exploit others only very slightly. All the petty bourgeoisie besides the peasants can generally support the revolution and are good allies of the proletariat. Their weakness is that some of them easily come under the influence of the bourgeoisie and this is why special attention must be devoted to carrying out propaganda and undertaking revolutionary organizational activities among them.

The peasants account for 60%–70% of the population of Indonesia, they make up the biggest group and together with their families number tens of millions of people. The peasants are basically divided into the rich peasants, the middle peasants and the poor peasants. There are indeed some persons among the rich peasants that lease out a part of their land, carry out money lending and brutally exploit the peasant laborers and they are by nature semi-feudal, but besides this, they themselves generally participate in labor, and in this sense they make up a part of the peasantry. Their productive activities will continue to be utilized for a certain period to come and they can also help the struggle against imperialism. They can adopt an attitude of neutrality in the revolutionary struggle against the landlords. This is why we cannot consider them as part of the landlords. The middle peasants are independent economically, they generally do not exploit others and do not earn interest on money, on the contrary, they suffer from the exploitation of the imperialists, the landlords and the bourgeoisie. Some of them do not own sufficient land for them to work it themselves. The middle peasants can not only become part of the anti-imperialist revolution and the agrarian revolution, but they can also accept Socialism. This is why they are one of the important forces pushing the revolution forward and are a reliable ally of the proletariat. Their attitude towards the revolution is a decisive factor for victory or defeat because the middle peasants comprise the majority in the countryside after the agrarian revolution. The poor peasants together with the agricultural laborers comprise the majority in the villages in our country, prior to the agrarian revolution. The poor peasants do not have any land or do not have sufficient for them to work it themselves; they are the village semi-proletariat, they are the largest force pushing the revolution forward and it is natural for them to be the most reliable of the allies of the proletariat and a basic part of the forces of the Indonesian revolution.

The poor peasants and the middle peasants can only attain their emancipation under the leadership of the proletariat, and the proletariat can only give leadership to the revolution if it has made a firm alliance with the poor and middle peasants. What we mean when we use the term "peasants" is mainly the poor and middle peasants that make up the majority of the inhabitants of the villages. In leading the people's struggle in the countryside, the Party must always strive to be able to draw in and mobilize 90% of the village inhabitants and must firmly base itself on the poor peasants and the peasant laborers as well as make an alliance with the middle peasants.

The Indonesian proletariat consists of about 500,000 workers in modern industry (transport workers, factory-workers, repair-shop workers, mine-workers, etc.). The workers in small industry and the handicrafts in the towns number more than 2,000,000. The agricultural and forestry proletariat and other groups of workers make up a very large number. All this amounts to about 6,000,000 or, together with their families, some 20,000,000 which is about 25% of the entire population of Indonesia. Besides this town and village proletariat, there are also in the villages of Indonesia millions of peasant laborers, those village inhabitants who generally own no land and agricultural implements and who make a livelihood out of selling their labor power in the villages. The peasant laborers are the group which suffers most in the village and their position in the peasant movement is just as important as that of the poor peasants.

As is also the case with the proletariat in other countries, the Indonesian proletariat has very fine qualities. Their work makes them unite in the most advanced economic forms, it gives them a strong understanding of organization and discipline, and because they do not own any means of production, they are not individualistic by nature and apart from this, since the Indonesian proletariat is exploited by three forms of brutal exploitation, that is, imperialism, capitalism and feudalism, they become more firm and more thoroughgoing in the revolutionary struggle than the other classes. Since Indonesia is not fertile soil for social-reformism as is the case in Europe, the proletariat is in its entirety very revolutionary indeed, of course with the exception of a small number who have become the scum. It is because the Indonesian proletariat has been led by its revolutionary political party, the Communist Party of Indonesia, ever since it appeared on the arena of the revolutionary struggle that it is politically the most conscious class in Indonesian society. Since a large part of the Indonesian proletariat consists of bankrupt peasants, it has natural bonds with the broad masses of the peasants, a fact which facilitates its alliance.

Although the Indonesian proletariat contains within it certain unavoidable weaknesses, such as for example its smallness in number by comparison with the peasants, its youth by comparison with the proletariat in capitalist countries and the low level of its culture by comparison with the bourgeoisie, it is nevertheless the basic force pushing the Indonesian revolution forward. The Indonesian revolution will not succeed unless it is under the leadership of the Indonesian proletariat. . . .

It must be understood that although the Indonesian proletariat is the class which has the highest political consciousness and organizational understanding, the victory of the revolution can never be achieved without the revolutionary unity under all circumstances with all other revolutionary classes and groups. The proletariat must build up a revolutionary front. Of the classes in society, the peasants are the firmest and most reliable ally of the working class, the urban petty bourgeoisie is a reliable ally, and the national bourgeoisie is an ally under certain circumstances and within certain limits: this is the fundamental law which has already been and is being proven by Indonesia's modern history. . . .

Based on the above analysis of the classes in Indonesian society, it is clear which classes and groups are the pillars of imperialism and feudalism, that is, the landlords and the compradores. They are obstacles standing in the way of the revolution and that is why they are the enemies of the people. The above analysis also makes it clear which classes and groups are the basic driving force of the revolution, that is the working class, the peasants and the petty bourgeoisie. It makes clear too which classes can take part in the revolution, that is, the national bourgeois class. This is why the workers, the peasants, the petty bourgeoisie and the national bourgeoisie are the People, and make up the forces of the revolution, the forces of the united national front.

65
"The Philippines First"

Ramon Magsaysay achieved recognition while Secretary of National Defense (1950–1953) by organizing the campaign that destroyed the Hukbalahap, the Communist-led guerrilla movement in the Philippines. As third President of the Philippine Republic (1953–1957) he negotiated the Laurel-Langley Agreement (1955), which essentially continued the depend-

ence of the Philippine economy on the United States until 1974. The following speech was delivered by Magsaysay before the Philippine-Columbian Association in Manila, July 4, 1955.

I welcome this opportunity to come before this distinguished club and speak at this time.

These are not just the empty words of a politician.

I welcome this opportunity because this club, the Philippine-Columbian, has always been renowned as a gathering place for those who believe in the principles of liberty and justice that typify our nation.

Thus I believe that this is a most fitting place—among the nationalists of this association—and certainly a most fitting time—the ninth anniversary of our glorious independence—for me to review a few basic principles for which I stand.

When I was campaigning for the sacred office of President of the Philippines, I made myself clear on the most vital issue affecting our independence.

I promised our people that I would take all possible steps to preserve our independence and to insure our national security, both from within and from without.

I defined not only our objectives, but how we were going to attain them.

In the matter of preserving our national security from outside threats, we recognized, in the light of the plans and objectives of the aggressive imperialism which then threatened and still threatens us, that there was no safety in standing alone and holding aloof.

We recognized the impossibility, in this world of modern arms, of organizing and providing for our own defense with the limited resources at our command.

We have, therefore, sought and secured the safety of alliance with more powerful nations.

Specifically, we have entered into close alliance with the most powerful nation on the face of the earth—the United States.

Ramon Magsaysay, "The Philippines First," *Department of Foreign Affairs Review* (Manila), Vol. II, No. 2 (January, 1956), pp. 2–3.

We have become part of the Southeast Asia pact, better known as the Manila Treaty.

We have done these things for the sake of no other country except our own country and for the sake of no other people except the Filipino people.

For this—the Philippines first—has always been and always will be the guiding principle of my administration.

We have served and will serve no other interest except our own national self-interest.

We have entered into these alliances to strengthen our own defense, secure our own independence, preserve our own freedoms.

We now find our own defenses augmented by the free world's collective strength and by the actual presence here of America's great fighting power.

I have also adhered to my promise of protecting our freedom from internal attack.

You will remember I broke with the Liberal administration because it just wanted me to fight and kill Huks. I felt that this gave only half the answer to this problem, and I wanted to do more.

I wanted to give our discontented a new life, to correct the abuses from which so many of them had suffered, to give them confidence in the honesty of our free and democratic institutions. I wanted to welcome those who were truly repentant and show them the meaning of our independence, the ninth anniversary of which we are celebrating today.

I believe that considerable progress has been made in that direction in the one-and-a-half years since I was given your mandate.

The leader of the Huk movement himself, Luis Taruc, has surrendered to the government.

The administration's policy of benevolence continues to attract surrenderees from the Huk ranks.

At the same time, the reforms we have instituted, the confidence that we have restored in the government's sense of justice, have prevented those with grievances from becoming Huks, or from turning to the Huks. They turn to us now, confident that they will get justice and redress of grievances.

An examination of Communist propaganda will bring out the fact that its greatest enemy in this country today is this administration.

Thus have we strengthened our independence against threats and attacks both from without and within, since I was elected to office.

We have done this—to repeat—by always serving foremost the interest of our country and people, by always thinking of the Philippines first. We have also gained added prestige and honor for our independence in this way.

When we sent a delegation to Bandung, to the Asia-African conference there, it was freely forecast by some that we would merely be looked upon as puppets of the United States.

I never shared that fear. We proved at Bandung how wrong were the prophets of puppetry.

Under the able leadership of our chief delegate, Ambassador Carlos P. Romulo, we made a deep impression upon our fellow Asians and upon the African nations at Bandung. Instead of finding ourselves labelled as puppets, we found ourselves as one of the leading advocates of the high principles of dignity for mankind in which all Filipinos believe.

It was not our delegation which had to retreat at Bandung. It was the representative of Communist China who was obliged to retreat. He found out that the desire for freedom and the hatred of Communism had inspired more nations to resistance than he had imagined.

Let me say here and now that we cannot flirt with Communism if we want our independence to remain real and secure.

When I say that, I am saying it because I am thinking of the Philippines first.

I am amused by those who try to put forward this slogan as some kind of new concept. To me, there certainly is nothing new in the idea. I do not know, and I could not practice, any policy but Philippines first. I cannot see how any Filipino who loves his fellow countrymen and the land of his birth can ever think in any terms other than Philippines first.

Only on this basis can we shape and build the kind of Philippines that you, here in this room, and the millions who have agreed with the principles I set forth during the campaign, want for yourselves and your children.

Our people want a Philippines strong and stable internally and able to preserve its hard-won independence against external threats, in firm alliance with our great and good friend the United States of America.

I am determined to see to it that our people continue to get what they want.

66
A Communist View of American Rule in the Philippines

> *Luis Taruc (1913–) joined the socialist movement in the Philippines during the 1930s and became Supremo (head) of the Hukbalahap, or People's Army Against Japan, in 1942. In the postwar years he led the peasant insurrection against the Manila government until his capture in 1954 and subsequent imprisonment. Assisted by William J. Pomeroy, an American Communist, Taruc completed his Born of the People in 1949. Passages from this work are presented below. It is one of the few autobiographies ever written by a Southeast Asian Communist, and has since abandoned Communism.*

For over half a century the Philippines has become largely the private landed estate of a handful of big businessmen who live ten thousand miles away in the United States. They acquired possession by taking us away from a previous owner, Spain, as the spoils of war in 1898, and they made sure of their possession

Luis Taruc, *Born of the People*. Reprinted by permission of International Publishers, Co. Inc. Copyright © 1953. Pp. 265–271, 274–275, 277–279.

by using the iron fist in 1899 to crush with blood our revolutionary movement for real independence. Since then, posing as our friends and benefactors, they have robbed and plundered our wealth, and they held back the achievement of our democracy and freedom. When they pretended to give us independence, in 1946, it was only as a smokescreen to hide an even greater domination.

The American imperialists used many excuses to justify their taking of the Philippines. President McKinley said that he had been advised to do so by God. Some said that it was the duty of the United States to civilize the Filipino. Others said that it was their duty to teach us how to govern ourselves. None mentioned publicly that they could make huge profits in our country.

To guarantee those profits, American imperialism has kept us a backward, colonial people, with the majority living in the misery of poverty and ignorance. It has prevented our growth as an independent nation, forcing us to act according to its own wishes, both in our internal and in our external affairs. It has stood in the path of our free economic development, compelling us to endure the narrow, outworn system of feudalism and keeping us from using our own means and our own energies to advance the welfare of the people.

It has boasted that it "educated the Filipinos," but today nearly fifty per cent of our people are still illiterate and a large proportion of the rest can barely read or write. It has said that it raised our standard of living to the highest in the Orient, yet today tens of thousands of Filipinos die each year of tuberculosis and beriberi, the diseases of poverty. It has claimed that it trained us in the ways of democratic government, but today the most corrupt regime in our history, with American approval, massacres the people and conducts itself like the worst emperors of pagan Rome.

It has allowed all of these things to exist because ignorance, poverty and corruption are weapons used by imperialism to maintain its rule. . . .

The American imperialists did not want our country to become industrialized because they wanted our people to buy only the products made in American factories. Our country was to be a market for their goods. It was also supposed to remain a source of raw materials needed by the American factories: unrefined sugar, copra, abaca, metallic ore, lumber, tobacco. Under our backward system of economy such raw materials could be obtained cheaply because our workers were paid very low wages. The raw materials were converted into finished products by the American factories and then sold back to us, by American import companies. All the Filipino ever received from this process, which involved the exploitation of the resources of his country, were very low wages.

The Filipino moves about in an American-made world. The clothes he wears, the cigarettes he smokes, the canned food he eats, the music he hears, the news of the world he reads (and the books and the magazines) are all American, although his own country has the ability to produce all these. He eats pineapple canned in California, but he grows it in the Philippines. His country grows millions of coconuts, but he has to buy toilet soap made in New Jersey out of coconut oil. He buys sugar refined in American mills, but grown on his own island of Negros; if he wants to buy Filipino-made sugar he must be content with *muscovado* [brown, unrefined sugar] or *panotsa* [brown sugar cakes]. He rides on American-made busses or an American-made train. On the radio, made in New York (if he is one of the very few who have a radio) he listens to recorded American programs. American movies dominate his theaters. His schools use American textbooks that explain science, economics, history, and politics from an American standpoint. . . . And finally, of American make, are the guns, the tanks, the planes, the artillery, the vehicles, and even the uniforms of the troops that have been used to shoot down the Filipino people who would like to see a Filipino-made future for their children. . . .

The clever American imperialist! He came into our country with his talk about democracy and about the superiority of the American way of life, painting a picture in colors about his big cities and his luxuries and his opportunities, dazzling the humble Filipino who lived on rice and fish, telling him that he too could be fortunate if he would just trust in the American way. He would pat Juan de la Cruz ["John Doe"] on the back and say: "You should feel proud. You are the only Christian nation in the Orient. Look at all the sugar and copra you produce and all the gold you dig and all the abaca you grow. One of these days, too, you'll be independent and then you too can be like your Uncle Sam."

The Filipino peasant, who slept on the floor and whose chair was an empty box, plastered the walls of his nipa hut with American magazine illustrations of mansions in the country and hotels and advertisements of luxurious beds and furniture. In the city the laborer who lived in a *barong-barong* [makeshift hut] that became flooded when it rained, went to the American movies and saw the well-dressed glamorous characters moving around in the handsome drawing-rooms and the modern kitchens that had refrigerators and washing machines and electric toasters.

How long did the purveyor of this kind of civilization think that he could convince the Filipino that poverty was ennobling in a Christian and that subservience was admirable in one whose skin was brown? . . .

The Americans soon realized they could not rule forever with an iron hand; it was too expensive. They solved their problem by getting Filipinos to rule for them. A group of Filipinos stood ready and willing to play such a role, the landlord-*ilustrado* class, the landed gentry. A large number of this group had not even joined the struggle against Spain. Their own fortunes were derived from the exploitation of the masses and they were content to have a strong external power upon which to rely, to help them maintain their exploiter's position. They were afraid the revolution would go too far and would get rid of them as well as of the Spaniards. The Americans were stronger than the Spaniards; they were even more reliable. The American Civil Government, operating through the Philippine Commission, at first based itself upon this class of Filipinos. . . .

American rule brought into prominence a new economic group, the compradores, the middle-men through whom raw materials left our country and finished products entered. The compradores had been a weak group under Spain but htey grew and flourished under the United States. . . . Owing their fortunes to the operations of imperialism, they became the right-hand men of foreign rule.

The whole process of "training to govern," about which American imperialism has boasted so much in the Philippines, has been built around the training of these groups to govern in the interests of American imperialism. One reason for perpetuating the feudal system of landowning that had functioned under the Spanish regime was to keep the big landlords in power because they were an integral part of the new American pattern of rule.

In the old Spanish universities, as well as in the new University of the Philippines and in the other higher schools of learning established by the Americans, the theory of the "intellectual aristocracy" was driven home to the students. The school system grew less and less adequate the closer down it got to the masses until, in the barrios [villages], it was mere perfunctory instruction. The gap between the educated and the uneducated or poorly educated was a sharply accentuated class difference. In addition, American textbooks were moved from the United States into Philippine schools without a line of revision, regardless of how great a difference existed between the two countries. The sociology of the American big city and of the American rural community was clamped grotesquely upon the mind of the Filipino student, to whom the cacique [rich landlord] and the governor-general were the symbols of authority. . . .

What happened in 1945 was almost a duplication of what had happened in 1898. The American army, on both occasions, landed to find a revolutionary movement fighting against the common enemy. On both occasions they took steps to crush it, and on both occasions they found allies in the exploiting classes of Filipinos. In 1945, however, there was a difference: the revolutionary movement was not led by vacillating elements who would sell it out; it was led by the working class leadership of Communists.

Within three years after the end of the war, the operation of American imperialism had resulted in converting the Hukbalahap guerrilla struggle into a national liberation movement.

At the beginning of our struggle in Central Luzon many observers referred to it as a movement for agrarian reform, just as they had referred in similar terms to the revolutionary movement of the Chinese people. They pointed out that centuries of feudal relations had brought our movement into being. What they said was correct, but they did not carry their observations far enough. They failed to see that our struggle, as well as that of the Chinese people, took place within the setting of imperialist relations. Our feudal agrarian economy was one of the mainstays of imperialist control in our country, and any movement to change it was inevitably bound to conflict with imperialist interests that were determined to perpetuate the age-old system. Our movement, therefore, could not be merely a movement for agrarian reform; it had to develop into a struggle against imperialism. . . .

The final pages of this book are being written in a very small nipa hut, somewhere on the slope of a mountain above the central plain of the island of Luzon. It is a temporary shelter, newly built, and it may have to be abandoned quickly, perhaps today, perhaps this afternoon. Perhaps even as I sit here writing, an alarm will come. The enemy is not far away.

There is no furniture in the hut. I balance my notebook on my knee. The roof is so low that I must bend my head where I sit. Bits of sun come through the branches overhead and through the nipa roof and fall on this page. It is very quiet in the forest. Down the slope, below the hut, I can hear the water on the rocks in the little stream from which we drink. The tuko [bird] calls from the tall trees in the sun. Crickets are chirping incessantly, and frogs sing, deep-voiced. These are the sounds of peace.

They are deceptive. At any time may come the sound of guns.

This hut is big enough to hold five sleeping men, lying close. Its sides are open, so we can roll out fast, if need be. It sits under dense trees, to escape aerial observation. Washed clothes drying in the sun are pulled from sight when a plane is heard. Cooking, when there is something to cook, is done in the early morning and after dark, so the smoke of the fire will not be seen. To the enemy, from above and below, there must be only the trees. The mountain is a friendly mother sheltering us....

This mere act of sitting on the rough floor of a hut in the forest is not an isolated incident today. It is being duplicated by the armed men of liberation movements in Indo-China, in Indonesia, in Malaya, in Burma, and wherever the masses of Asia are stirring themselves. The facts and the men are everywhere, and towering over them all is the enormous fact of the Chinese people, who have emerged from their mountains, and from their huts in the forests, into the towns and the cities, into their own.

On the corner poles of this hut hang all my possessions: a light, packed knapsack, and a carbine. Both are the unintentional gifts of American imperialism. None among us has more. Something else, however, is ours: the love and comradeship of each other and of thousands more like us in a thousand huts across our country, and of the masses of people to whom we are the hope of the future. That is more than enough to keep alive a man's body and his spirit—indefinitely if necessary.

67
The Declaration of Independence of the Republic of Vietnam

Following the establishment of the new republican regime in Vietnam after the abdication of Bao Dai, the new state formally declared its independence from the French during the period when a power vacuum existed after the collapse of imperial Japan. It was signed at Hanoi by the President of the Republic, Ho Chi Minh, on September 2, 1945, the very day of the Japanese surrender on the battleship Missouri.

"All men are created equal.... They are endowed by their Creator with certain inalienable rights. Among these are life, liberty, and the pursuit of happiness."

These immortal words are from the Declaration of Independence of the United States of America in 1776. Taken in a broader sense, these phrases mean: "All peoples on earth are born equal; all peoples have the right to live, to be free, to be happy."

The Declaration of the Rights of the Man and Citizen of the French Revolution of 1791 also proclaimed: "Men are born and remain free and with equal rights."

These are undeniable truths.

Nevertheless for more than eighty years the French imperialists, abusing their "liberty, equality, and fraternity," have violated the land of our ancestors and oppressed our countrymen. Their acts are contrary to the ideals of humanity and justice.

In the political domain, they have deprived us of all our liberties.

They have imposed upon us inhuman laws. They have established three different political regimes in the North, the Center, and the South of Viet Nam in order to destroy our historic and ethnic national unity.

They have built more prisons than schools. They have acted without mercy toward our patriots. They have drenched our revolutions in rivers of blood.

They have subjugated public opinion and practiced obscurantism on the broadest scale. They have imposed upon us the use of opium and alcohol to weaken our race.

In the economic domain, they have exploited us without respite, reduced our people to the blackest misery and pitilessly looted our country.

They have despoiled our ricelands, our mines, our forests, our raw materials. They have retained the privilege of issuing banknotes and a monopoly of foreign trade.

They have invented hundreds of unjustified taxes, condemning our countrymen, especially the peasants and small merchants, to extreme poverty.

They have prevented our capital from fructifying; they have exploited our workers in the most barbarous fashion.

Harold R. Isaacs, ed., *New Cycle in Asia: Selected Documents on Major International Developments in the Far East, 1943–1947* (New York: Macmillan for the Institute of Pacific Relations, 1947), pp. 163–165. By permission of the author and W. L. Holland, American Institute of Pacific Relations, University of British Columbia.

In the autumn of 1940 when the Japanese Fascists, with a view to fighting the Allies, invaded Indochina to organize new war bases, the French imperialists, on their knees, surrendered our country.

Since then, under the double Japanese and French yokes, our people have literally bled. The result has been terrifying. From Quangtri to the North, two million of our countrymen died of famine in the first months of this year.

On March 9, 1945, the Japanese disarmed the French troops. Once again, the French either fled or unconditionally surrendered. Thus they have been totally incapable of "protecting" us; on the contrary, in the space of five years they have twice sold our country to the Japanese.

Before March 9, the League of Viet-Minh several times invited the French to join it in struggle against the Japanese. Instead of responding to this appeal, the French struck all the harder at the partisans of the Viet-Minh. They went as far as to murder a large number of the political prisoners at Yen Bay and Caobang during their rout.

Despite all this, our countrymen have continued to maintain a tolerant and human attitude toward the French. After the events of March 9, the League of Viet-Minh helped many Frenchmen to cross the frontier, saved others from Japanese prisons, and besides protected the lives and property of all Frenchmen.

In fact, since the autumn of 1940, our country has ceased to be a French colony and became a Japanese possession.

After the surrender of the Japanese, our entire people rose to regain their sovereignty and founded the democratic Republic of Viet Nam.

The truth is that we seized our independence from the hands of the Japanese and not from the hands of the French.

The French fleeing, the Japanese surrendering, Emperor Bao Dai abdicating, our people broke all the chains which have weighed upon us for nearly a hundred years and made our Viet Nam an independent country. Our people at the same time overthrew the monarchical regime established for tens of centuries and founded the Republic.

For these reasons we, members of the Provisional Government, representing the entire population of Viet Nam, declare that we shall henceforth have no relations with imperialist France, that we cancel all treaties which France has signed on the subject of Viet Nam, that we abolish all the privileges which the French have arrogated to themselves on our territory.

All the people of Viet Nam, inspired by the same will, are determined to fight to the end against any attempt at aggression by the French imperialists.

We are convinced that the Allies who have recognized the principles of equality of peoples at the Conferences of Teheran and San Francisco cannot but recognize the independence of Viet Nam.

A people which has obstinately opposed French domination for more than eighty years, a people who during these last years ranged themselves definitely on the side of the Allies to fight against Fascism, this people has the right to be free. This people must be independent.

For these reasons, we, members of the Provisional Government of the Democratic Republic of Viet Nam, solemnly proclaim to the entire world:

Viet Nam has the right to be free and independent and is, in fact, free and independent. All the people of Viet Nam are determined to mobilize all their spiritual and material strength, to sacrifice their lives and property, to safeguard their right to liberty and independence.

Hanoi, September 2, 1945

(Signed)   Ho Chi Minh, *President*.
Tran Huy Lieu, Vo Nguyen Giap, Chu Van Tan, Duong Duc Hien, Nguyen Van To, Nguyen Manh Ha, Cu Huy Can, Pham Ngoh Thach, Nguyen Van Xuan, Vu Trong Khanh, Pham Van Dong, Dao Trong Kim, Vu Din Hoc, Le Van Hien.

68

Ho Chi Minh Interprets the Geneva Conference

> *Founder of the Communist party of Indochina, prominent Comintern agent in Asia, and at one and the same time the most powerful spokesman for Vietnamese nationalism in modern colonial times, Ho Chi Minh (known as Nguyen Ai Quoc in his younger years) became president of the Democratic Republic of Viet Nam in September, 1945, and has retained that office in the northern part of the country, temporarily separated at the Geneva Conference of 1954. The following speech, in which Ho obviously tries to render the terms of that Conference acceptable to his followers in the North and South, was pronounced on July 22, 1954.*

Compatriots all over the country,

Armymen and cadres,

The Geneva Conference has come to an end. It is a great victory for our diplomacy.

On behalf of the Government, I cordially make the following appeal:

1—For the sake of peace, unity, independence and democracy of the Fatherland, our people, armymen, cadres and government have, during these eight years or so, joined in a monolithic bloc, endured hardship and overcome all difficulties to resolutely carry out the Resistance and have won many brilliant victories. On this occasion, on behalf of the Government, I cordially congratulate you, from North to South. I respectfully bow to the memory of the armymen and people who have sacrificed their lives for the Fatherland, and send my homages of comfort to the wounded and sick armymen.

This great victory is also due to the support given us in our

Ho Chi Minh, *Selected Works* (Hanoi: Foreign Languages Publishing House, 1962), Vol. IV, pp. 17–20.

just struggle by the peoples of our brother countries, by the French people and the peace-loving people of the world.

Thanks to these victories and the efforts made by the delegation of the Soviet Union at the Berlin Conference, negotiations were opened between our country and France at the Geneva Conference. At this conference the struggle of our delegation and the assistance given by the delegations of the Soviet Union and China have ended in a great victory for us: the French government has recognized the independence, sovereignty, unity and territorial integrity of our country; it has agreed to withdraw French troops from our country, etc.

From now on, we must make every effort to consolidate peace and achieve reunification, independence and democracy throughout our country.

2—In order to re-establish peace, the first step to take is that the armed forces of both parties should cease fire.

The regroupment in two regions is a temporary measure; it is a transitional step for the implementation of the armistice and restoration of peace, and paves the way for national reunification through general elections. Regroupment in regions is in no way a partition of our country, neither is it an administrative division.

During the armistice, our army is regrouped in the North; the French troops are regrouped in the South, that is to say, there is a change of regions. A number of regions which were formerly occupied by the French, now become our free zones. Vice versa, a number of regions formerly liberated by us, will now be temporarily occupied by the French troops before they leave for France.

This is a necessity; North, Central and South Viet Nam are territories of ours. Our country will certainly be unified, our entire people will surely be liberated.

Our compatriots in the South were the first to wage the war of Resistance. They possess a high political consciousness. I am confident that they will place national interests above local interests, permanent interests above temporary interests and join their efforts with the entire people in strengthening peace, achieving unity, independence and democracy all over the country. The Party, Government and I, always follow the efforts of our people and we are sure that our compatriots will be victorious.

3—The struggle to consolidate peace and achieve reunification, independence and democracy, is also a long and hard struggle. In order to carry the day, our people, armymen and cadres from North to South, must unite closely. They must be at one in thought and deed.

We are resolved to abide by the agreements entered into with the French Government. At the same time we demand that the French Government should correctly implement the agreements they have signed with us.

We must do our utmost to strengthen peace, and be vigilant to check the manoeuvres of peace wreckers.

We must endeavour to struggle for the holding of free general elections throughout the country to reunify our territory.

We must exert all our efforts to restore, build, strengthen and develop our forces in every field so as to attain complete independence.

We must do our utmost to carry out social reforms in order to improve our people's livelihood and realize genuine democracy.

We further tighten our fraternal relations with Cambodia and Laos.

We strengthen the great friendship between us and the Soviet Union, China and other brother countries. To maintain peace, we enhance our solidarity with the French people, the Asian people and people all over the world.

4—I call on all our compatriots, armymen and cadres to strictly follow the lines and policies laid down by the Party and Government, to struggle for the consolidation of peace, and the achievement of national reunification, independence and democracy throughout the country.

I eagerly appeal to all genuine patriots, irrespective of their social class, creed, political stand and former affiliation, sincerely to co-operate with us and fight for the sake of our country and our people so as to bring about peace and achieve reunification, independence and democracy for our beloved Viet Nam.

If our people are as one, if thousands of men are like one, victory will certainly be ours.

Long live a peaceful, unified, independent and democratic Viet Nam.

69

Problems of Nation-Building in Independent Burma

> *Aung San (1914–1947), politically active in the Thakin Movement in British Burma, became commander of the Burma Independence Army and founder of the Anti-Fascist People's Freedom League. He was the first Prime Minister of the Union of Burma, but on July 19, 1947, he, together with several of his cabinet colleagues, was assassinated in Rangoon. The document presents excerpts from his address to a public meeting in Rangoon, six days before his death.*

A FEW PAINFUL TRUTHS

This meeting was originally convened so that we might report, as members of the Constituent Assembly, to you as electors, on what we have so far accomplished in the Assembly. It is the traditional practice in a parliamentary democracy for a member to go back to his electors, when a session is over, and report on progress and events.

Even though we were elected in April, we became the Constituent Assembly only on the 10th June, when the session started in due form. This is an Assembly which is unique in our history, for we are writing the constitution of independent Burma, and even though in strict law the Assembly does not enjoy sovereign powers, it is going through the process of creating a sovereign nation. Our present status in strict law is complicated, but the important thing is that we are moving on to our goal.

I am a great one for uttering the brutal truth, or the painful

Maung Maung, ed., *Aung San of Burma* (The Hague: Nijhoff, 1962), pp. 139–142. By permission of the publisher.

truth, as Thakin Nu calls it. He has warned me occasionally that I should refrain from uttering these truths too frequently. But I have some to utter today; I am so full of them, I cannot contain them, and I only wish I had the time to tell them all.

Independence is coming, but it is not going to bring a heaven on earth. Some of you may dream fondly that once we are independent, there will not be the need to work, and the good things will spout out of the earth to take as you wish. That is not so.

Our people are inclined to believe that independence would mean a free-for-all. I remember visiting Henzada during the war, during the believe-it-or-not-independence that we had then. I saw people putting out tobacco leaves in the streets to dry, obstructing traffic. They thought they were independent and could do what they liked. That is not what independence means; liberty is not license.

In a free country the people must be free to develop their individual personality and follow their own occupations in free and equal opportunity, but they must not infringe on the freedom and the rights of others.

You must also remember that you cannot have something for nothing in life. You have to work and earn what you want. You may dream of a new state like the Soviet Union, like America, or England, but dreams will not bring you the new state, you must work and build it.

Years of toil lie ahead of you. Maybe 20 years, at the least, will pass before you see the fruits of your toil. You must work with perseverance, with unity and discipline, always conscious of your duties as citizens of a free country. Rights carry responsibilities; you cannot enjoy the rights without discharging the responsibilities.

Britain is an inspiring example. We may not like the British, because they have been our rulers, but they do show many qualities as a nation which we must admire. How they fought, with back to the wall, during the war, and now after they have won they are still having to go through severe austerity, to rebuild their economy Britain makes a lot of things, but at this point the country needs to sell them abroad, and her own people have to produce while denying themselves those goods. We too must plan our economy for the long future and persevere with our plans. There is no substitute for work.

We must build and preserve unity between the peoples in our country, people of the frontier areas and other peoples, and in unity we must work together to build our national strength. Without unity and strength, independence will be meaningless; the nation will be weak and vulnerable, whichever party may be in office. Behave like the lion, I therefore say. The lion, the king of the forest, exerts his full strength in hunting down his prey, however small or big the animal may be. We must all, therefore, put forth our very best in our endeavours to build the new nation.

Our people lack stamina and the sporting spirit. I watched a boat race during the war at Bassein; the winning crew relaxed, put up their oars and started to sing their victory songs even before the goal was reached. The crew behind could have exerted and put up a good fight then, but no, they relaxed too, giving up before the race was over. That, I thought, was a national trait. In football games the losers like to play foul, kick and break the limbs of their opponents, instead of putting up a good clean fight in the proper sporting spirit. We must mend our ways.

You have to go abroad and study the lives of other peoples to discover how lax we have been. I visited Japan during the war and saw how their peoples took hardship and self-denial in their war effort. They did not have enough to eat or to wear. I thought, at that time, that perhaps their economic system was at fault to cause such hardship to the people. But I was in India after the war, and there also people had to take restrictions in many ways. One could not entertain more than 24 people to dinner; food was rationed. The same situation prevailed in Britain. In Burma we are lavish; we eat what we want and throw away the rest. There is a lot of wastage, but agricultural production is down, and rice is being looted by lawless gangs in the bargain. Political tensions have eased now, but there is general lawlessness, these lootings and dacoities and destruction, and all patriotic citizens should unite to put them down.

There is a lot of nation-building to be done, and you must remember that you are building over the ashes of the war. Everywhere, we are behind, and to catch up with the world we must work far harder than other nations. Some say we should improve our education by introducing free compulsory education; make laws for that, they say. But what good are laws if we do not have the money, the teachers and the men. It will take another 20 years of persistent effort to turn out the teachers, to build the schools in every village, and have compulsory education.

Then have a look at defence. Every citizen must give his service in the defence forces. Under British rule people got into the habit of thinking that the government would do the needful, and if anything went wrong they could blame the government. That is not the spirit in which you can build a free country. The needs for the defence of Burma are stupendous. We do not have an adequate Army, Air Force or Navy, and with the forces that we have we cannot stand against a modern enemy even for a few hours. The defence expenditure will be heavy if we want our defence to be adequate, and you have to remember that when we are tested here and there by aggressive powers we must be able to reply in no uncertain terms.

All these lead us back to this: you must work hard, be united and disciplined. Otherwise, the fruits of freedom will not be yours to enjoy, whether you have a Communist government or a Socialist government. You must mend your ways and build a New Burma together. These words I leave with you today.

70

Malayan Independence

Malayan political integration has been gradual and peaceful, from the British-created Federated Malay States in 1895 to the Federation of Malaya, established in 1948 and, ultimately, to the independent Federation proclaimed in August, 1957. In marked contrast to the revolutionary anticolonialism that accompanied independence in many other parts of Southeast Asia, Prime Minister Tengku Abdul Rahman's speech, reprinted below, is a graphic expression of a moderate, evolutionary nationalism. The speech was made at the proclamation of independence in Kuala Lumpur on August 31, 1957.

Your Majesties, Your Royal Highnesses, Your Highnesses, Your Excellencies, People of Persekutuan Tanah Melayu [Federation of Malaya]:

I am indeed proud that on this, the greatest day in Malaya's history, it falls to my lot to proclaim the formal independence of this country. Today a new page is turned, and Malaya steps forward to take her rightful place as a free and independent partner in the great community of Nations—a new nation is born and though we fully realize that difficulties and problems lie ahead, we are confident that, with the blessing of God, these difficulties will be overcome and that today's events, down the avenues of history, will be our inspiration and our guide. It is therefore with a feeling of particular solemnity that we have listened to the eloquent words of His Royal Highness and in particular to the moving message he has conveyed from Her Majesty the Queen. We are indeed honoured that Her Majesty should have deputed her own uncle, His Royal Highness, to be with us on this occasion particularly when we remember that he is no stranger to this land: we recall too with pleasure his previous visit to Malaya and happy recollections of his stay have remained with us.

His Royal Highness has spoken in moving words of the past associations of our two countries. We in Malaya have a long history, but we do not lightly forget old relationships. For many years past our fortunes have been linked with those of Great Britain and we recall in particular the comradeship of two world wars. We remember too the products of our association; justice before the law, the legacy of an efficient public service and the highest standard of living in Asia. We shall therefore always remember

Text from the government of the Federation of Malaya.

with gratitude the assistance which we have received from Great Britain down our long path to nationhood; an assistance which culminates today with the proclamation of Malaya's Independence. But the long standing friendship between our countries does not cease with independence: rather it takes on a new form. As you have heard in the gracious message from Her Majesty the Queen, Malaya will henceforward take her place in the great Commonwealth of Independent Nations whose members are found in all parts of the world, and as an equal partner in that great association. We in this country will do all in our power to promote its wellbeing in the interests of mankind in general and in the particular service of world peace.

Thus today a new chapter opens in our relationship with Britain; our colonial status has given place to full equality but we are confident that, fortified by old associations, and linked by old memories, our ties with Britain will grow ever stronger and more durable. Britain will ever find in us her best friend, and it is a source of much gratification to my Government that British civil servants will continue to serve in this country to assist us in the solution of the many problems which independence will present.

But while we think of the past, we look forward in faith and hope to the future; from henceforth we are masters of our destiny, and the welfare of this beloved land is our own responsibility. Let no one think we have reached the end of the road: independence is indeed a milestone, but is only the threshold to high endeavour—the creation of a new and sovereign State. At this solemn moment therefore I call upon you all to dedicate yourselves to the service of the new Malaya: to work and strive with hand and brain to create a new nation, inspired by the ideals of justice and liberty—a beacon of light in a disturbed and distracted world.

High confidence has been reposed in us; let us unitedly face the challenge of the years. And so with remembrance for the past, and with confidence in the future, under the providence of God, we shall succeed.

71

Thai Foreign Policy in the 1960s

> *Ever since the end of the Second World War, Thailand has steered a decidedly pro-Western course in international affairs, playing a prominent role in the Southeast Asia Treaty Organization (SEATO), whose headquarters are located in the Thai capital. This document consists of excerpts from the translation of an address to the Thai armed forces, delivered by the Supreme Commander of the Armed Forces, Field Marshal Thanom Kittikachorn, Prime Minister of Thailand, on November 8, 1964.*

The strength of the Armed Forces is recognized by all civilized nations to be not only the dignity of a free nation but also the staying power determining foreign policy as well as national defence.

Only independent nations can possess military strength and the Armed Forces. Thailand has its own Armed Forces that have played an important role in safeguarding the country's independence for several hundred years. Brave warriors of old made to their credit a great impression in our miiltary history.

It is, therefore, national pride that all servicemen should gratify [rejoice?] as long as they have the Armed Forces of their own with the illustrious record of our ancestors. It is also for you, my fellow Thais, who are patriots holding national independence so dear, to give your country's Armed Forces every support deserving the dignity of the independent country.

The dominant policy of this Government regards the safeguarding of national independence and sovereignty of vital importance. It is the life and death of the nation necessitating constant guard

Thanom Kittikachorn, "Importance of Armed Forces to Free Nations," *SEATO Record* (Bangkok), Vol. III (December, 1964), pp. 40–41.

and not a moment's relaxation. For once we lose our independence, we shall not be able to carry out national development and shall be deprived of personal freedom and happiness. . . .

At present the deadliest enemy of Thailand is Communism. This is because through the use of force the Communists are endeavouring to impose their evil policies on the free nations. Their forces of aggression and the tactics of infiltration and subversion are the courses of action they primarily resort to.

Communist aggression in South-East Asia has once again become an active problem. Laos and South Vietnam are already in the thick of battle. Although direct aggression against Thailand has not yet taken place, the presence of Communist forces in the vicinity is the immediate threat to our security because of the close proximity of the countries involved.

Already, we have had some infiltration and subversion by the Communists in Thailand, which appears to be increasing despite strong counter-measures by the Government. This looming danger which is besetting Thailand every moment cannot be scorned or laughed at. The current situation in our neighboring countries and the crisis after crisis occurring here and there are most unfavourable and must be coped with.

We traditionally mark this day an important day in our profession of arms when members of the three Services assemble to take the oath before the colours. I would like to take the opportunity to call upon all my fellow servicemen and my fellow citizens to strengthen our efforts in guarding against and eliminating this ever-impending danger. I ask you all to bind in harmonious unity in our service of the nation and to be careful not to allow internal rivalry to divide us as that would be detrimental to national security.

The history of Thailand shows that if and when we remain dedicated to unity, no other aggressive nations can deprive us of our freedom and independence. This valuable lesson which our ancestors established with patriotic sacrifice must not be forgotten. . . .

Men-at-arms like you who guard this beloved land of ours must always be on the alert and be prepared. Yours is the profession of arms and you are trained to fight and to defend your country. In your training you must acquire combat experience as much as you can in order to be ready for any eventuality. Always bear in mind that combat readiness is the only guarantee for the safeguarding of our country. To be qualified for this task, you must be courageous, well-trained, well-informed, in good physical condition and well-disciplined, and must stand ever prepared to truly lay down your lives for your motherland and the Throne. By so doing you are upholding the true hallmarks of the Armed Forces of Thailand and following in your illustrious ancestors' footsteps.

As for myself I pledge my word to you, officers and men of His Majesty's Forces, that if and when our Thai nation is imperiled, you will readily find me in close company with you personally in the struggle for freedom. Only death that ensues can detach me from you at that difficult time, but national independence must be upheld above every other consideration even at the cost of our lives.

In my capacity as your Supreme Commander I most heartily welcome all of you who have taken the oath before the colours today to the glorious company of the nation's warriors. I am confident that you will keep your words of allegiance like the sacred oaths, and maintain unity and harmony among your companions with no discrimination against any of the three Services.

PART VI

The Modern Traveler

THE FINAL PART of this volume contains selections
from the writings of a group of contemporary anthropologists. In a real sense they are the successors of the
early travelers. The anthropologist visits Southeast Asia,
records observations which reflect his own interests, and
yet remains aloof from involvement in the affairs of the
indigenous community.

Unlike the early traveler, however, the modern anthropologist explores inland communities as well as the
coastal ports. His major scientific interest centers on peasant populations rather than on governing elites. Again, unlike his precursors, he usually brings to his work solid
training in methodology and languages, and he also stays
long enough in a particular region to see beyond the day-
to-day events occurring around him. If his scope is more
limited than that of the early onlooker, his understanding
goes much deeper.

The passages that follow have been chosen from a wide
variety of available writings with two specific purposes in
mind. In the first place, they explore the basis dichotomies
that exist throughout Southeast Asian societies. Phya Rajadhon and Judith Djamour examine the differences between urban and rural environments (Documents 72 and
73), while E. R. Leach and Peter Goethals look at the

287

division between lowland and upland communities (Documents 78 and 80). Raymond Firth discusses the separate roles of foreign and native communities in Southeast Asia (Document 75), and Clifford Geertz describes the differences between traditional Javanese religious worship and modern Islamic orthodoxy (Document 77). Secondly, the selections present information about communities and peoples hitherto mostly neglected in this book. Gerald Hickey writes about village life in modern South Vietnam and Joel Halpern writes of a village in Laos (Documents 74 and 76). Finally, Harold Conklin describes the daily life of a Hanunóo girl living on Mindoro, one of the Visayan Islands in the Philippines (Document 79).

Most of the selections deal with the "little tradition" in Southeast Asia, the society of the peasant, rather than the "great tradition," the life of the court and national government. The little tradition, or rather, little traditions, are shown to be influenced here and there by modern developments; yet on the whole, they remain rather firmly based on older loyalties and customs. Even these loyalties and customs, however, vary from place to place and they have little in common with the abstract stereotypes about peasant societies often encountered in less scientific writings. For this reason, the "modern traveler" is providing future generations of historians with reliable source materials not available to those of the past.

72
City and Country in Modern Thailand

Life and Ritual in Old Siam *evinces much of the flavor and style of a modern ethnographic treatment. Of its author, Professor William Gedney has written: "Phya Anuman Rajadhon occupies, or rather has created for himself, a position in the field of Thai letters and scholarship which is unique and paradoxical. Though he is not an academician by training, his scholarly attainments have placed all younger teachers and students at his feet and made him one of Thailand's most highly respected university professors. Though he is not a trained anthropologist, no one has made so great a contribution as he to the study of traditional Thai culture" (Preface to* Life and Ritual in Old Siam). *The following passage introduces a study of the daily life of the Thai farmer.*

Not too far out from the city, one sees great vacant space as far as the eye can reach; clumps of trees rise at irregular intervals. In the extreme distance one sees the treetops looking as if placed in orderly rows. The sky is clear to the distant horizon. The scene is quiet and lonely, with only the sound of crows and the sound of the wind blowing from time to time. At long intervals one sees a few people in the distance. The air one breathes feels pure and fresh. This is the condition of the meadows and fields outside of town; their characteristics are just the opposite of those of the city. In the city there are many people; whatever places are gathering points for people are crowded with thronging humans. There is a deafening din of people and of cars almost all the time. One cannot see anything at a distance, for buildings and shops and houses intervene almost everywhere. The atmosphere is hot and oppressive and impure; one breathes with difficulty. Foul and

Phya Anuman Rajadhon, *Life and Ritual in Old Siam*, trans., William Gedney (New Haven, Conn.: HRAF Press, 1961), pp. 7–9. By permission of Human Relations Area Files Press.

rotten odors assail the nose frequently. Some places are disgustingly dirty and cluttered. Life in the city and life in the country offer sharp contrasts. One is close to nature; the other is remote from nature. One is the source of food and health; the other is a place where people gather to share their food, and disease germs. To say only this much makes it appear that in the city there is only evil, not to be compared with the country. Actually if one were to speak of the good points, the city has many advantages over the country, because the center of progress is in the city. If this progress spreads to the country in appropriate proportions, one can say that the nation, both city and country, achieves prosperity. If the city is selfish to too great a degree—seeking only to accumulate wealth to provide entertainment and comfort for itself, becoming remote from nature and never glancing toward the country—the progress of the city will be like a light that flares up only for a moment and then goes out for lack of fuel, that is to say, food. The country has the function of producing food to feed the city. Therefore the city has to depend upon the country for sustenance. To speak of the country, people living too close to nature will have the living conditions of nature. Whatever life is like, it continues so, with no progress upward and forward, because the country must depend upon the wealth, intelligence, and power of the city for maintenance and improvement in order that the country may advance and grow toward prosperity. World civilization and progress in the history of various nations depend upon both city and country. Each depends upon the other, and neither is better or worse than the other. If there are tools but no rice, or rice but no tools, there is hardship. Therefore in Thai it is said that nation and possessions (the expression for "possessions" is literally "rice and things") go hand in hand; if separated, neither nation nor possessions exist fully.

City people call people outside the city "countryfolk." When one speaks the word "country" he thinks at once of backwardness both in wealth and in knowledge, but if city people did not have country people to help them, they could not live, for they would have no rice to eat, and would have no riches or happiness. For this reason we should share our knowledge and our wealth with the country people; thus we help the nation and help ourselves at one and the same time, for the people together form the nation. If one divides them broadly as I do, there are only two groups, the city people and the country people. . . .

When we say that the country people constitute the largest part of the population of the country or, as they say, the backbone of the country, this is usually an end of the matter. No one is interested in knowing about country people, except to have them farm much and produce much rice, to feed the centers of population, namely, the cities. As for the life of country people and the difference between their conditions and beliefs and amusements and those of city people, no one seems much interested, for it is a question of country people, who could not possibly have anything better than city people. Whatever the country people think or believe is old-fashioned, unchanged with the times. This is true, but the majority of country people live in small groups, not large groups like city people, because none of them has an opportunity to become acquainted with other people to open his ears and eyes, surrounding circumstances limiting him. Whatever country people have done and believed in the past with satisfactory results, they continue to do and believe, not changing readily. It is as if we had always used our own tools until we are handy with them; if we replace them suddenly with new tools it is like an about-face; we have not sufficient time to adapt ourselves. Such change causes confusion among the country people, for the old familiar tools are destroyed before use of the new tools has been learned; this amounts to destroying good things without providing anything better, so that the only door is broken. For this reason the country people advance slowly. Alone, they do not dare change the old for the new because they are unsure, differing from the city people who have seen things of various kinds and so advance quickly; but sometimes they misstep, because of advancing too fast. . . .

73

Patterns of Malay Life in Singapore

Judith Djamour, a British-trained anthropologist, studied marriage customs among the Malays of Singapore in 1949 and 1950. In the following excerpts she explores some of the differences between urban and rural Malay communities on the island.

In Malay villages in the rural areas of Singapore, the inhabitants formed a community in the sense that a village was a territorially compact group of people performing a wide range of functions. The villagers [in Tanjong] knew each other personally, being often related by birth or affinity among themselves. They had been born in the house built by their parents or grandparents, and would probably be buried in the village cemetery; their children went to the same school and were taught to read the Koran by the same religious teacher; the same local midwife delivered all the babies. On religious festivals the men assembled at the local mosque to pray. If the village well fell into disrepair every household contributed towards the cost of the necessary materials and the able-bodied men set to work on the job. When there was a death, every household contributed towards the expenses of the burial ceremonies. . . .

In the urban areas of the Colony where there was a concentration of Malays, I knew of no comparable example where community feeling was as intense as in villages of the type of Tanjong. Although there was often a local mosque, a local vernacular school, and sometimes also one local midwife, the Malay inhabitants of any urban district did not appear to feel closely bound to each other, and certainly they rarely acted as a group. There

Judith Djamour, *Malay Kinship and Marriage in Singapore* (London: The Athlone Press, 1959), pp. 19, 21–22. By permission of the author and The London School of Economics and Political Science and The Athlone Press.

were obvious reasons for this. Urban districts were not often de-limited by visible boundaries which could compare with the bare patches of land surrounding a Malay village. There might be Chinese or Indians living in the next house, or in the next street. The Malay inhabitants themselves, at least the adults, were usually born in another district of the Colony and had rarely lived in the house they now occupied for more than a few years. As a rule, they did not own the house but rented it from a Chinese or from an Arab. They would move out if the head of the household changed his job and found it more convenient to live within closer proximity of his new place of work. In the villages, men sought jobs which were easily accessible to their homes. In the town they sought homes which were near the area in which they found employment.

One significant aspect of the lack of a strong community tie in urban districts was that whereas membership of a death-benefit association in a Malay village was limited to the inhabitants of that particular village, in the town these associations were based, not on common residence, but often on common occupation. Thus there were death-benefit associations for Malay drivers, for fitters, policemen, etc.

On the other hand, although community feeling was intense only in small villages and practically non-existent in urban and suburban areas, and although there were neither hereditary nor elected leaders acting specifically as representatives of Singapore Malays, yet that segment of the Colony's population was more than just a census category. One Malay identified another by certain explicit and implicit criteria. Malays are not a race in the strict sense of the term, but there was usually enough physical difference between them and other elements in the Colony's population to make them distinguishable on physical grounds. These physical characteristics were reinforced by peculiarities of dress, gait and posture. In addition there was language: Malay as spoken by the Malays among themselves was distinct from the varieties spoken by the local Chinese, the Indians, the Eurasians, and the Euro-peans. Apart from these immediately perceptible traits, Singapore

Malays had many other points in common. They had rites and ceremonies connected with childbirth, circumcision, marriage and death which were peculiar to them not only as Muslims, but as Malays.

However, the most important point in this context was that Malays felt considerable in-group solidarity. This feeling found expression in their phrase *kita orang Mělayu* (we Malay people) which they used to refer to themselves as a discrete section of the Island's population. Singapore Malays attempted to form themselves into voluntary associations for charitable purposes and for economic co-operation. Malay women of the Colony started organizations for the purposes of helping destitute mothers and widows and of providing financial help for the sick. The rules of these organizations specifically stated that recipients of the services must be Malays resident in the Colony.

The majority of Malay charitable associations were of recent (postwar) origin. They had not accumulated much capital by 1950; membership fluctuated; suitable premises were not always available; and committees did not always work smoothly. However, their formation was an undeniable attempt by Singapore Malays to give concrete expression to the fact that they considered themselves to be one unitary body.

74
A Village in Contemporary South Vietnam

> *This description of the village of Khanh Hau in the Mekong River delta is excerpted from the concluding chapter in the first comprehensive anthropological study of Vietnamese peasant culture undertaken by an American scholar. Chicago-trained, Hickey studied the village in the late 1950s, and has since then often returned to Vietnam for additional field work.*

The old proverb "Phep vua thua le lang" (The laws of the emperor yield to the customs of the village) is known by all Vietnamese, and in many respects it characterizes the village in Vietnam as a self-contained homogeneous community, jealously guarding its way of life—a little world that is autonomous and disregards (if not disdains) the outside world. . . .

. . . In southern Vietnam, historical events since the end of the nineteenth century have rendered the image implicit in the proverb less and less applicable to the village. The isolation of the village has steadily grown less, and the ways of the village have been more and more encroached upon by the ways of the world. This situation is very much reflected in Khanh Hau where the little-community qualities exist but are perceptibly dwindling.

There is, for example, homogeneity in the attitudes and values of many of the Khanh Hau villagers. They share a cosmological view deeply rooted in the Buddhist-Taoist-Confucianist ideology of the Chinese Great Tradition, with Vietnamese alterations and additions, which underlies the amalgam of beliefs and practices that make up village religion, and it influences all other aspects of village society as well. Adherence to it is manifest almost daily in behavior—even in the behavior of Catholics, followers of the Minh Chon Ly sect (who consider themselves emancipated from the traditional religious beliefs), and villagers who for whatever reason have rejected some of the traditional ways. Belief in universal order, and the related concepts of harmony with this order and human destiny within it, are reflected in the conformity of all villagers to guidance by the lunar calendar and reliance on individual horoscopy, and in the respect of most villagers for the principles of geomancy. The notion of harmony is involved in many practices and rituals—observance of taboos, use of amulets or talismans, preparation of medicines, consultation with healers, propitiation or expulsion of spirits, invocations to deities, and veneration of ancestors. The aim of these is to preserve or restore harmony and, with it, well-being.

Before the advent of Cao Daism, and with the exception of a small group of Catholics, all villagers identified themselves as Buddhists. Although the homogeneity of formal affiliation (or ex-

Gerald Cannon Hickey, *Village in Vietnam* (New Haven, Conn. and London: Yale University Press, 1964), pp. 276–279. By permission of the author and Yale University Press.

pressed association) consequently has diminished as several hundred villagers became Cao Daists, homogeneity of belief in Buddhist doctrine and deities (all incorporated in Cao Daism) has continued. This also is true of popular beliefs and practices which are admitted by all Cao Daist sects except the Minh Chon Ly (some twenty adherents in Khanh Hau). Veneration of ancestors (Catholics specify that they honor rather than venerate ancestors) is almost universal in the village. The altars are the same and rituals are performed according to prescribed form.

There also is homogeneity in the social expectation. The drive to provide well for one's family combined with some of the basic beliefs associated with the Cult of the Ancestors contributes to the strong motivation for economic gain that characterizes the Vietnamese peasant (which in turn has contributed to the expansionism that marks Vietnamese history).

It is the desire of most villagers to improve their lot, which means having land, a fine house, material comfort, and education for one's children. One of the dreads of poverty is that the family may disintegrate as members quit the village to seek a livelihood elsewhere. For the villager it is extremely important that the family remain together: in addition to the comfort of having kinfolk about, immortality lies in an undying lineage.

There is homogeneity in the villagers' style of life. Variations are not great enough to warrant stratification into social classes. Rather, they are variations on a common theme which amount more to elaborations than to substantive differences.

There also is a great deal of homogeneity in livelihood activities, with practically everyone in the village directly or indirectly engaged in rice cultivation. All farmers cultivate rice, and all laborers are farm laborers. Village leaders—those in the sociopolitical elite and/or the Village Council—as well as rice millers and rice merchants own paddy land and describe themselves as farmers and most specialists also are farmers. . . .

The homogeneity of values, style of life, and some behavior patterns, as well as the functional interrelationships that exist among the various aspects of village society, implies communal personal associations. . . . These communal personal associations, however, cannot be said to exist for the whole of Khanh Hau society. Cultural values and social behavioral patterns are shared because the inhabitants have a common tradition, which in this case is the Vietnamese tradition as it exists in southern Vietnam. It does not necessarily follow that members of village society have strong social bonds or a sense of social solidarity. These qualities are found within the village but cannot be attributed to the village.

Several outstanding factors relating to this lack of communal personal association can be isolated. First, the settlements that make up Khanh Hau are widely dispersed; sections of Ap Cau and Ap Nhon Hau are 5 kilometers from the northern part of Ap Dinh-B and, unless he has kin or acquaintances in such a distant place, a villager is not likely to visit there. Villagers often remark that they do not know fellow villagers from other hamlets—they may know them by sight, but they have never spoken. On the other hand, those living in the string settlements of Ap Cau and Ap Nhon Hau literally are a stone's throw from string hamlets along the opposite banks of the streams separating Khanh Hau from the neighboring villages of Tan Huong and An Vinh Ngai. . . .

The effect of this dispersion is compounded by the fact that there are no real focal centers to attract sizable segments of the village population, giving them the opportunity for social interaction. The *dinh* [communal temple] often is described as the social and religious center of the Vietnamese village, but this is true in only a limited sense in villages of southern Vietnam. There are four rituals held at the dinh in the course of the lunar year, but participation is expected only of the cult committee members. Although attendance is compulsory for all male household heads, there is very little interaction among the audience either before, during, or after the meetings. Undoubtedly, having two dinh and two cult committees diminishes the importance of each, but had the village only one, its primary importance would still be that of ritual center for some of the village men.

The Council House does not function as a focal center. Most villagers visit there only occasionally to take care of some administrative necessity. The Buddhist pagoda in Ap Moi (the village pagoda) and that in Ap Cau draw a relatively small attendance at rituals, and their active congregations are from the locale rather than from the whole village. Although both the Tien Thien and Ban Chin Dao Cao Daist sects have sizable congregations, their temples actually function as social centers more for the residential groups surrounding them than for any significant segment of the village. . . .

One might speculate that if Khanh Hau had a market it would serve as a center for social intercourse in the village. Marketing, however, is done by the women, and the proximity of the Tan Huong market to the southern portion of the village, combined with the attraction of the large Tan An market 4 kilometers from the northern edge, would reduce the significance of any market within Khanh Hau. Finally, the political events of the past several decades have greatly disrupted village life. Whereas war may have the effect of generating solidarity among a people, the guerrilla type of hostilities characteristic of the Indochina War bred only conflict and suspicion. Without battle lines, without an identifiable enemy, the war was everywhere. Pro-Viet Minh and pro-French factions existed in the village, and although most villagers did not take sides actively, accusations of being on one side or the other were rampant. This pattern continued as the Viet Cong movement against the national government reached Khanh Hau, and the effect has been to turn many villagers inward. They now are primarily concerned with survival for themselves and their families.

75
The Plural Society in Malaya

Raymond Firth undertook research among the Malay communities of the east coast of Malaya, focussing attention on fishing, a much neglected but very important industry in Southeast Asia. His monograph, a section of which is presented below, remains the most complete and informative study of a Southeast Asian fishing community. Professor Firth teaches Anthropology in the London School of Economics and Political Science of the University of London.

The Perupok area, as a cross-section of the Kelantan coastal region, is not isolated, and there is considerable movement of population into and out of it.

The resident population consists of three elements. Most important are the local Malays, describing themselves as "people from here" *(orang sini),* that is, born in the area roughly from the north of Bachok coastwise of the Kemassin River to its mouth. Of next importance are the non-local Malays, specified by their origin —Jelawat people, Tumpat people, "inland people" *(orang darat),* etc. In this category are a few Malays from Trengganu and from Patani in southern Siam, which has a Malay population closely allied to that in Kelantan. There were in all about 5 Malays from outside Kelantan and 20 from other areas in Kelantan, as permanent residents. There were no Malays from the west coast living in the area. These non-local Malays are easily absorbed, but their immigration has certain economic results for them. One or more of their children may be adopted by their kinsfolk in their original home. Adjustments are necessary for them to maintain income from rice, coco-nut and rubber lands there; such lands must be worked by their kin (and the proceeds shared) or leased, or visited periodically. They suffer when they hold a circumcision or marriage feast, since they cannot hope to assemble such a large body of kinsfolk contributors as a local person can, and they may be at a disadvantage for other types of economic coöperation as well. These points are mentioned to show that while Perupok is a comparatively new development as a coastal settlement, the shift of population has been quite local, and that there are solid reasons for this.

The third element in the area is non-Malay, mainly Indian and Chinese, and numbers about a score in all. . . . There was one Siamese, an old woman who had married a Malay long ago and had

Raymond Firth, *Malay Fishermen: Their Peasant Economy*, 2nd rev. ed. (London: Routledge and Kegan Paul Ltd.; Hamden, Conn.: Archon Books, 1966), pp. 67–69. By permission of the author and Routledge & Kegan Paul Ltd. and The Shoe String Press, Inc.

become a Muslim. She was accepted as a full member of the community and was regarded as the head of the little group of houses where we lived. The Indians, known generically as *orang Kĕling,* are mostly from South India. They are Muslims, and as such they are socially more acceptable than Chinese. They all wear the Malay sarong—though retaining the Indian shirt—and speak tolerable Malay. They tend to congregate together, but of about ten in the census area two were married to Malay women and two others were living with Malay women, in separate dwellings. The children of the former were completely accepted into Malay society. Nearly all were shop-keepers or coffee-shop proprietors, though one, who used to sell nuts on the beach as a hawker, went out fishing for a time. The Chinese, also numbering about ten, remain separate in most social affairs, though some Kelantan Chinese of long standing in the State have assimilated a great deal of Malay speech and customs. These people wear Chinese dress and speak poor Malay. One old man, however (said locally to be possibly a Japanese), did embrace Islam, mainly, it appeared, in order to be able to marry a Malay woman; it was easier to change his religion than his domestic life. The Chinese keep a couple of shops, selling general merchandise, and a coffee-shop and eating-house; there is also a Chinese bus-owner.

In the Perupok area these foreign elements had no great economic importance, and they had Malay competitors in each occupation. This is the case in many of the coastal villages. Inland, however, especially in the towns and new villages at cross-roads, Indians and Chinese provide most of the shop-keepers. Elsewhere in Kelantan, too, there are some Siamese communities. One, a few miles to the north of Perupok, had a temple and a seminary staffed by Buddhist monks, with a settlement of Siamese rice-cultivators, who also made tiles and did plastering and other construction work.

76

Lao Rice Planting Rituals

> *In 1957 Joel M. Halpern, presently on the faculty of Bran-*
> *deis University, served as field representative for the Ameri-*
> *can aid mission in Luang Prabang. The following passage is*
> *taken from the second of two monographs based on his field*
> *research at that time.*

Various means, sacred as well as secular, are taken to ensure the water supply and fertility of the crops. The sacred are connected with the dominant belief in *phi* or nature spirits which exists throughout Laos. In April, just before the rains, an elaborate New Year's celebration is held by the Lao, a prominent feature of which is reciprocal water dousing everyone gives everyone else.

On an auspicious day in the sixth month of the Lao calendar, chosen by consulting the proper sacred manuscript or a local astrologer, villagers make offerings of a boiled chicken, rice alcohol, and sometimes a pig to the protective spirits of the village. The phi are then beseeched to protect the villagers during their work, to keep destructive animals and insects out of the rice fields, especially the small crabs which can destroy the crop, and to provide adequate rain and a good harvest. In addition to this ceremony each worker presents an offering to the spirits of the fields, who live in the trees and in the rice fields. The belief in the efficacy of these phi is still very strong and the villagers have been known to refuse to work in certain fields if they think the spirits are angry.

In traditional Thai-Lao culture rice is not regarded simply as a

Joel M. Halpern, *Economy and Society in Laos: A Brief Survey* (New Haven, Conn.: Yale University Southeast Asia Studies, Monograph Series No. 5, 1964), pp. 26–29. By permission of the author and Southeast Asia Studies, Yale University.

food but as a sacred substance presided over by a guardian spirit. . . .

Among the Lao each stage in the cultivation of rice, after the initial planting, is accompanied by appropriate rituals. Formerly, when it came time to start work in the fields, the king turned the first ceremonial spade of earth since there was believed to be a degree of kinship between the royal family and the protecting spirits. The rite of Lieng Phi Ta Hek ("feeding the Phi Ta Hek") is held at transplanting time. Altars for Phi Ta Hek, the leading spirit of the rice fields, are built in a corner of the paddy field to receive offerings of glutinous rice mixed with grains of paddy and shaped into ears of rice to symbolize abundance. Also placed on the altar are four banana leaves rolled into horns to contain betel. The transplanting starts after the recitation of chants that accompany the planting of the first seven shoots of rice.

I plant the rice shoot; may you be green as the Thao.

I plant the second shoot; may you be green as the grass of the ninth month.

I plant the third shoot; may the gong of nine *kam* [measure of diameter] be mine.

I plant the fourth shoot; may the ninety thousand pounds of gold be mine.

I plant the fifth shoot; may ninety thousand baskets of rice be mine.

I plant the sixth shoot; may I have a wife to sleep by my side.

I plant the seventh shoot; may a rare elephant saddled in gold and silver be mine.

Glory! Prosperity!

The transplanting finished, further offerings usually of boiled chicken, alcohol, and cigarettes are made to Ta Hek to ensure protection of the fields. During the threshing, four guardian symbols wrapped in white cotton thread are placed on the threshing floor at the cardinal points to form a barrier against the possible entry of evil spirits who might make off with the rice.

A celebration known as Khoun Lane takes place in connection with the storing of the rice in raised storage sheds. At dawn the souls of the rice are informed that food is about to be presented and a meal is offered to the bonzes [monks] at the threshing ground before a gathering of the villagers. After the meal a bonze climbs on top of the rice pile and reads a traditional text. This recitation is followed by villagers calling together the souls of the rice where-ever they may have wandered. Taking a basket of hard-boiled eggs and other delicacies they walk through the fields intoning: "Spirit of the Rice, here are tubers for thee, here are the buds of the areca palm and good alcohol made from your grain. Spirit of the Rice, come down to earth! Come and preside over the festivities I am giving in your honor." The basket, which now carries the spirit of the rice, is brought back to the village by the owner to be suspended from a beam of the storage loft. The old women of the village come to welcome the Rice, speak familiarly to it and compliment it, all the while running the paddy through their wrinkled fingers. The owner brings a small figure made of straw and, just as a friend would be greeted on his return from a jour-ney, the women tender the figure a *sukwan,* tying white cotton threads on the straw wrists. The spirit of the rice is congratulated on having returned to the village, made welcome in the most affec-tionate manner, and begged never to leave the granary.

There is even a special rite for the re-opening of the storage sheds—Boun Khay Pa Tou Lao, which is celebrated on the third day of the waxing moon of the third month. A platter of offerings for the souls of the rice is brought to the loft where, crouching and holding candles, the people recite: "Today is an auspicious day. We take you. We draw you out. When we eat of you, you shall still remain undiminished. May you always be plentiful." Then they tell the souls of the rice not to fear the rhythmic sounds and heavy weight of the pestles that will soon come to break up the rice.

In recent years these rites have been modified. Bouns [celebra-tions] such as Khoun Lane and Khay Pa Tou Lao, which were formerly exclusively religious, have gradually tended to become profane—more a time for relaxation and amusement than an occasion on which to pray and thank the spirits. Yet by no means has rice cultivation become a secular process, for great respect is still paid to the guardian phi of the rice fields and their altars can be seen frequently in the paddy fields of Lao villages. Bonzes continue to participate in the ceremonies, particularly those rites connected with harvesting and with ensuring a good yield the following year.

For the Lao, then, raising paddy rice is not simply an economic activity, subsistence or otherwise, but rather a way of life closely interwoven with the supernatural. Intensive wet-rice cultivation as practiced by the Lao and Black Tai is capable of yielding a surplus beyond the need of the farmers and thereby provides the basis for the establishment of an elaborate hierarchy of political and religious specialists, as reflected in the rituals described. In the case of the Lao prominent ceremonial roles are given to the Buddhist priests (and formerly the king with his ritual plowing); among the Black Tai these roles go to hereditary priests and leaders. Such specialization does not exist in cultures relying primarily on dry-rice cultivation.

77
Religious Life in Java

The Islamization of island Southeast Asia has been a gradual process, in the course of which older religious beliefs and forms have been slowly changed without necessarily disappearing. But side by side with these older forms, "purer" versions of Islam have penetrated to many parts of the area, often leading to more or less pronounced cleavages between old and new. In the following excerpts, Clifford Geertz, an anthropologist at the University of Chicago, examines such a cleavage in a central Javanese community which includes both rural and urban inhabitants. Based on Javanese usage, he calls the two religious orientations abangan *and* santri, *denoting the syncretically traditionalist and the consciously*

Islamic groupings, respectively. His study is based on field work carried out in the early 1950s. Geertz has given the community he studied the fictitious name of Modjokuto.

Comparing the *abangan* and *santri* variants of the Modjokuto religious pattern, two very striking general differences, other than their differential evaluation of Islamic orthodoxy, are immediately apparent. In the first place, *abangans* are fairly indifferent to doctrine but fascinated with ritual detail, while among the *santris* the concern with doctrine almost entirely overshadows the already attenuated ritualistic aspects of Islam.

An *abangan* knows when to give a *slametan* [ritual communal feast] and what the major foods should be—porridge for a birth, pancakes for a death. He may have some ideas as to what various elements in it symbolize (and as often he may not, saying that one has porridge because one always has porridge on such an occasion), but he will be little upset if someone else gives a different interpretation. He is tolerant about religious beliefs; he says, "Many are the ways." If one performs the correct passage rituals, one is not an animal; if one gives the *slametans* in the Fast, one is not an infidel; and if one sends a tray off to the "cleansing of the village," one is not a subversive—and that is enough. If one doesn't believe in spirits or if one thinks God lives in the sun, that's one's own affair.

For the *santri* the basic rituals are also important—particularly the prayers, the conscientious performance of which is taken by *santris* and non-*santris* alike to be the distinguishing mark of a true *santri*—but little thought is given to them; they are simple enough in any case. What concerns the *santris* is Islamic doctrine, and most especially the moral and social interpretation of it. They seem especially interested, particularly the urban "modernist" *santris,* in apologetics: the defense of Islam as a superior ethical code for modern man, as a workable social doctrine for modern society, and as a fertile source of values for modern culture. In the countryside the doctrinal aspect is less marked; there the *santri* ethic remains somewhat closer to the *abangan*. But even in the countryside a *santri* differs from an *abangan* not only in his self-declared religious superiority to the latter, but also in his realization, if only vague, that in Islam the main religious issues are doctrinal; and in any case the rural *santri* follows an urban leadership. For the *santri* the dimensions have shifted. It is not the knowledge of ritual detail or spiritual discipline which is important, but the application of Islamic doctrine to life. The kinds of *santris* vary from those whose difference from their *abangan* neighbors seems to lie entirely in their insistence that they are true Moslems, while their neighbors are not, to those whose commitment to Islam dominates almost all of their life. But, for all, a concern for dogma has to some extent replaced a concern for ritual.

One result of this difference of emphasis is that the curiously detached unemotional relativism that *abangans* evince toward their own religious customs, an attitude not entirely unlike that of the dilettante ethnologist collecting quaint customs among the heathen, tends to be replaced among the *santris* by a strong emphasis on the necessity for unreserved belief and faith in the absolute truth of Islam and by marked intolerance for Javanese beliefs and practices they take to be heterodox. . . .

The second obvious way in which the *abangan* and *santri* religious variants differ from one another is in the matter of their social organization. For the *abangan* the basic social unit to which nearly all ritual refers is the household—a man, his wife, and his children. It is the household which gives the *slametan* and it is the heads of other households who come to attend it and then carry home part of the food to the other members of their families. Even the *bersih désa,* the "cleansing of the village" ceremony, the closest thing to a public or super-household ritual that one can find within the *abangan* system, is but little more than a compound of separate *slametan* contributions from each of the village's households rather than a ritual of the village as a whole; it is food from separate kitchens brought together, rather than food from a common kitchen divided up. Aside from coming with their food, there is little that the participants are called upon to do. . . .

For the *santri,* the sense of community—of *ummat*—is primary. Islam is seen as a set of concentric social circles, wider and wider communities—Modjokuto, Java, Indonesia, the whole of the Islamic world—spreading away from the individual *santri* where he stands: a great society of equal believers constantly repeating the name of the Prophet, going through the prayers, chanting the Koran. . . .

This concern with the community means that, despite their tremendous interest in doctrine, Modjokuto Moslems never see their religion as a mere set of beliefs, as a kind of abstract philosophy, or even as a general system of values to which as individuals they are committed. Instead, they always conceive of it as institutionalized in some social group: the *santris* in their neighborhood, or all those they consider such in the Modjokuto area, or all Indonesian Moslems, or "the Islamic world." When they speak of Islam, there is almost always in the back of their minds a social organization of some sort in which the Islamic creed is the defining element. It may be a charitable organization, a woman's club, the village mosque committee, a religious school, the local office of the religious bureaucracy, or their political party at either the local, regional, or national level.

These two distinguishing features of the *santri* religious pattern —a concern for doctrine and apology and for social organization— crosscut one another to produce the internal structure of the Moslem community in Modjokuto. On the doctrinal level there is only one major distinction of importance, rather less marked now than it was in the years before the [Second World] war: that between the "modern" *(modèren)* and the conservative or "old-fashioned" *(kolot)* variants of the creed. From 1912 almost until the war the conflict between those Indonesian Moslems who had been influenced by modernist Islamic reform movements originating in Cairo, Mecca, and, to a far lesser extent, in parts of India, and those who reacted against this influence, was indeed a sharp and bitter one. Today, this once entirely religious conflict has been transformed in part into a political one as the leaders of both groups have come to accept a general and watered-down version of modernism and have shifted their interest more and more towards the ever intriguing question of how they are going to get into power. But the old division still remains. Although many of the leaders of the "old-fashioned" group have abandoned the extreme reactionary position, many of the rank-and-file members have not; and the general distinction between modern *santris,* who accept the twentieth century with enthusiasm and see its complexities as but a challenge to be dealt with, and those who are at best resigned to it and its pitfalls for the pious, is still of fundamental importance within the Modjokuto *unmat.*

78

Upland and Lowland in Modern Burma

> *E. R. Leach, now of King's College, Cambridge, conducted much of his research in northern Burma while also perform-ing military duties there during World War II. Although his primary work was among the Kachins, a hill group, he had ample opportunity to observe their lowland-dwelling neigh-bors, the Shans.*

Before proceeding further it is necessary to give some general indication of the kind of economic life that is led by Kachins and their Shan neighbours. . . .

Along the river valleys irrigated rice cultivation is easy and cart tracks are readily constructed, but in the mountains which separate the valleys the construction of either roads or rice terraces is a feat of major engineering. It is hardly surprising, therefore, that

E. R. Leach, *Political Systems of Highland Burma* (London: G. Bell & Sons, 1954; Cambridge, Mass.: Harvard University Press, 1954), pp. 18, 20–22. By permission of the author and The London School of Economics and Political Science.

the technical and economic organisation of the hill-dwelling peoples is very different from that of the peoples of the valleys, nor is it very surprising that the hill peoples in different parts of Burma all resort to much the same kind of technical device to overcome the difficulties of their environment.

The contrast between the highlanders and the lowlanders is thus in the first place ecological. Even if the two categories of population spoke the same language one might well expect to find marked cultural differences between the two groups and, on analogy with countries such as Scotland and Northern Italy, one might also anticipate a jealous and mutual contempt between the rival parties. And such is the case. The only peculiarity about Burma is that the cultural contrast between the highlanders and the lowlanders is so very marked. The two groups do not share a common language and they share few traits of material culture. In matters of household and technical equipment, almost the only objects which are common to both groups in the Kachin Hills Area are such things as iron cooking-pans and tripods which both parties purchase from the Chinese. Yet this is understandable enough, for technological equipment is necessarily adjusted to the conditions of life, and the highland and lowland mode of living is sharply contrasted. . . .

The valley-dwelling peoples, that is the "Burmese" and the "Shans," mostly practise wet rice cultivation with moderate though adequate efficiency. This permits a system of continuous cultivation and continuous settlement even in areas where the annual rainfall is relatively slight. Nearly all these valley peoples make use of animals for cultivation and transport. . . . Under normal conditions—that is in the absence of war and epidemics and similar disasters—the valley peoples can always easily raise more rice than is immediately required for the consumption of the actual cultivators. This secure economic basis permits the development of trade and small scale urbanisation and a moderate degree of general cultural sophistication. As a broad generalisation it may be said that the valley peoples constitute a semi-literate peasantry. In an economic sense they live at a considerably "higher" level of organisation than their neighbours in the surrounding mountains.

In contrast, the normal shifting cultivation techniques practised by the hill peoples can only be expected to yield a surplus under exceptional conditions of low population density and specially favorable terrain. Wherever this technique proves inadequate, the hill peoples are forced into expedients of various kinds. Some groups, such as the Central Chins, have developed quite elaborate schemes of crop rotation; others, notably the Angami Nagas and certain Kachin groups, have gone in for the construction of irrigated rice terraces cut out of the mountainside; others again have found a solution to their difficulties by achieving some form of political and economic alliance with their more prosperous neighbours of the plains. This latter kind of symbiosis has assumed a variety of forms at different times in different places. For example, the mountaineers are sometimes regarded as the political overlords of the valley, so that the valley people pay a feudal rent to the hill chieftains; sometimes the hill peoples merely exploit the fact that they control the cross-country communications between the valleys and levy a toll on passing caravans; sometimes the valley peoples have been willing to pay "blackmail" provided the hillmen agreed not to raid the valley crops; sometimes the valley chieftains have engaged the hillmen as mercenaries on a large scale.

All such transactions are related to the fact that as a general rule the valley peoples are producers of rice surplus to their own requirements, while equally, as a general rule, the hill peoples suffer from a rice deficiency which must somehow be made good from outside. This crucial economic fact is of the utmost importance for the understanding of all long term social developments throughout the Burma area. . . .

79

Among the Hanunóo of Mindoro

In 1953, Harold C. Conklin, presently Professor at Yale University, undertook research among the Hanunóo, a hill group living on Mindoro island in the central Philippines. He wrote the following passage about Maling, a seven-year-old Hanunóo girl.

One day Maling was sent by her parents to see if the door had been finished on a nearby rice granary which was being built for the family by one of her uncles. She said she wasn't going to be gone long and wondered if I wouldn't walk along with her. On reaching the bamboo and wood storehouse which was hidden from our house-yard clearing by a few yards of low scrub and jungle, we climbed the inclined pole ladder and sat down on the door ledge.

Maling seemed to be in a talkative mood.

"Mother went down to the stream to bathe today," she began, "and left the baby all alone with Hanap [an older sister]. We were awfully worried that something might happen, but nothing did. He is six days old, and he doesn't have a name yet. Our grandparents are coming up here in a day or two and I suppose we will decide on a name then."

"What do you think would be a good name for your brother?" I queried.

"There are a lot of names that are good for boys, but some we don't like because they sound too much like those used by the *damū'ung* (lowland Christians). Others we can't use because

Harold C. Conklin, "Maling, A Hanunóo Girl from the Philippines," in *In The Company of Man: Twenty Portraits by Anthropologists*, ed. Joseph B. Casagrande (New York: Harper & Row, 1960), pp. 110–112. Copyright © 1960 by Joseph B. Casagrande. Reprinted by permission of Harper & Row, Publishers.

they belonged to relatives who have been dead only a few years. I think the best name would be the one Father has suggested, Gawid. My great-great-grandfather's name was Gawid. See that peak beyond Alyun? I've never been there, but they say that's where old Gawid once shot two deer with the same arrow. When my brother gets Grandfather Andung to prepare some hunting medicine for him, he should be a good hunter too.

"You know, we used to have a brother, who was several years younger than Hanap, but he died of a sudden illness two rice harvests ago. It was really too bad. He was just learning how to trap and shoot. If he had lived we would now have fish and game to eat with our rice or bananas almost every day. And there are so many things he could have helped Father do. He could have operated the bellows while Father worked at the forge, and he could have built this granary. As it is now, Father will have to forge two bolo blades to repay my uncle for this job. And look there, the cogon [wild grass] thatch seems a bit thin over in that corner, and the lashing here on the floor is poorly knotted. It just isn't the same as having one's own son for a helper.

"With Mother it is different. Hanap already can do most household chores including cooking, and she is pretty good at spinning and weaving baskets. I haven't learned to do all these things yet, but by the time Hanap gets married, I'll be able to take her place."

Our conversation was interrupted at this point by Hanap's call for Maling to go with her to fetch water. As we walked down to the main settlement clearing, Maling asked if girls in America also carry water like the Hanunóo, and whether their brothers ever helped them. Before I had time to answer she had joined Hanap and two other Parina [Maling's village] girls on their way to the spring.

The infant's ears were pierced the following day and, not unimpressed by Maling's (and her father's) enthusiasm, the family decided to name him Gawid. Sukub [Maling's mother] was now able to gather firewood, cook, harvest bananas and beans, and work in the family fields—never, however, without Gawid slung at her side, or in Hanap's care.

During the second week, Maling helped her mother tie small circlets of red and white beads around Gawid's wrists and legs, and a tiny medicinal amulet about his neck. He was now well on his way to becoming accepted as a full-fledged member of the community and Parinans stopped calling him "the infant" as they began to use his proper name. . . .

80

A Sumbawan Village

This selection is from Peter Goethals' study of Rarak, a village on the island of Sumbawa in the Lesser Sunda group of Indonesia. Located midway between mountain and lowland communities, Rarak exhibits some of the characteristics of both. The author is on the faculty of the University of North Carolina.

. . . This settlement of some four hundred people is situated in the northernmost tier of the western peninsula's foothills about thirteen miles from the island's capital town in the lowlands. The frame houses of the village are typically nucleated around the small community mosque, and much of the villager's social rounds as well as periodic ritual activities are centered in this important community building. Economically the villager depends for his often meagre subsistence upon shifting-field rice cultivation on the slopes surrounding the village. Yet with his occasional extra income the average farmer from Rarak is able to make the short trip to town and there purchase such essentials for his up-

Peter R. Goethals, "The Sumbawan Village," in *Local, Ethnic, and National Loyalties in Village Indonesia: A Symposium,* ed. G. William Skinner (New Haven, Conn.: Yale University Southeast Asia Studies, Cultural Report Series, No. 8, 1959), pp. 15–18. By permission of the author and Southeast Asia Studies, Yale University.

land household as sugar, kerosene and cotton cloth. There he encounters not only the Chinese and Arab merchants of the lowland shops but also the crescendo and increasing apparatus of the new national government. Garish political posters printed in the national language that he usually cannot read, burgeoning new white stucco office buildings, jeeps and weapons carriers loaded with khaki-clad government officials—these are a few of the clues by which the villager apprehends yet a new horizon to his identity: that of citizenship in the new Indonesian state. This horizon remains but dimly perceived, for the villager has had few opportunities to realize loyalties in national terms. The matrix of his most compelling loyalties, lies, rather, within and around his upland community. It is to this essentially conservative subsociety that one must look to comprehend the most central of the modern villager's ties. From it derives the bulk of his historically precipitated and still cautiously extended loyalties.

All the villagers at Rarak share a characteristic concern for the niceties of local *adat* [custom]. Those who have married into the village—whether from Bima, Lombok, or even from closely neighboring villages of the highlands—have usually achieved at best a somewhat begrudged general acceptance. At times of argument one will occasionally hear the taunt: "Since you don't like the way things are done here, why don't you go back to where you came from?" Especially with marriage negotiations and in land inheritance those of different *adat* may be at a distinct disadvantage. It seems that the first-generation villager of alien *adat* almost never overcomes the slight stigma of his origin, even if it be in a village no more than thirty miles distant. Despite this the villagers well realize that the origins of their own families in the village are both recent and diverse. Accounts are numerous as to who first came to Rarak to settle and the reasons for doing so. In all likelihood the villages of the immediate area were established soon after the Tambora holocaust [volcanic eruption in 1815] but arguments can still rage over the actual identity within family lines of the first settlers. The people of the village have had considerably less contact with westerners than have villagers of the lowlands and, since the former Dutch colonial officers were almost never seen in the village except in the company of the sultan of Sumbawa, the older villagers tend, even today, to identify the westerner with legitimate indigenous political authority.

Naturally and inevitably the villager's strongest loyalties are confined within the groups of which he has traditionally been a member. In the scattered villages of the Rarak area these groups are one's family, the several primary groups important within the village for religious, social and economic functions and the village community itself. In addition each villager is a member of a loosely knit group of kin whose members are found in many other villages near and far distant. These various groupings, comprising the social structure of the village in its regional setting, channel most of the individual's activities. Yet it is the village that stands out as the prime focus of the individual's identification. This is expressed in a variety of ways: traditions accounting for the development of individual villages are well remembered as are the associated tales of former competition between villages for control of land and the seduction of pretty women. Familiar also from the cognate Malay phrase is the aphorism commonly cited in Rarak: *lén dèsa, lén adat,* "another village, another custom." Apprehension of small deviations from the villager's own *adat* is also apparent at intervillage soccer contests, drumming and singing contests at wedding feasts, and from the allegations of witchcraft following visits to distant communities. This primary identification with a particular local community also shapes the Rarak villager's attitude toward, and trust in, local leadership.

Formal village authority is composed essentially of two simple hierarchies of leaders, one to provide guidance in matters of *adat,* or civil custom, and the other to supervise matters of religious law and belief. These leaders, together with the village's more active elder men, are explicitly accorded the trust and confidence of the individual villager when considered advice, counsel or representation becomes necessary. In Rarak, as in the neighboring villages, there have never been residents of aristocratic status; all the villagers are commoners, and claim to local leadership has never rested upon formally inherited rank. The core group of senior village leaders commands almost automatic respect among their fellow villagers by virtue of their generational seniority as well as the formal authority of office. Nevertheless local leaders individually maintain continual face-to-face contact with their fellow villagers, and personal characteristics and abilities become important criteria for positions of leadership. Although a villager may privately express his doubt—or even scorn —about the mosque head's ability to read the Friday scripture or the village head's capacity to arbitrate disputes effectively, these reservations are usually offset by the extraordinary or even charismatic qualities attributed to each important leader. In Rarak in 1955 it was a striking fact that no member of the village hierarchies lacked some highly specialized ability as either curer or diviner.

Beyond the immediate village horizon lies the discernible, though indistinctly bounded, circle of communities familiar to the villager. These half dozen settlements which lie scattered mostly within a six to eight mile radius tend to be somewhat smaller than Rarak, yet share the same economy, problems of subsistence and lack of aristocratic tradition. Furthermore their families are in many instances linked to those at Rarak by ties of marriage or close kinship. Largely through frequent visits to these related households for purposes of sociability, work assistance or trade, the Rarak citizen keeps abreast of gossip or news in one or several of the neighboring settlements. There is a tendency for all villagers within this circle to share a common orientation toward fellow islanders of the adjacent regions. They consider themselves distinct from the villagers of the more prosperous and urbane lowlands, on the one hand, and from the mountaineer rustics of Sumbawa's hinterlands, on the other.

Traditionally these people of the Rarak circle of villages have looked to the lowlands not only for their trickle of goods from market and shop but also for the ultimate authority in government. In the large lowland houses amid extensive rice terraces live the titled and affluent lieutenants of the former sultanate. As the aristocratic "arms and legs" of the sultan they have always provided the immediate link in authority between the village headman and the sultan's court. If, figuratively speaking, the villager looks up to the lowlands, he tends to look down on the mountain population. A day and a half's journey upland from Rarak live people whom he sees as basically uncouth, wild-eyed mountaineers. Such people in occasional trading parties pass the village en route to the town market with their horseloads of woven mats and baskets. Their dialect is barely intelligible, their clothing is often in rags and, had not their distant villages produced several of Sumbawa's better known *hadjis* [pilgrims to Mecca], their claim in Rarak as *tau semawa,* or bona fide Sumbawans, would indeed be dubious.

Suggested Readings

BIBLIOGRAPHY

Hay, Stephen N. and Margaret H. Chase, *Southeast Asian History: A Bibliographic Guide* (New York, 1962). A useful compilation for the beginning student. Includes also important articles in learned journals.

GEOGRAPHY

Atlas of South-east Asia. With an introduction by D. G. E. Hall (London and New York, 1964). A very useful volume for the historian.

Fisher, Charles A., *South-east Asia: A Social, Economic, and Political Geography* (London and New York, 1964). A comprehensive survey.

HISTORY

Cady, John F., *Southeast Asia: Its Historical Development* (New York, 1964). A standard text.

Coedès, Georges, *The Making of South East Asia*, trans. H. M. Wright (Berkeley and Los Angeles, 1966). A clear presentation of the major facets of the history of mainland Southeast Asia, by the most renowned scholar. Main emphasis on the pre-European period.

Hall, D. G. E., *A History of South-East Asia*, 2nd rev. ed. (London and New York, 1964). A carefully executed synthesis. Has an excellent bibliography.

Harrison, Brian, *South-East Asia: A Short History*, 3rd ed. (London and New York, 1966). A useful, short volume.

319

Kahin, George McTurnan (ed.), *Governments and Politics of Southeast Asia,* 2nd ed. (Ithaca, N.Y., 1964). An indispensable reference work for the contemporary scene. Individual chapters on each country.

Tarling, Nicholas, *A Concise History of Southeast Asia* (New York, Washington, London, 1966). A thoughtful work by a British scholar, emphasizing the modern era.

Toussaint, Auguste, *History of the Indian Ocean,* trans. June Guicharnaud (Chicago, 1966). Penetrating study which places Southeast Asia in the wider context of the Indian Ocean area as a whole.

BURMA

Cady, John F., *A History of Modern Burma* (Ithaca, N.Y., 1958). Comprehensive, well-presented.

Maung Maung, *Burma in the Family of Nations* (Amsterdam, 1958). A lucid presentation by one of Burma's leading writers in English.

Tinker, Hugh, *The Union of Burma: A Study of the First Years of Independence,* 3rd ed. (London and New York, 1961). A careful analysis.

Trager, Frank N., *Burma from Kingdom to Republic: A Historical and Political Analysis* (New York, Washington, London, 1966). A detailed and thoughtful study.

INDOCHINA (VIETNAM, LAOS, CAMBODIA)

Buttinger, Joseph, *The Smaller Dragon: A Political History of Vietnam* (New York, 1958). The only volume in English on the premodern period.

Fall, Bernard B., *The Two Viet-Nams: A Political and Military Analysis,* rev. ed. (New York and London, 1965). Careful and comprehensive, by a leading student.

Halpern, Joel M., *Government, Politics and Social Structure in Laos: A Study of Tradition and Innovation* (New Haven, Conn., 1964). Includes important statistical materials, collected by an American anthropologist.

Isoart, Paul, *Le phénomène national viêtnamien: De l'indépendance unitaire à l'indépendance fractionnée* (Paris, 1961). Very insightful and useful study.

Lê Thánh Khôi, *Le Viêt-Nam: Histoire et Civilisation* (Paris, 1955). The only one-volume history, based on exhaustive research. By a Vietnamese scholar resident in France.

LeBar, Frank M., and Adrienne Suddard (eds.), *Laos: Its People, Its Society, Its Culture* (New Haven, Conn., 1960) A useful compilation.

Steinberg, David J. *et al., Cambodia: Its People, Its Society, Its Culture,* rev. ed. (New Haven, Conn., 1959). A useful compilation.

INDONESIA

Furnivall, J. S., *Netherlands India: A Study of Plural Economy* (Cambridge and New York, 1944). Penetrating study of colonial rule in Indonesia, by a British student and former administrator in British Burma.

Legge, J. D., *Indonesia* (Englewood Cliffs, N.J., 1964). A highly useful short volume by an Australian scholar. Emphasis on problems in Indonesian history and historiography.

McVey, Ruth T. (ed.), *Indonesia* (New Haven, Conn., 1963). A comprehensive survey of the country by a number of specialists.

Vlekke, Bernard H. M., *Nusantara: A History of Indonesia* (The Hague and Bandung, 1959). Well-written synthesis by a leading Dutch scholar.

Wertheim, W. F., *Indonesian Society in Transition: A Study of Social Change,* 2nd ed. (The Hague and Bandung, 1959). A searching analysis.

MALAYSIA

Gullick, J. M., *Malaya,* rev. ed. (New York and Washington, 1964). A succinct survey.

Roff, William R., *The Origins of Malay Nationalism* (New Haven, Conn. and London, 1967). A pioneering study.

Tregonning, K. G., *A History of Modern Malaya* (Singapore and London, 1964). Vividly presented survey.

Wang Gungwu (ed.), *Malaysia: A Survey* (New York, Washington, and London, 1964). Comprehensive series of essays by leading experts.

Winstedt, Sir Richard, *A History of Malaya,* rev. ed. (Singapore, 1962). By the leading British scholar.

PHILIPPINES

Agoncillo, Teodoro A. and Oscar M. Alfonso, *A Short History of the Filipino People* (Quezon City, 1960). A standard text devoted to the modern period, by well-known Filipino historians.

Corpuz, Onofre D., *The Philippines* (Englewood Cliffs, N.J., 1965). A searching interpretation by a younger Filipino political scientist.

Phelan, John Leddy, *The Hispanization of the Philippines: Spanish Aims and Filipino Responses 1565–1700* (Madison, Wis., 1959). Valuable study of culture contact.

Schurz, William Lytle, *The Manila Galleon* (New York, 1959). A classic study of the economy under Spanish rule.

Zaide, Gregorio F., *Philippine Political and Cultural History*, 2 vols., rev. ed. (Manila, 1957). Detailed treatment by a senior Filipino scholar.

THAILAND

Ingram, James C., *Economic Change in Thailand since 1850* (Stanford, Calif., 1955). Authoritative treatment.

Landon, Kenneth P., *Siam in Transition: A Brief Survey of Cultural Trends in the Five Years Since the Revolution of 1932* (Shanghai, 1939; reprinted Ann Arbor, Mich., 1966). Important study by an American expert on the spot.

Riggs, Fred W., *Thailand: The Modernization of a Bureaucratic Polity* (Honolulu, 1966). A penetrating analysis.

Vella, Walter F., *The Impact of the West on Government in Thailand* (Berkeley, Calif., 1955). Careful pioneering work.

Wilson, David A., *Politics in Thailand* (Ithaca, N.Y., 1962). By a leading American political scientist.

Index

Page numbers in italics refer to the main discussion

Abad Santos, José, 199
Abad Santos, Pedro, 198, 199
Abdul Rahman, Tengku, 217, *281–282*
Abdullah bin Abdul Kadir, *149– 152*
Acheh, Achehnese, 5, 30, *59–62*, 90
Adran, Bishop, 105, 106, 107
Agung, Sultan, 52, 193
Aidit, D. N., *254–260*
Alaungsithu (Lansu I), 34
Albuquerque, Afonso de, 74, *77– 80*
Amangkurat II, *98–101*
America, Americans, 121, 122, 123, 195, 205, 213, 216, 229, 233, 238, 239, 240, 243, 261, 262, 263, 264, 271
in the Philippines, *264–270*
Ammerapoora, 108
Angrok, King, 37–39
Annam, 46, *47–49*, 104, 115, *128–132*, 137, 153, 154, 179, 243

Anti-Fascist People's Freedom League (Burma), 277
Arabs, 19, 149, 155, 293, 314
Aranyik, 42, 43, 44
Aung San, 216, *277–280*
Ava, *108–110*
Avalokitesvara, 3, 4
Ayuthia, 19, 40, 92

Ba Maw, 227, 229, *230–234*
Bagyidaw, King, 68
Bali, 190
Bandung, 263
Bangkok, 186
Bantam, 80–84, 89, 134–137, 193
Bao Dai, Emperor, 179, 270, 272
Barrow, John, 74, *104–107*
Basco y Vargas, José, *102–104*
Basma (Pasai), Kingdom, 12–13
Batavia, 31, 74, 94, 99
See also Jakarta
Bengal, 19, 20, 21, 109, 110, 116, 143
Bengal Revolutionary Party, 143

325

Bintara, 54, 55, 56, 193
Bodawpaya, King, 62, 108
Borneo, 7, 23, 97, 190
Borobudur, 195
Bra-Widjaja, Prince, 53–56
Britain, British, 73, 74, 75, 89,
    96, 104, 105, 111, 113, 119,
    130, 190, 205, 227, 229,
    251, 279, 281, 282
    See also East India Com-
    pany (English)
Brunei, 26
Buddhism, Buddhists, 210–211,
    222, 300
    in Burma, 30, *34–37*, 64–68,
    141–142, 160–164
    in Java, 38
    in Laos, 304
    in Sumatra, 1, 3–6
    in Thailand, 42–44, 73, 118–
    119, 120–122
    in Vietnam, 295–297
Bulacan, 102
Burma, 20, 21, 29, 31, 34, *62–*
    67, 68–71, 74, 75, *108–110,*
    111, 114, *141–144,* 146,
    157–160, 199–202, 202–
    204, 215, 216, *227–234,*
    241, 244, 270, *277–280,*
    308–310
Burma Round Table Conference,
    199–202, 202–204

Cairo, 78, 79, 307
Cambodia, 18, 20, 21, 46, 90,
    115, 116, 131, 145, *152–*
    154, 190, 243, 276
Cao Daism, 295–296, 298
Caram, Fermin, 235, 238

Carpentier, Pieter de, *87–90*
Caung-Shung, *see* Gia-Long
Cebu, 24
Ceylon, 3, 5, 110
Champa, *10–12,* 18, 20, 21, 22,
    46, 105, 190
Chao Ju-kua, 1, *7–10*
Cheng-Ho, 14, 15
Ch'eng-tsung (Timur Khan), 47,
    48–49
Chettiars, 200, 201
China, Chinese, 1–7, 10–13, 14,
    15, 17, 21, 22, 23, 29, 30,
    46, 106, 110, 130, 147, 193,
    221, 241, 263, 269, 270,
    275, 276
    in Burma, 162, 309
    in Indonesia, 81, 83, 88, 314
    in Malaysia, 133, 293, 299–
    300
    in the Philippines, *211–214*
    in Thailand, 18, 19, 20, 119,
    204–211
    in Vietnam, 116
    relations with Vietnam, *47–49,*
    107
Christianity, Christians, 210, 211,
    247
    in Indonesia, 245
    in the Philippines, *90–91,* 213,
    214, 267
    in Thailand, 93–94, 121
    in Vietnam, 74, 106–107, 295,
    296
Chulalongkorn (Rama V), 119,
    146, *169–173*
Cochinchina, 18, 20, 21–23, 73,
    75, 90, 105, 107, *114–116,*
    123, *128–132,* 152

Coen, Jan Pieterszoon, 87
Communism, Communists, 216,
    244
  in Burma, 280
  in Indonesia, 134, 136, 252–
    253, *254–260*
  in the Philippines, 260–264,
    264–270
  in Thailand, 284
  in Vietnam, 274
Confesor, Tomas, 235, *238–242*
Confucius, Confucianism, 106,
    107, 295
Cowasjee, N. M., *200–202*
Cox, Hiram, 109, 110
Crawfurd, John, 73, *114–119*
Çrivijaya, 190, 192
Cultivation System (Indonesia),
    124–128

Decoux, Jean, 216, *242–244*
Dedel, Jacob, *87–90*
Diponegoro, Prince, *157–160*
Douwes Dekker, E., *124–128*
Dutch, 45, 73, 75, 94
  in Indonesia, 56–58, 80–84,
    87–90, *134–137*, 157, 224,
    226, 253, 315
  in Siam, 94–97
  relations with Mataram, *98–
    101*
Dutch East India Company, 53,
    56–58, 74, 89, 92, *94–97*,
    98
Dutch East Indies, 75, 87, 98,
    114, *124–128*, 130, 135

East India Company (English),
    110–113, 114

  in Cochin China, 114–116
  in Malaya, *110–113, 132–
    134*
  relations with Burma, 108–
    110, *141–144, 160–164,
    199–202*, 202–204, 230–
    234, 277, 278–279, 280,
    281, 282

Fa-hsien, 1, *3–5*
Federated Malay States, *132–
    134*, 280
Federation of Malaya, *280–282*
Fei-Hsin, 2, *14–15*
Ferlec (Perlak), Kingdom, 12–13
France, French, 75, 84–87, 104,
    105, 106, 110, 128, 129,
    130, 138, 139, 140, 152,
    180, 181
  in Indochina, *128–132, 137–
    141, 179–181, 182–185*,
    216, *242–244*, 271–273,
    275, 276, 298

Gandasubrata, S. M., *224–227*
Garnier, Francis, 75, *128–132*
General Council of Buddhist As-
    sociations (G.C.B.A.), 142,
    143, 160, 161
Geneva Conference, 274–277
Gia-Long, Emperor, 74, *104–107*
Giri, 53–56
Goens, Rijklof van, *98–101*
Greater East Asia Co-Prosperity
    Sphere, 220–223, 228, 233,
    235, 242–244
Guided Democracy (Indonesia),
    250, 255

Hanoi, 270, 273
Hanthawaddy, 62–63
Hanunóo, 288, *311–313*
Hayam Wuruk, 45
Hinduism, 4, 6, 34, 37, 38, 53, 68, 155, 211
Ho Chi Minh, 216, *270–273, 274–277*
Houtman, Cornelius van, 80
Hué, 131, 153
Hukbalahap, 260–261, 262–263, 264, 269

India, Indians, 3, 5, 6, 18, 19, 23, 29, 46, 60, 65, 74, 77, 78, 83, 94, 108–110, 143, 147, 149, 162, 279, 293, 299, 300, 307
    in Burma, *199–202*
    See also Bengal
Indochina, 75, *137–141*, 179, 216, *242–244*, 270
    See also Annam; Cambodia; Cochinchina; Laos; Tonkin; Vietnam
Indonesia, 18, 59–62, 124, *134–137, 189–193*, 196, 215, 216, 219, 220, 224–227, *244–250, 250–254, 254–260*, 270, 307, 313–317
    See also Dutch East Indies
Innes, Charles, *141–144*
Irian Barat (West New Guinea), 194
    See also New Guinea
Isa Anshari, K. H., Muhammed, *250–254*
Iskandar Muda, Sultan, 59
Islam, 13, 73, 77, 83, 93, 134, 145, 211, 216, 245, 247, 292, 294
    in Indonesia, *250–254*
    in Java, *53–56, 155–157, 157–160*, 195, 288, *304–308*
    in Malaya, *149–152*, 300
I-tsing, 1, *5–6*

Jakarta, 57, 74, *87–90*, 224
    See also Batavia
Japan, Japanese, 96, 166, 190, 215, *219–223*, 270, 279, 300
Japanese occupation of Burma, *227–234*
    of Indochina, *242–244*, 272
    of Indonesia, *224–227*, 250, 253
    of the Philippines, *235–242*
Java, Javanese, 10, 12, 17, 29, 30, 31, *37–39*, 45–46, *52–58*, 61, *80–84, 87–90*, 98, 111, 124, 125, 126, 127, 128, 134, 146, *155–157, 157–160*, 195, *224–227*, 288, *304–308*

Kachins, 308–310
Karens, 63, 147, *202–204*, 228
Kedah, 20, 74, *110–113*
Kediri, 37–39, 193
Kelantan, 299, 300
Khmers, 33–34
Konbaung Dynasty, 62
Korea, 190, 244
Kuala Kangsar, *see* Perak
Kuala Lumpur, 132–134, 281
Kublai Khan, 10, 11, 12, 13, 47
Kwang-tung, 6

Laguna de Bay, 102
Laos, 106, 115, 243, 276, 284, 288, *301–304*
Laurel, José P., *235–238*
Lefebvre, Father, 84–85
Le-Hoan, General, 47–48
Leonowens, Anna, 73, *119–123*
Le-Tac, *47–48*
Light, Francis, 111, 112, 113
Ligor, 96, 97
Locsin, Teodoro M., *211–214*
Lodewijcksz, Willem, *80–84*
Lombok, 45, 314
Louis XIV, 74, *84–86*
Luang Prabang, 301
Luzon, 9, 18, 23, 26, 164–169, 196, 269

Magsaysay, Ramon, 216, *260–264*
Ma-Huan, 2, 14, *15–17*
Majapahit, 37, 45–46, *53–56*, 190, 193
Malabar, 79, 90
Malacca, *13–17*, 18, 19, 20, 21, 22, 23, *49–52*, *77–80*, 94, 149, 190
Malaya, Malays, *49–52*, 74, *110–113*, *132–134*, 145, *149–152*, 190, 192, 219, 244, 270, *280–282*, 292–294, *298–300*
    See also Federated Malay States; Federation of Malaya
Manila, 102, 211, 261, 262, 264
Manuel, D., King, 78, 79, 80
Mataram, *52–58*, 73, 74, *98–101*, 193

Maung Gyi, Joseph, 141
Mecca, 56, 78, 79, 159, 307, 317
Mekong, 42, 294
Minangkabau, 193–194
Mindanao, 24–27, 90–91
Mindoro, 8, 288, *311–313*
Moluccas, 190, 194
Mongkut (Rama IV), 119, *119–123*
Moors, 19, 21, 77, 78, 79
    See also Islam
Moros, 26
Muhammed Shah, Sultan, 52
Multatuli, *see* Douwes Dekker, E.
Muslims, *see* Islam

Nationalism, Nationalists, 75, 136, 146, 173, 196, 199
    in Burma, *160–164*, *202–204*, 281
    in Indonesia, *189–193*, *244–250*, *250–254*
    in Vietnam, *179–181*, *182–185*, 274
Negri Sembilan, 132–134
Negros, 266
Netherlands, 81, 87, 88, 94, 98, 124, 125, 127, 157, 189, 190, 194
Netherlands East Indies, *see* Dutch East Indies
New Guinea, 241
    See also Irian Barat
Nguyen-Anh, *see* Gia-Long
Nguyen Dynasty, 74, *104–107*
Nguyen-Thai-Hoc, 146, *182–185*

Pagan, 29, 30, *34–37*
Pahang, 18, 19, 20, 132–134

Palawan, 8, 26–27
Palembang, 5–6, 14, 20, 82, 83, 90
Pampanga, 102, 196
Panay, 235, 238, 239
Pantja Sila, 216, *245–248*, 252
Partai Nasional Indonesia (PNI), 191, 192
Pase, 19, 20
Pasquier, Pierre, *137–141*
Patani, 299
Pedir, 19, 20
Pegu, 18, 19, 20, 62–67, 96
Penang, 110–113
People's Party (Thailand), 185–189
Perak, 132–134
Persia, Persians, 19, 84, 193
Perupok, 299, 300
Pham Quynh, 146, *179–181*
Philippine Revolution, 173, 268–269
Philippines, *7–10*, 23, *24–27*, 74, *90–91*, *102–104*, 146, 147, *164–169*, *173–179*, *196–199*, *211–214*, 215, 216, 220, *235–242*, 244, *260–264*, *264–270*, 288, *311–313*
Pigafetta, Antonio, 2, *24–27*
Pires, Tomé, 1, *18–23*
Polo, Marco, 2, *10–13*
Pomeroy, William J., 264
Portugal, Portuguese, 1, 18, 73, 74, *77–80*, 81–84, 93, 94, 96, 114, 115
Prajadhipok (Rama VII), *185–189*
Prapança, *45–46*
Pulau Pandjang, 81, 82, 83, 84

Quezon, Manuel Luis, 146, 164, *196–199*

Raffles, Thomas Stamford, 149
Rajadhon, Phya Anuman, 287, *289–291*
Rām Khamhāēng, King, *40–45*
Rangoon, 109, 160, 200, 234, 277
Rarak, 313–317
Reynaud, Paul, 179–181
Rice planting, in Burma, 308–310
  in Laos, *301–304*
Rizal, José, 146, *173–179*
Romulo, Carlos P., 263

Saigon, 105, 130
Sakdal Movement (Philippines), *164–169*
San Nicolas, Fray Juan de, 90–91
San-sü, 8, 9, 10
Saya San rebellion (Burma), *141–144*, *160–164*
Schouten, Joost, *92–94*
Selangor, *see* Kuala Lumpur
Shans, 228, 308–310
Siam, Siamese, *see* Thailand
Singapore, 219, *292–294*
Singosari, 37–39, 193
Sjahrir, Sutan, 146, *193–196*
Soekarno, *see* Sukarno
Southeast Asia Treaty Organization, 283
Spain, Spaniards, Spanish, 74, 75, 90, 95, 102, 190, 264
  in the Philippines, 90–91, 102–104, *173–179*, 267, 268
Spices, 12, 13, 20, 21, 22, 77, 78, 79, 81, 90, 127

Sra Shwe Ba, *202–204*
Sukarno, 146, *189–193*, 216,
    244–250, 251–252, 253, 255
Sukothai, 29, *40–45*
Sumatra, 1, *3–5*, *5–6*, 10, 12–13,
    30, 59, 60, 80, 82, 90, 124,
    190, 194, 195
Sumbawa, *313–317*
Sunda, 20, 61, 80–84
Suryavarman I, 29, *33–34*
Swettenham, Frank, *132–134*
Symes, Michael, *108–110*

Taruc, Luis, 216, 262, *264–270*
Tenasserim, 95, 96
Terung, 54, 55
Thailand, Thais, 14, 15, 18–20,
    21, *40–45*, 46, 73, 90, *92–
    94*, 94–97, 111, 112, 113,
    114, *117–119*, *119–123*,
    146, 152, 153, 154, *169–
    173*, *185–189*, *204–211*,
    217, 244, *283–285*, *289–
    291*, 299, 300, 301
Thakins, 216, 277
Thanom Kittikachorn, *283–285*
Tharawaddy district (Burma),
    141, 142, 160, 163
Tōjō, Hideki, *227–230*
Tonkin, 74, 75, *84–87*, 115, 137,
    182, 183

Trengganu, 299
Tydings-McDuffie Act, 164–165

U Nu, 278
United States of America, *see*
    America, Americans

Varenne, Alexandre, 183
Viet Cong, 298
Viet Minh, 179, 272, 298
Vietnam, Vietnamese, 30, *47–49*,
    74, *104–107*, 110, 137, 145,
    152–154, *179–181*, *182–
    185*, 217, 244
    Democratic Republic of Viet-
    nam, 216, *270–273*, *274–
    277*
    South Vietnam, 216, 284, 288,
    294–298
        See also Annam; Cochin-
        china; Tonkin
Vietnamese Nationalist Party
    (VNQDD), 137, *182–185*
Visayan Islands, 24–27, 288

Wachirawut (Rama VI), *204–211*

Yavadvipa, 4
Yen-Bay revolt (Vietnam), 137,
    182, 184
Yung-lo, 14, 15